Efficient
Memory
Programming

To my wife Jill and my daughter Kira

Efficient Memory Programming

David Loshin

McGraw-Hill

New York   San Francisco   Washington, D.C.   Auckland   Bogotá
Caracas   Lisbon   London   Madrid   Mexico City   Milan
Montreal   New Delhi   San Juan   Singapore
Sydney   Tokyo   Toronto

Library of Congress Cataloging-in-Publication Data

Loshin, David, 1963–
    Efficient Memory Programming / David Loshin.
        p. cm.
    Includes bibliographical references and index.
    ISBN 0-07-038868-7
    1. Memory management (Computer science). I. Title.
QA76.9.M45L647   1998
005.4 ' 35—dc21   98-31719
                                                    CIP

McGraw-Hill

*A Division of The **McGraw·Hill** Companies*

1 2 3 4 5 6 7 8 9 DOC/DOC 9 0 3 2 1 0 9 8

ISBN 0-07-038868-7

*The sponsoring editor of this book was Michael Sprague, the editing
supervisor was Ruth Mannino, and the production supervisor was Claire
Stanley. It was set in Times Roman by Kim Sheran and Michele M. Zito of
McGraw-Hill's Hightstown Professional Book Group composition unit,
Hightstown, N.J., in cooperation with Spring Point Publishing Services.*

 This book is printed on recycled, acid-free paper containing
a minimum of 50% recycled de-inked fiber.

Printed and bound by R. R. Donnelley & Sons Company.

McGraw-Hill books are available at special quantity discounts to use as
premiums and sales promotions, or for use in corporate training
programs. For more information, please write to the Director of Special
Sales, McGraw-Hill, 11 West 19th Street, New York, NY 10011. Or
contact your local bookstore.

Contents

Acknowledgments

I would like to thank Michael Sprague at McGraw-Hill for his enthusiasm in putting this work together. Special thanks also go to the following people, who added significant advice during the writing process: Mary Treseler, Alan Broder (who was always available as a sounding board), Mike Schmit, Steve Taylor, David Eliezer (both for his comments and for his encouragement), and especially Jonathan Sandberg, whose insightful comments helped guide me through a good part of the way. Thanks also go to Dennis Shasha, Bob Morgan, and a host of compiler-writers out there who keep pushing the performance envelope.

I would also like to thank my brother Peter, who helped me move this book in a forward direction when help was most needed. I especially would like to thank my wife Jill, whose constant encouragement kept me at work, and very especially, my beautiful daughter Kira, who has inspired me to complete this work so that I can spend more time being a daddy.

Introduction

Speed

Speed—that is the name of the game when designing computer applications. In our world of the information superhighway, three-dimensional graphics, computer movies, high-performance scientific applications, business applications, etc., the faster the computer can return the answer, the better. As processor speeds have increased, so have the opportunities to bring high-performance applications to the desktop. Yet, the tiny physical distance spanning disk drives through memory chips to the processor's registers hides a wide chasm of performance traps and pitfalls that can hamper your program's performance.

With the propagation of high-performance microprocessors down to the desktop level, it is necessary for programmers of all levels to achieve an understanding of how the structure of a computer's memory hierarchies affects the performance of applications. While this insight has been learned by many high-performance system applications developers, operating systems designers, and compiler writers, the secrets to efficient memory programming are not known to the average programmer. This book is meant to introduce these difficult topics in a way that is both understandable and comprehensive.

In the struggle for better performance, there are many traditional methods for increasing the speed of an application. Because of the difference in speeds between processors and memories, simple programs may exhibit disastrous performance—but that can be easily fixed if the programmer understands how caches and memories work. This book will describe how to bridge the performance chasm by elaborating on the memory hierarchy embedded in most computers, and how to write programs that make efficient use of this hierarchy.

There are four events that have led me to write this book. The first occurred in the early 1990s, when I was working on an optimizing compiler for an interesting microprocessor produced by Intel called the i860. As this was my first experience with a RISC (reduced instruction set computer) microprocessor, I was astounded at its performance characteristics. My previous experience with optimizing compilers had been with more traditional CISC (complex instruction set computer) processors, such as the VAX and the Motorola 68000 series of computers.

In the compilers for the earlier computer organizations, optimization techniques were applied to reduce computation. The CPU was seen as the performance bottleneck, and any way that computations could be reduced would increase the execution time of applications.

But in the i860, the benefit of these traditional optimizations reached a limit. The amount of computation could be reduced only to a certain point, after which further optimizations had no effect. Evidently, the RISC processor performance was so good that the performance bottleneck had migrated out of the CPU and out to the memory system. In other words, the application was running slowly because the CPU had stalled waiting for data to be delivered from the memory system!

What my team members and I had discovered was that, when performance is gauged on the i860, computation is effectively free. The main performance cost was moving data operands from memory to the CPU, and results from the CPU back to memory. Thus, our eyes having been opened to the vagaries of the memory bottleneck, we began to study and understand the performance characteristics of the memory hierarchy.

The second event occurred a few months later. I was attending a talk about compiling for symmetric multiprocessor machines. The speaker considered how computation of a program would be distributed across the multiple processors in the system. This talk was my first advanced introduction to dependence analysis (a technique that we will cover in this book). During this talk, the speaker elaborated on the method of distribution of the iterations of a matrix computation algorithm across the processors based on the memory access patterns of the computation. What the speaker had described was a way to transform the code that allowed the different processors to share the computation. What occurred to me at the time was the similarity between the multiprocessor "computation distribution" problem and the RISC processor blocked-pipeline problem—that of keeping the rate of data flowing into the processor the same as the speed of execution of the processor.

The third event took place a few years later. I was working on compiler design at Thinking Machines Corporation, which at the time was a manufacturer of massively parallel processing (MPP) supercomputers. As we will discuss later in this book, an MPP computer consists of a collection of individual processors linked by a high-speed interconnection network. Our team had been concentrating on the performance bottlenecks that appeared when data were broadcast between processors.

What we had learned was that while the processing units chugged along at a fairly high speed, the whole computation bogged down while the processors waited for data to be transferred over the network. Our desire was to come up with a way to overlap the computation at each processor with the communication of data between processors. Apparently, the problem was the same—there was a performance bottleneck at the point of moving data from one location to where it was needed for computation.

The fourth event took place some time later, when I was working on a large-scale data mining project. In this application, large amounts of transaction data were under investigation for recurring patterns. Between the amount of data being processed and the amount of processing that was required, performance was the key. Yet in this instance, data were flowing into a disk array, only to be redirected to a set of cooperating networked processors. A performance bottleneck in this application was moving the data from the disk array to the processing nodes in a way that kept up with the CPU processing speeds—apparently, the same problem again!

The problems discussed in these four instances shared some similarities:

- They involved moving data from a slow device to a faster device.

- The performance of the application or system depended on the ability to access data quickly.

- The applications under investigation performed some amount of computation on a set of data, provided a set of results, and then continued on with another set of data.

- The problems dealt with moving data through different levels of a memory hierarchy.

And these problems shared one more similarity: careful analysis of the access patterns and methodically rewritten code allowed the applications to take advantage of locality of reference to achieve better performance. Most of these code transformations were eventually incorporated into some compiler or another. Yet while many compilation systems can perform these optimizations, many do not provide this level of performance, and many code fragments are not well suited to these kinds of automatic optimizations, as we will see.

The result of these realizations led to this book—an attempt to discuss the notions of application performance and code optimization in the presence of the memory hierarchy. By understanding the architectural and organizational structure of modern computers, the programmer can avoid performance pitfalls, and create "memory-aware" applications.

The Memory Hierarchy

To summarize our discussion above, with the significant amount of computing power available in today's compact and complicated multiple-instruction-issue computers, the benefit of the super performance of the microprocessor is limited by the ability to provide data to the processor for computation. The difference in speed of data delivery from the main memory and the processor reveals a performance bottleneck. The effect of this bottleneck can be measured and evaluated by examining the computer's memory hierarchy.

A hierarchy is a collection of ranked levels, each of which is subordinate to the one above it. In any computer system, the different types of memories are collected together into a hierarchy that is ranked by a combination of speed of delivery, capacity, and cost. For example, most computer systems will have at least three levels of memory in a hierarchy. The highest level in that hierarchy contains the processor registers, the second level consists of the dynamic, temporary memory storage [usually random access memory (RAM)], and the third level consists of the static storage (which is often made up of disk storage systems).

In this typical configuration, the processor registers are the most expensive (and limited) resource, and also provide the fastest access time. The dynamic memory level is less expensive (and more available) than the processor registers, but the memory access time is slower than that of the registers. The static disk memory is available in greater quantity at much lower cost, but the time to retrieve data from disk greatly lags the RAM access time.

While this configuration represents a typical memory hierarchy, there are many different possible types of memories that can occupy levels in the order, such as different kinds of caches, CD-ROMs, magnetic tape, and in multiple processor systems, even remote processors' memories. These types of memories will be discussed in greater detail.

An Example of a Data Hierarchy

To get a feel for the nature of a computer's memory hierarchy, let's examine a simple real-life example that exhibits the same kind of behavior. Consider a tax accountant with many clients. Our accountant has a fancy desk with a relatively wide desktop, enough to hold the folders of five clients. In general, the client folders for the past year are kept in a file cabinet across the office. At the end of the year, all the current folders are boxed up and moved to a separate storage building across the street.

When the accountant wants to work on client A's accounts, he goes to the file cabinet, removes client A's folder, and brings it to the desktop. At some point, the accountant needs to begin work on the sixth client's taxes, but his desktop is full. Now the accountant needs to return one of the open folders to the file cabinet to make room for the next folder. As April 15 nears, the accountant begins cycling many folders back and forth from the file cabinet to the desktop.

When the accountant tires of this constant bouncing up and down, he realizes that it might make sense to buy a smaller side table on which to stack the most recently used folders that need to be moved from the top of the desk. This way, instead of going back and forth to the file cabinet to look up the information, he has the folders handily available on the side table. While this helps the accountant, there is a limit to the number of folders that may be piled on the side table.

One morning, the accountant learns that one of his clients is being audited. In order to prepare for the audit, the accountant must retrieve the tax folders from the previous 7 years. This requires going to the long-term storage folders in the building across the street, searching for the particular client's information, and carrying it back to the office.

Computer systems act the same way when reading data in and out of memory. Clients' tax folders are representative of data that need to be available for computation. The accountant's desktop corresponds to the processor registers; the access to the data is the fastest, but there is a limit to the amount of data that can be available at one time. The file cabinet represents the main memory; during the tax year, all the data that are needed are readily available, at the cost of getting up from the desk and going to the file cabinet, similar to the cost of fetching data from memory into the processor registers.

The accountant's new side table corresponds to a processor's cache. The cache is a temporary storage location for recently used data. Just as the accountant can grab a folder from his side table quickly, data that has been placed in the cache can be accessed quickly. And, just as the side table can hold a larger, but still limited, number of folders, the cache can hold a limited amount of data.

The folders that need to be recovered from the storage facility across the street correspond to data that are stored in a long-term storage medium, such as a floppy disk. Like the storage facility, the disk may hold a much larger amount of data, but the cost of accessing that data is much greater than the cost of accessing main memory.

As can be seen, if the accountant wants to make best use of his time, he can decide ahead of time the order of work for the day, and arrange his access time accordingly. Obviously, it would be absurd to walk across the street to grab a set of folders, then repeat that process 2 hours later.

Instead, it is better to determine at the beginning of each day which folders need to be brought back to the office from the storage facility, and go across the street only once. In addition, if the accountant thinks about which of his clients will get his attention during the day, he can remove those folders from the file cabinet at the beginning of the day and set them all on his side table. This way he may be able to limit the number of times he needs to go back and forth to the file cabinet.

This corresponds to a program that carefully arranges its data accesses to bring data in from different areas of memory in a way that minimizes the memory access delays. Bringing folders from the file cabinet to the side table is similar to prefetching data from main memory into a cache. Being able to control how data move in and out of the cache is particularly important to the idea of memory hierarchy management, and so a brief history of cache memories is in order.

A Brief History of Caches

The idea of a temporary area of fast memory known as a cache first appeared in computers in the early 1960s. The first commercial machine that had a cache memory was the IBM 360/85. Later, the PDP-11 from Digital Equipment Corporation was the first offering from that company to have a cache memory. Later VAX machines from DEC also had caches, and much work was done on evaluating the usefulness and efficiency of caches.

Caches moved to the desktop when Sun placed a Motorola 68020 microprocessor in the 3/260. At this point, there begin to appear machines with dual caches: one for machine instructions and one for data. Other companies using caches in their machines at that time were Silicon Graphics, MIPS, and IBM.

This book will describe the evolution of the architecture of the cache and the algorithms used for accessing data in the cache, bringing data into the cache, replacing data in the cache, and cache coherency protocols.

Other Hierarchy Levels

Caches are not the only centers of data movement; data items ebb and flow throughout different kinds of memory: main memory, disk drives, networks, etc. As computer architectures and organizations develop, the details of the way the hardware is connected may differ, but the issues will remain the same. The issue that we will deal with in this book is that of efficiency of data movement, and optimizing computation and data delivery.

Because data delivery is the bottleneck, a lot of work has been done to try to alleviate the sources of the delays. We will look at attempts to solve this problem using both hardware solutions and software solutions. The goal is to gain an understanding of the memory bottleneck and ways that an application can be built to address that problem.

Organization of the Book

The book consists of two parts. Part 1 discusses a general outline of performance processor computation. This part elaborates on microprocessor organization, memory systems, caches, paging, registers, and other parts of the memory hierarchy. Part 2 covers performance optimization, traps and pitfalls of certain kinds of code, some general philosophies about efficient memory access, and how to evaluate a program's access behavior. Part 2 also contains practical power tips for optimizing programs for memory efficiency. There will be many examples throughout the book, mostly in C++ (or in a simple representative assembly language). Because we will use the Intel P6 architecture for illustrative purposes, programmers targeting Pentium Pro or Pentium II-based machines will reap an extra benefit.

Part 1: Architecture and Organization

Chapter 1 is a review of modern processor computation basics. In Chapter 1 we look at processor organization and the instruction execution sequence in modern processors. We also look at the instruction pipeline and introduce some hardware optimizations for performance such as superpipelining, superscalar processors, and branch prediction.

Chapter 2 introduces the memory hierarchy and discusses its importance. A focus of the chapter is the concept of locality of reference, which refers to the relationship between "nearness" of computation and performance within the memory hierarchy. The range of different kinds of memory systems that are connected in a computer make up a memory hierarchy.

Chapter 3 contains details on the structure of caches. There are a number of ways that data are moved in and out of caches, and consequently there are many ways in which a program—and how it is written—can affect the movement of cached data. This chapter elaborates on the architectural structure of a cache, and then elaborates on the algorithms used to control the cache, such as algorithms for bringing data into the cache and writing it back out, and cache line replacement strategies.

On the basis of a clear description of how the different levels of memory interact with each other hardwarewise (from Chapter 1), Chapter 4 describes paging, paged memory systems, and details about how pages are kept track of in memory. In particular, Chapter 4 covers how the page table held in a translation lookaside buffer (TLB) works, and the costs of using paged memory.

Chapter 5 covers disk systems and the interaction between memory and disks.

Part 2: Performance

Performance programming begins with an understanding of the different kinds of optimizations that can take place. Chapter 6 is an introduction to optimization basics, and covers the kinds of transformations that optimizing compilers perform.

In Chapter 7, we will look at tools and techniques to help with performance analysis, including a look at profiling and application timing. We see how analysis and timing can help pinpoint program trouble spots, and concentrate on learning how to choose the best opportunities for improvement. In particular, we look at some frequently used algorithm paradigms and their memory access behavior.

Chapter 8 follows with a collection of tips for writing optimizable code.

Chapter 9 elucidates dependence analysis (enough to give a beginning programmer a good basic understanding), using examples of linked lists and other loop-oriented code such as vector and matrix operations to show different kinds of dependencies. We also look at ways to discover data dependencies.

Chapter 10 discusses advanced optimization and covers some interesting cache-optimization techniques. In particular, topics such as cache blocking, software prefetch, cache tiling, cache images, and multi-level blocking are covered.

In Chapter 11, we introduce the concepts of concurrency and parallelism, and the differences between heavy processes and lightweight threads. We look at scheduling for processes and threads, and how thread scheduling interacts with memory allocation and data distribution. We show how transformations from Chapter 10 are applied to identify and separate opportunities for concurrency, as well as how dependence analysis can be used to find fine-grained parallelism at the instruction level, including instruction scheduling for superscalar processors and software pipelining.

Part 3: Final Thoughts

Chapter 12, the conclusion, discusses the future of caches and memory hierarchies, compiler optimizations, and some novel ideas for automatically improving application performance. One example is new ways in which instructions are executed, including software prefetch, cache-control instructions, stream registers, out-of-order execution, and VLIW chips with separate memory access instruction streams. Also, this chapter discusses how compilers are written to take advantage of these hardware innovations. In addition, multiple processor architectures and their specific memory issues are covered.

Architecture
and
Organization

1

CPU Execution Basics

The General Structure of Computer Systems

High-performance programmers rely on a good understanding of the nature of application computation. To this end, it is useful to review some basics of computer architecture and organization. For the sake of clarity, we will distinguish between "new" processor architectures that have been developed over the past 7 to 10 years (including, for example, RISC, superpipelined, and VLIW) and what we will call "traditional" processor architectures developed prior to 10 years ago (e.g., CISC architectures). Traditional computers are organized around three logical parts: the computational engine, an area of transient storage embodied as the main memory (and virtual memory), and a set of interfaces to the outside world (see Fig. 1.1). These three logical parts are respectively embodied by the CPU, main memory, and various I/O devices for controlling the machine and reporting results. All computer applications, ranging from PC apps to mainframe projects, manipulate input data to compute solutions that are presented to the application users. These data necessarily must flow through the different parts of the computer.

As a matter of abstraction, we can safely say that the flow of data in any application is encapsulated in the way that the program is stored, loaded, and executed. A programmer writes a program and then passes it through a compiler, which generates a sequence of executable instructions. These instructions are assembled into an executable file. The executable file is then stored on the disk to await invocation. When the user invokes the program, the executable file is accessed from the disk and loaded into main memory, and execution begins at the first

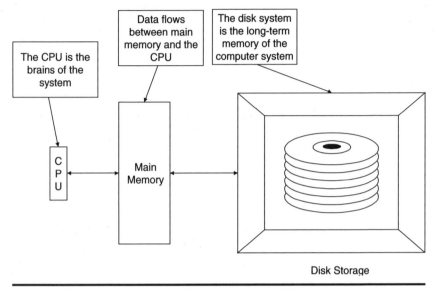

Figure 1.1   The organization of a traditional computer architecture.

instruction in the code sequence. As the program executes, both instructions and data are read from different levels of memory (as well as through some levels of cache) into the CPU. Data items are loaded into registers, values are computed, and the results are stored back to memory. As the program completes its result, the resulting solution is piped through an output device, typically to a CRT terminal or to a file on disk.

CPUs and Computation

In older complex instruction set computers (CISC) machine organizations, the functionality of the chip is encompassed by a large number of instructions in the assembly language instruction set. Instructions will typically make use of a flexible set of *addressing modes.* Addressing modes are used to represent different ways to access operands. These include constants, registers, memory (i.e., directly addressed references), and even memory-deferred addressing (i.e., a double reference such as the contents of the address stored in a memory address). The increased flexibility comes at the expense of predictability and performance. In CISC machines, instruction lengths are not of a standard length; one instruction could take up 4 bytes or 9 bytes. Operation timings are also unpredictable (to some extent) because the same operation with different addressing modes may take drastically different times.

Modern processor architects tend to more predictable operations, both in instruction size and execution time. Even in more modern reduced instruction set computers (RISC) microprocessors, there is usually still a healthy set of instructions. With the reduced set of instructions, though, the same computations that had been performed on a CISC machine using a small number of specialized instructions will require a larger number of instructions on the RISC machine.

The load/store execution model

Modern machines make use of a *load/store* execution model. In this model, the flexible addressing modes are eliminated. Instead, the only operands allowed are constants or registers. A data value operand in memory must first be loaded into a register before it may be used in an instruction. Similarly, a result value must be explicitly stored into a memory location.

All RISC assembly instructions look vaguely similar. Because the execution model is so simple, the instruction sets tend to reflect this simplicity. Since our goal is to investigate performance optimizations, we will choose a representation of assembly instruction execution. The following pseudo-instruction set will serve our purposes, as it conveys the "look and feel" of microprocessor execution.

A simple assembly language

For the sake of clarity, we will distinguish between different classes of operations that the CPU can perform. For the sake of generality, we will use a simplified assembly language that easily maps high-level source code to the same instructions on most RISC machines. These classes of operations are:

- *Integer operations,* including integer arithmetic operations such as *add, subtract, multiply, divide;* logical operations such as *and, or, exclusive or, shift right, shift left;* operations that cast integers into floating-point operands; and comparison operations

- *Floating-point operations,* including arithmetic operations on floating point operands such as *fadd, fmul, fdiv, frcp* (reciprocal)

- *Memory operations,* such as *load* and *store*

- *Branch operations,* which change the instruction pointed to by the instruction pointer

All operations will be represented by a quadruple format, in which (other than memory and branch operations) all instructions consist of four components: an operator, at most two source operands (constants or registers), and a target operand register. The final register is always the target operand. A simple example, integer add, would look like this:

    add r1, r2, r3

which means add the values in register r1 and register r2 and store the result in register r3.

Memory operations always have two operands—a memory location and a register. In a *load* instruction, the memory location is the first operand and the destination register is the second operand. In a *store* instruction, the source register is the first operand and the destination location is the second operand. For example,

    load (r2), r4

will load the value stored in the memory location referenced in register r2, and bring it into register r4. The instruction

    store r6, [0x7fff0012]

stores the value in register r6 into the absolute memory address 0x7fff0012.

Branch instructions use the CPU comparison flags and jump the execution pointer to the new location. The branch instruction

    bge LOOP1

will branch to LOOP1 if the previous instruction set the greater than or equal flags.

Programs written into all high-level languages should reduce to the same assembly language. Consider this assembly language example:

```
LOOP1:    load (r1), r2       ; load from array a
          load (r3), r4       ; load from array b
          add r2, r4, r5      ; add the values
          store r5, (r6)      ; store the result into array c
          add r1, 4, r1       ; increment the pointer into array a
          add r3, 4, r3       ; increment the pointer into array b
          compare r1, r7      ; have we finished?
          ble LOOP1           ; if not, execute again
```

In BASIC, the code would look like this:

```
            DO 100 I = 1, 100
               C(I) = A(I) + B(I)
    100     LOOP
```

In C++, the code would look like this:

```
        for (i = 0; i < = 100; i ++ )
           c(i) = a(i) + b(i);
```

In Fortran, the code would look like this:

```
        FOR I = 1,100,1
           C(I) = A(I) + B(I)
```

The fact that different programming languages should be transformed into the same assembly language indicates that the ideas we discuss will apply to all these languages. We will use C++ as the language of choice, but remember that the optimizations will apply in other languages.

The CPU

The CPU (or processor) consists of two critical pieces: the datapath and the control. The datapath contains the "brains" of the processor: the arithmetic logic unit (ALU), other computational units, the registers, and the mechanism to carry communication between them. The control contains the hardware to control the execution of instructions. An internal clock cycle time, usually measured in megahertz (MHz), is determined by the slowest time it takes for control information to flow to the required locations in the processor. A processor with a speed of 350 MHz will have a clock that counts 350,000,000 cycles each second. The control is designed to organize the different phases of instruction execution.

The stages of execution

Instructions are executed as a sequence of stages. Each of these stages, which together complete the execution of a single instruction, may take one or more clock cycles. While the number of specific stages in different processor implementations may vary, there are generally five classes of stages. In a RISC architecture, these stages are:

1. Instruction fetch
2. Instruction decode/register fetch
3. Execution

4. Memory reference

5. Write-back

During the first stage, called the instruction fetch stage, the next instruction is fetched from memory and loaded into an instruction register. As soon as the instruction arrives at the processor, the CPU must determine what kind of instruction it is, how many arguments the instruction takes, and from where to get those arguments. This occurs during the instruction decode stage. During the same stage, the processor also detects which registers from the collection of registers known as the register file will be used as arguments to the instruction (see Fig. 1.2). As soon as the source registers have been determined, the data in those registers are brought into the CPU. When the arguments have arrived, the CPU enters the next stage of instruction processing, called the execution stage. During this stage, the desired computation is performed. If the instruction is an arithmetic or logical operation, the ALU computes the value. If the instruction is a memory operation, the data address registers are prepared for the memory reference. If the instruction is a branch operation, the destination branch address is computed. During the fourth stage, called the memory reference stage, the data value residing in memory at the specified address is either loaded or stored (depending on the instruction). The final stage, called the write-back stage (Fig. 1.3), is when a result computed by the ALU is shunted back to the register file.

Execution pipelining

Because the execution of an instruction is separable into distinct phases, as soon as the current instruction enters its second stage it is possible to begin the first stage of the execution of the next instruction. In fact, it is possible to have a different instruction executing in each of the stages all at the same time. Each instruction advances a stage at the end of each clock cycle. This is known as an instruction pipeline (Fig. 1.4). As such, in a five-stage instruction pipeline computer, it may be possible for five instructions to be executing simultaneously. This form of instruction-level parallelism is commonly found in most modern microprocessors. More advanced forms of instruction-level parallelism (in particular, those forms that are controlled by the programmer) will be discussed in Chapter 11.

Hazards

It is important at this point to understand that the instruction pipeline continues in an efficient manner only as long as there are no

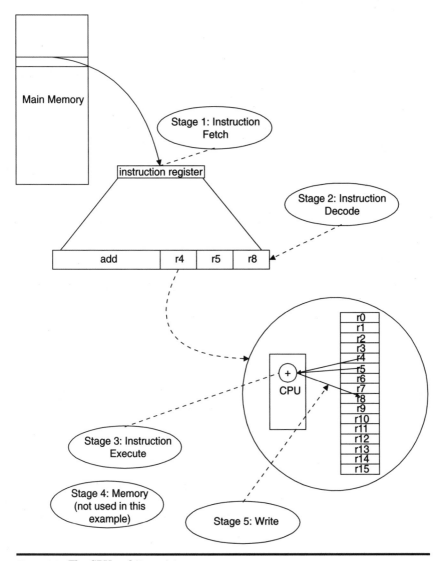

Figure 1.2 The CPU and its registers.

hazards or stalls that break the pipeline. A hazard is a situation that prevents the instruction pipeline from executing instructions in their specific cycle. There are three types of hazards:

- Structural hazards
- Control hazards
- Data hazards

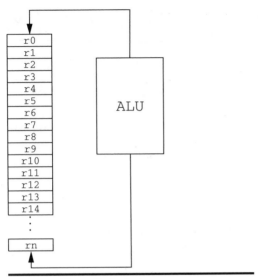

Figure 1.3 The write-back stage.

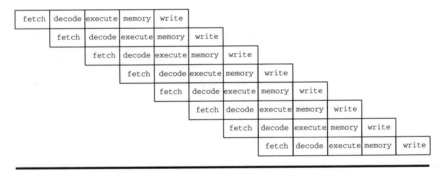

Figure 1.4 The instruction pipeline.

A *structural hazard* occurs when two instructions cannot execute in their appointed cycle because of a hardware conflict preventing the simultaneous execution. A *control hazard* occurs when jumps or branches break the instruction stream and begin execution at another point in the program. A *data hazard* occurs when one instruction uses data operands that are the result of a previous instruction (or instructions) that have not yet completed.

Structural hazards

A structural hazard is a hazard due to the need of a specific resource by more than one instruction at the same time. For example, a load instruction may need to send an address through the bus in two parts when data are requested from a memory location. If one load instruction follows another, the first load may be in its second bus transaction when the next load attempts to initiate its first bus transaction. Because the bus is currently being use by the first load, this structural hazard will force the second load to wait until the bus resource is free.

A good analogy is that of two railroad trains traveling along the same track in opposite directions. It is structurally impossible for the two trains to travel over the same piece of track at the same time—that is indeed hazardous! To handle this structural hazard, there are occasional track spurs where one train will wait while the other passes.

Control hazards

Because the instruction execution stream is pipelined, the CPU will load instructions prior to their execution. Hopefully, preloading the instructions will ensure a smooth instruction execution sequence. But when a branch appears in the code, different instructions than those already preloaded will be executed, and the preloaded instructions will be ignored. When this control hazard occurs, the instruction pipeline must be flushed and restarted by fetching instructions from the destination location. Hardware optimizations for branching help to get around the problems of some control hazards.

Data hazards

Data hazards appear either because a computed value is not yet ready (i.e., the value has not been written to the register file), or data values fetched from memory have not yet been delivered to the register file. The stalling of an instruction execution sequence due to the inability to deliver a stream of data from memory to the CPU exposes what is called the memory bottleneck. Any time that a stream of instruction requires fetching data from main memory, the instruction pipeline will stall because of a data hazard. Because there is a speed difference between accessing data in registers and accessing data in main memory, if the arguments come from memory instead of from registers, then the instruction pipeline must stall until the requested data is brought in from memory. When CPUs execute instructions at a faster rate than the data delivery rate, an attempt must be made to accommodate the bottleneck. These attempts are usually encapsulated by hardware improvements to the memory levels or by programming application code in a memory-aware manner.

Superscalar Architectures

In modern microprocessors, classes of different operations are different enough to separate the actual computations into different execution units that compose the CPU. Remember that we talked about integer, floating-point, memory, and branch operations. As an example, a processor may have an integer and logical computation unit, a floating-point computation unit, a memory unit to handle memory instructions, and a branch unit to deal with branches. Often, the floating-point unit may be in turn composed of multiple functional units, such as separate floating-point addition and floating-point multiplication units (see Fig. 1.5).

By separating the computations into different functional units, the processor can separate the instructions that are executed on each of these units, effectively turning a single instruction stream into multiple instruction streams. With multiple functional units, the processor can initiate more than one instruction on every clock cycle. An architecture that allows multiple instruction issue is called a *superscalar* architecture. Superscalar means that the processor can achieve better than scalar performance if the multiple instruction units can be kept busy.

Superpipelining

Some architectures optimize the pipelining of instruction execution by increasing the number of the pipeline stages while decreasing the amount of work that is performed during each pipeline stage. By doing this, more instructions can be in execution ("in flight") simultaneously. At the same time, since less work is being done in each stage, the processor clock rate can be increased, thereby achieving a greater overall throughput. An architecture that makes use of a deep pipeline, or uses pipelines for all the execution units, is called a *superpipelined* architecture.

What may not be clear right away is that when processors have a longer instruction pipeline, the sequence of instructions being executed must be long enough to warrant the pipeline optimization. In other words, if instruction sequences are short, then the pipeline cannot be kept filled at all times, which then negates the parallelism effect.

Branch Optimizations

Instruction sequences can be short when the sequence is interrupted by branching. When a branch takes place, the sequence is broken, and any instructions that were in the pipeline are to be ignored. The pipeline will need to be restarted when instructions are loaded from the branch target location.

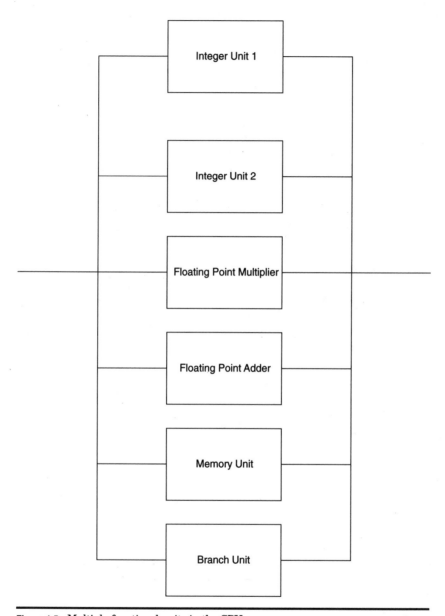

Figure 1.5 Multiple functional units in the CPU.

Branch prediction

To get around this problem, another hardware optimization called *branch prediction* is used to keep the pipeline filled as much as possible. When a branch instruction is seen, the processor "guesses" which way the execution will continue—either the branch is taken or it is not taken. When the processor guesses, it will continue to load and initiate instructions along the guessed instruction sequence. If the guess was right, the execution pipeline continues uninterrupted. If the guess was incorrect, the penalty is no different than if no branch prediction had taken place.

The branch target buffer

Instruction pipelines work well as long as the instruction sequence continues unbroken. If the sequence is broken by a branch, the instructions in the pipeline need to be flushed, and the pipeline needs to be refilled.

One way this interruption is avoided at a branch is to feed instructions from the branch target address into the instruction fetch buffer. A branch target buffer keeps track of the branches that have already been seen along with their targets. Every time a branch instruction is executed, the address of the branch and the target of that branch are inserted as a pair into the branch target buffer.

Branches that have been seen are predicted dynamically and those that have not been seen are predicted statically. An example of a branch prediction algorithm is based on the previous behavior of the code. A branch can be predicted to be *taken* or *not taken.*

The simplest form of branch prediction is encapsulating the branch history in a single bit buffer associated with each entry in the branch target buffer. If the branch is predicted to be taken, when the branch is executed the instructions are loaded from the branch target. If the branch is correctly predicted to be taken, execution may continue uninterrupted. If the branch is incorrectly predicted, the filled instruction prefetch buffer must be flushed and restarted at the correct instruction pointer location, thereby causing a significant processing delay. The prediction bit is then inverted, indicating that the next prediction is for that branch to be not taken.

The Intel P6 Architecture

The Intel P6 architecture is the basis for the Intel Pentium Pro and the Pentium II processors. The P6 architecture is an example of an organization that is both superscalar and superpipelined. Even though the assembly language for the P6 is based on the x86 architecture assembly language, the P6 architecture transforms Intel x86 assembly macro-instructions into simple microinstructions called micro-ops. The P6 architecture makes use of a dynamic execution framework that allows *out-of-order execution*. Out-of-order execution, which we will detail below, allows a more flexible hardware instruction scheduling, where instructions may be initiated out of their original sequence, but are guaranteed to complete in the original order. There are several instruction pipelines, and different execution units (e.g., integer or floating-point units) may share a pipeline.

The execution sequence of the P6 architecture is broken into three logical phases: the fetch/decode phase, the dispatch and execute phase, and the retirement phase (see Fig. 1.6). During the fetch/decode phase, instructions are streamed into the CPU (the same way as described above). To allow the optimized out-of-order execution, the execute stage is broken into two substages. One stage is the dispatch and execute stage, where instructions are chosen for initiation, and a retirement stage where instructions wait to complete until the preceding instructions have completed. Decoded micro-ops are forwarded to an *instruction pool*. The dispatch unit then schedules the micro-ops in the instruction pool on the basis of their dependencies. As long as an instruction is not waiting on a hazard, it may be scheduled and executed. If an instruction's data dependencies have been satisfied, or if there are no resource constraints, the instruction may be executed. This allows the dispatch unit to schedule instructions out of their original sequence.

Once an instruction is executed, its result must be reserved until the instructions preceding it in the original sequence have been committed. The instructions awaiting retirement are stored back in the instruction pool, where the retirement unit commits instructions in their correct sequence.

Out-of-order execution

Allowing out-of-order execution coupled with a deep instruction pipeline sequence will increase performance as long as there is a steady stream of instructions coming into the execution phase of the CPU. Out-of-order execution can be seen as a hardware solution to a memory latency problem. Consider this instruction sequence:

```
(1) load  (r2), r1; load contents of memory address in r2 into r1
(2) add   r1, r3, r4
(3) add   r5, r7, r6
(4) sub   r9, 21, r8
```

In instruction (1), a memory location is fetched. If the data are not readily available in the cache, the access will require a load from main

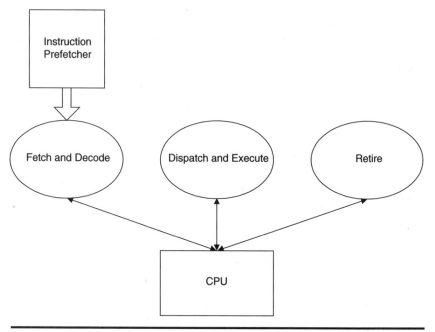

Figure 1.6   The three phases of execution for the P6 architecture.

memory, which will incur a small delay. Instruction (2), however, uses the result of the load (the value in register r1). In a traditional architecture, the execution of instruction (2) stalls while the cache miss is serviced.

But a processor with dynamic execution may initiate any subsequent instructions with no pending dependencies. So, in this example, both instructions (3) and (4) may begin execution out of order. Since the completion sequence of the instructions must be the same as the original specified order, the results of executing instructions (3) and (4) may not be committed until instructions (1) and then (2) complete. Instead, the instructions are shuffled to the retirement pool to await the appropriate retirement order.

P6 branch prediction

The dynamic branch prediction of the P6 architecture makes use of a 4-bit branch prediction history. If a branch is not in the branch target buffer, the execution is predicted to continue without branching (i.e., to fall through). Branches that are not in the branch target buffer are predicted using a static branch prediction algorithm. The algorithm states that

1. Unconditional branches are predicted to be taken.

2. Backward conditional branches are predicted to be taken.

3. Forward conditional branches are predicted to be not taken.

Item 1 is logical in that unconditional branches should always be taken, since an unconditional jump statement (such as GOTO) will always be executed. Items 2 and 3 are suitable for loops; typically, the conditional branch statement at the bottom of a loop is to loop back to the beginning of the loop.

Summary

In this chapter, we introduced the general structure of computer systems, made up of the CPU, memory, and I/O devices. Our focus on the CPU led us to the distinction between CISC and RISC computers, and the load/store execution model. We introduced a simple assembly language that we will use to model execution on our target machines.

This chapter also looked at the CPU, registers, and the execution pipeline, including the fetch, decode, execute, and store stages. We introduced structural, control, and data hazards, superscalar architectures, superpipelined architectures, and branch optimization. Finally, we looked at an example of a modern processor architecture, the Intel P6 architecture.

2

The Memory Hierarchy

In Chapter 1, we looked at processor execution and the load/store execution models. Here, we will look at how the load/store model causes reverberations through the computer system and the effects on application performance. Since data values must be loaded into registers before computations may take place, the topic of data motion becomes important. Data values actually are present at different levels of memory locations during execution, and efficient movement between these levels, known as the *memory hierarchy,* becomes a driving force in performance programming. This chapter introduces the memory hierarchy. In particular, we will look at the movement of information across the different memory components of the computer system that make up the memory hierarchy.

What Is a Memory Hierarchy?

The word *hierarchy* evokes the notion of a series of graded or ranked levels. The memory hierarchy refers to the different levels of memory in a computer system. Memory levels in the system are graded by the memory's performance, price, and size. All computers have multiple levels in a memory hierarchy, and the differences in size and price will have an effect on the system's cost, as well as the system's performance.

In Chapter 1, we examined instruction execution, but we glossed over the details of how the instructions as well as the operands were accessed in memory. In fact, there is a significant difference between loading a program from disk into main memory, loading instructions from memory into the CPU, and loading data from memory into the registers used as operands during execution. The register file and the main memory are only two types of memory. The major features of a *memory hierarchy* are that data move between two adjacent levels in the hierarchy, and data movement is managed between two levels at a time. An upper level typically acts as a temporary buffer for data. Any two adjacent levels can be referred to as an upper and a lower level, and data that are stored in the upper level are reflected in the lower level also.

As an example, consider this simple program fragment:

```
x = 10;
for (i = 0; i < x; i++)
        cout << i << endl;
```

This example shows how certain data values can exist at different levels of memory. In the compiled code for this sample, which is stored on disk, the value 10 is stored in a text segment in the object file. When the program is invoked, the program is loaded into main memory, including the constant value 10. At execution time, the instruction corresponding to $x = 10$ will bring the value 10 from memory into a register.

Typically, the higher a memory unit is in the hierarchy, the smaller and more expensive the medium used for that level. As an example, the register file would be the highest level of a memory hierarchy, and magnetic tape may be the lowest level of that hierarchy. Other levels in the memory hierarchy are first-level caches, second-level caches, main memory, etc.

Memory hierarchy basics

These are the characteristics of the memory hierarchy:

1. In a memory hierarchy, there are different levels of memory.
2. The highest level of the memory hierarchy has
   - The greatest performance
   - The highest price
   - The smallest capacity

3. Moving down the hierarchy, the levels
   - Decrease in performance
   - Decrease in price
   - Increase in capacity

4. During execution, data values that are moved into a high level of the memory hierarchy are frequently shadowed in lower levels of the memory hierarchy.

5. Not all the data required during execution can exist in the memory hierarchy level closest to the CPU at the same time.

Item 1 indicates the existence of different kinds of memory in a computer system (see Fig. 2.1). Items 2 and 3 are the cost drivers for building high-performance computer systems: the greater the power needed during execution, the more money must be spent on the expensive high-performance components. This can be borne out by simple empirical evidence at the local Mega-Compu-Mart, where caches (the highest performing memory) are the most expensive per megabyte (MB), RAM SIMM modules are less expensive (at the time of this writing, about $8/MB), and hard-disk drives are extremely inexpensive (at the time of this writing, about $50/GB).

Item 4 on the above list is important in that it implies that when data values are shadowed in different levels, and there are multiple copies of the data item at the different levels, a modification to a copy at a higher level must be reflected somehow in the copies in lower levels. Item 5 points out that data values need to be shuttled between levels of the hierarchy, often requiring transfers of data between two components running at different speeds. These points drive our discussion of performance programming, which will be enhanced by an overview of memory hierarchy management.

Multilevel inclusion

Levels of a memory hierarchy share a property known as *multilevel inclusion*. This property indicates that a copy of some data sitting in an upper level of the memory hierarchy is shadowed by a copy at one

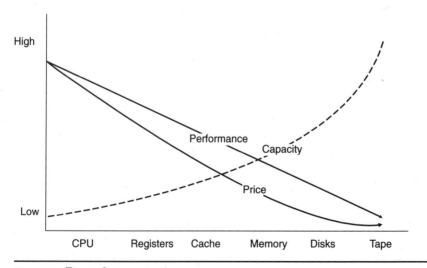

Figure 2.1 Types of memory.

or more lower levels in the hierarchy. When dealing with multilevel inclusion, it is important to remember that modifications to a copy of data at one level of the hierarchy must be reflected back at some point to the copies lying in lower levels. (See Fig. 2.2.)

Data blocking

The unit of measurement for data values in a memory hierarchy is called a *block*. A block is the smallest area of a memory hierarchy level in which a data value may be present. The size of a block is related to the level in the hierarchy. At the register level, a block may consist of a single word; at the cache level, a block may consist of four words, etc.

During execution, when a data value is requested, each level starting from the top of the hierarchy is searched to see if the value is sitting in a block at that level. If the block is found in a level of the hierarchy, the memory access is referred to as a *hit* at that level. If the block is not present, that is referred to as a *miss,* in which case the next subsequent levels are searched until the data are found. Finding a data value at a high level of the hierarchy is good, because as different levels of the hierarchy are searched, the amount of time the execution is stalled waiting for data increases. Therefore, ultimately our goal is to increase the number of hits and decrease the number of misses.

Characterizing Memory Performance Costs

Since our goal is to evaluate performance, it is important to characterize the cost of accessing data values at each level of the memory

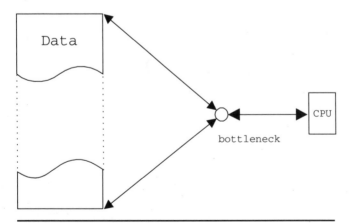

Figure 2.2 The memory bottleneck.

hierarchy. Doing this will allow us later to predict the expected performance of an algorithm based on its memory access patterns. There are four measurements that are important in gauging the cost of memory accesses at any memory hierarchy level.

The first measurement is the *hit rate*, which is the percentage of memory accesses for which a memory reference is found at a particular level in the hierarchy. The *miss rate* is the percentage of memory accesses for which a memory reference is not found at that level. The miss rate is equal to (1 − the hit rate).

The *hit time* is the time to reference and transfer a data item from the memory level at which it was hit. The *miss time* is the time to access a memory item when a miss has occurred. The miss time is mostly the penalty incurred in moving data from a slower device into the higher memory level. The miss time is the sum of the time to access the data at the lower level in the memory hierarchy (called the latency) and the time to transfer the entire data block to the upper level in the hierarchy. The transfer time is related to the amount of data that can flow at a particular rate. That rate is called the bandwidth. Once that block has been moved into the higher level, subsequent references to data in that block will hit at that level.

Example Let's go back to our example from the Introduction. Our accountant has three defined memory hierarchy levels: his desktop, his side table, and the file cabinet. When the accountant needs a file, he first looks for it at the highest level of his hierarchy, on his desktop. If it is there (i.e., it hits at the first level), he can continue working with no delay. If the file is not on the desktop (i.e., it misses at that level), he goes to the next level in the hierarchy, the side table. If the file is found on the table, it is switched with the one on top of the desk, causing a small delay in his ability to work. The amount of time the switch takes is the miss time. If the file is not found on the side table (i.e., a level 2 miss), the accountant must retrieve the file from the file cabinet, incurring an even greater miss time penalty.

Not all references will always hit at a given level, nor are all references misses. The average access time is computed as [the hit time + (the miss rate * the miss time)].

Increasing performance

Given the goal of increasing the performance by speeding the delivery of data to the CPU, it is important to lower the average access time. This can be done either by lowering the miss rate or by lowering the miss time. While a simple answer would be to improve the hardware, we will see that, to some extent, many aspects of these measurements may be brought under the programmer's control.

Locality of Reference

A guiding principle behind the idea for careful design of a memory hierarchy is the rule of thumb that programs spend 90 percent of the time executing 10 percent of the code. In other words, the bulk of any application's computing takes place in very small sections of code. The execution of a program is concentrated in a local area. This "local" area exists in the form of small snippets of code that are executed many times, or in the form of chunks of data that are subject to computation. This leads to the concepts of *locality of reference*. Locality refers to nearness of computation. There are two kinds of locality that we will discuss: *temporal* locality and *spatial* locality.

Considering locality of reference is important both in hardware design and in software design; the care in hardware design is evident by the construction of memory hierarchies in computer systems. The care for software design is needed to take advantage of the hardware! A cache is a hardware innovation designed for taking advantage of locality. We can see how this works by looking at a simple example.

Temporal locality

Temporal locality deals with nearness in time, and implies that items that are referenced will tend to be referenced again soon. For example, consider this function:

```
void function vector_add (double A[], double B[], int ARR_SIZE) {
    for (int i = 0; i < ARR_SIZE; i++)
        A[i] = A[i] + B[i];
}
```

This function, which computes a vector addition, contains one loop. The size of this code is relatively small; the vectors being added may have thousands, tens of thousands, or millions of elements, yet the instructions being executed are the same during each iteration of the loop. This loop is a good example of temporal locality as applied to instruction streams; all the time of the execution is spent in a small fragment of code, executing the same instructions many times.

Instructions must be loaded from memory into the CPU for decoding and execution. In the vector addition example, the amount of code to be read in is so small that it would be a shame to have to read it in from memory each time control is passed back to the beginning of the loop, which is where a cache comes in. An instruction cache will hold the instructions that have recently been executed; instead of loading the instructions from memory, those instructions are loaded from the cache. This saves the time to actually go out over the bus to memory to fetch the instructions. Thus, a cache is used to take advantage of temporal locality.

Spatial locality

Spatial locality deals with nearness in space. Spatial locality implies that if a data item is referenced, the chances are good that data items nearby will also be referenced. Again, the vector addition function can be used as an example. The execution of this code will fetch values from two source arrays in memory, add them and store the result in a destination array. The next iteration of the loop will take the next consecutive values from the two source arrays, add them, and store the result in the next consecutive location in the destination array. Throughout the execution, each iteration will operate on the next consecutive values; this is the spatial locality.

Again, this is where a cache comes in handy. Assuming that during each iteration the next elements in the array will be read, the computer can "read ahead," and read more than just the next value. Since only one value per array is needed per iteration, a cache is the perfect area to store those preread data. When a data item is fetched from the cache, it is brought into the CPU much faster than by reading it from memory.

In the vector addition example, each time a value is loaded, the cache is checked to see if the memory address referenced has already been "mirrored" in the cache. If it has, then the value is loaded directly from the cache. If not, a cache miss occurs, and the appropriate cache line is accessed in the lower hierarchy level, and is loaded into the cache. This protocol is based on the idea of spatial locality, and in the vector addition example, it will work well. If the cache line size is 4 items (meaning that each memory fetch out of cache will grab that item and three others also) the function will only need to go to memory once for every 4 iterations of the loop!

The anticipation is that by understanding the way locality of reference interacts with the movement of data between levels of the memory hierarchy, a programmer will be able to write code that effectively uses the hierarchy. Computer systems are constantly being improved, but the issues regarding data movement will always remain.

Unfortunately, programmers may assume that the hardware and compilers will take care of the memory hierarchy management. While the sophistication of hardware and compiler technology is impressive, it is always worthwhile to write programs that are well-tuned to the memory hierarchy.

Describing the memory hierarchy

There are four fundamental issues that are discussed in describing a level in a memory hierarchy:

- A strategy for *block placement,* which describes how and when an item is placed in a location in a memory hierarchy level.

- A strategy for *block identification,* which describes how an address is located in a memory hierarchy level.

- A strategy for *block replacement,* which describes how blocks are replaced when more space is needed at a hierarchy level.

- A *write strategy,* which describes what happens when a block is written.

We will address each of these issues with respect to specific levels of the memory hierarchy in the next few chapters.

Interlude: Optimizing Compilers

In the Introduction, we discussed the compilation of a program: the code is compiled into assembly language instructions, which are then assembled and linked into an executable object module. An optimizing compiler is a compiler that looks for opportunities to increase the execution speed of a program by applying functionality-preserving transformations to the code.

Optimizing compilers perform a number of code transformations, some of which we will profile in Chapter 6. A nice feature of an optimizing compiler is that it allows the programmer to make certain assumptions about how code is generated. For example, induction variables (variables used for loop indexes), unless passed by reference, are usually assigned to registers. As an example, consider this loop:

```
for (i = 0; i < 100; i++)
    a[i] = i;
```

This would typically be transformed into code that may look like this:

```
          mov  0, r1          ; induction variable i in r1
LOOP_1:   shl  r1, 2, r2      ; shortcut multiply by 4
          add  _a, r2, r2     ; add to base address of array a
          st   r1, (r2)       ; store i in a(i)
          inc  r1             ; increment i
          sub  100, r1, r3    ; still less than 100?
          Bgz  LOOP_1         ; jump back if i < 100
```

During code optimization, compilers make a determination as to whether program variables are assigned to memory or assigned to registers. Variables that are passed by reference to other functions, global variables, saved or static local variables, and all variables that are of a size greater than that of a register will all be assigned to memory. Variables that are local to a scope and will fit in a register will often be assigned to registers. As an example, consider this code:

```
{
        int i;
        float sum = 0.0;
        for (i = 0; i < N; i++)
                sum = sum + A[i];
        printf("The sum is %f\n", sum);
}
```

In this example, the variable i is defined inside the scope, and is only used locally as an induction variable within the for loop. Therefore, this variable would typically be assigned to a register, and not to memory. However, the referenced array A would require memory storage, because it is an array (and would not fit into a register). In fact, even though the array A requires storage, each of its elements actually is loaded into a register, since in our load/store model, data operand must be in registers before operations may be performed. During each iteration of the loop, the ith element of A (A[i]) needs to be loaded into a register before it can be added to sum.

Introduction to the Hierarchy

There are many levels to a memory hierarchy. In this section we will discuss the top levels of the memory hierarchy.

Registers

Registers represent the hierarchy level closest to the CPU. Registers are usually incorporated as part of the chip architecture; consequently, the time to access data from a register is the fastest. On the other hand, because the registers are incorporated into the chip, the "real estate" needed for registers is limited, thereby limiting the number of registers available.

In today's common RISC machines, a data item may be retrieved from a register into the CPU during a single cycle. Because the access time is the fastest, fetching data from a register will not cause a delay in the instruction pipeline (unless the value in the register is one that is still being computed). The fastest computer applications are written so that needed data reside in registers as often as possible. There are not too many computers that have more than 64 general-purpose registers.

In most programs there are more data items that are accessed or computed than there are registers to hold them. That is why optimizing compilers attempt to make sure that needed data are in registers as much as possible. This means trying to make sure the data are available when needed, but clearing out items from registers when those data will not be required for a while. This implies that registers are often spilled, or copied, to memory in order to make space for other data items. The problem of optimal register allocation, which is making sure the assignment of program variables to registers in a way that minimizes the amount of copying and spilling that needs to be done, is a problem that is known to belong to a class of problems that require an exponential amount of computation. Therefore, shortcuts are taken in optimizing compilers by applying heuristic algorithms to try to get a good register allocation which may not be the absolute optimal allocation.

Cache

A cache is a small buffer of relatively fast memory that is used to hold values that have recently been read from memory. The cache sits below the registers in the hierarchy, and above main memory. Caches are of limited size, but will hold more data than can fit into registers. Data values that have been loaded into registers will most often be in blocks that have already been loaded into the cache, and blocks that have been loaded into cache reflect blocks of data sitting in main memory.

Main memory is much larger than the cache, and subsequently will hold many more values. Because any address reference into memory must be able to be brought into the cache, memory addresses must be mapped into the cache space (Fig. 2.3). That means that each block address in the cache may reflect a number of different memory blocks at different times.

The access time for data from the cache is very fast when compared to main memory. Typically, data residing in the cache may be accessed in 1 or 2 clock cycles. A cache is designed to be a low-latency, high-bandwidth module. Caches are often engineered into the microprocessor chip; these caches are called on-chip caches. As with registers, chip real estate is expensive, and therefore on-chip caches are expensive. Caches may also be used to separate connected memory chips. In this case, a special type of memory is used to guarantee fast access time, which also raises the cost of the cache.

Often systems are organized with more than one level of cache. In these cases, there may be small caches (used for instructions, data, or both) called *level 1 caches* (or *L1* cache) located on the microprocessor

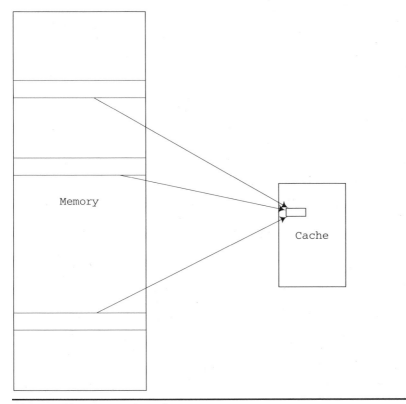

Figure 2.3 Mapping into the cache.

chip, and a much larger off-chip cache called a *level 2* (or *L2*) cache. (See Fig. 2.4.)

Main memory

The main memory level is the next level below the cache. Memory serves both as a repository for all the data and code in a program and as an interface for I/O for the applications. Memory has a higher latency than the cache, but will have a lower bandwidth.

Memory can be constructed from different kinds of memory chips: the dynamic RAM (random access memory) chip (DRAM) or the static RAM or (SRAM). Data are stored and referenced in a chip in blocks that are organized as a 2-dimensional array of rows and columns. The time to access memory is broken up into two parts: the access time, which is the time it takes to access a memory reference, and the cycle time, which is the time required between requests to memory.

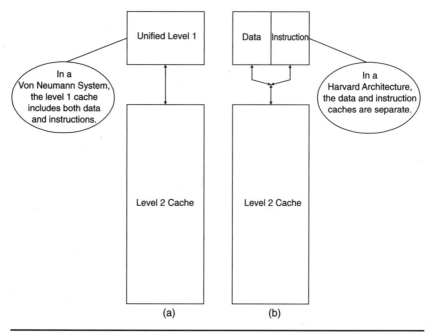

Figure 2.4 (*a*) A unified cache. (*b*) Separate data and instruction caches.

The "dynamic" part of a DRAM chip indicates the characteristic of the chip that each row in the memory must be accessed within a short time span or else the data are lost. This forces the DRAM chip to write back data after it is read. Thus the cycle time is increased, because the chips may be busy refreshing the data. This is opposed to the "static" RAM, which, through the use of more hardware, does not need to be refreshed. The additional hardware allows for a faster overall memory reference time, because there is a reduction in the cycle time. However, the cost of SRAM chips is significantly higher than that of DRAM chips. Also, SRAM chips hold much less data than DRAM chips.

DRAM chips are the most popular for main memory modules. SRAM chips are used in specialized hardware needing fast access memory and are the primary kind of memory chip used for caches.

Virtual memory

In a computer system that allows multiprocessing, many processes will be running simultaneously. Each process has its own memory requirements, and these requirements may exceed the amount of physical memory. Also, a single process may require a large memory area. Yet the amount of physical memory is limited. This constraint has led to the development of virtual memory. In a computer system that supports virtual memory, the physical memory area is shared, both between different processes and within the memory needs of a single process.

A process's memory is divided into blocks, called *pages*. Physical memory is divided into same-sized *page frames*. A process's pages are loaded into physical memory. Because the process's address space is only virtually contiguous, and not necessarily physically contiguous, there are no constraints as to where each page is loaded into memory. In fact, pages are relocatable, which means that a page may be removed from one page frame during the execution of a program and inserted into a different page frame later, in a way that is transparent to the process.

As the program runs, memory addresses are referenced. A referenced virtual address, which is a 0-based index into a specific process's address space, must be transformed into a physical address. This process, known as *address translation,* determines the physical location of a memory reference. This consists of determining the page in which an address lives, if that page has been loaded into memory, where that page has been loaded into physical memory, and transforming the address into a real offset into that page. A hardware page table is used to assist in the page lookup process.

But what if that page has not been loaded into memory? This page miss will cause a page fault. During a page fault, the needed page is found in the backing store, a loaded page is possibly "kicked out" of memory (referred to as *eviction*) and the needed page is loaded into memory. When the new page has finished loading, the internal page table is updated to reflect the current view of the memory map. The cost of a page fault is significant; we will examine these issues in greater detail in Chapter 4.

Disks

As virtual memory uses a secondary storage unit (usually a disk) to copy memory pages that are not currently held in physical memory, we must elaborate on the disk as the next level in the memory hierarchy. In line with its position in the memory hierarchy, disks are much slower than the previous hierarchy level (memory), but will hold a large amount of data.

A disk itself is organized as a hierarchy of storage units. A disk consists of a collection of *platters,* each of which contains one or two *surfaces* on which data are written. Like a vinyl record or a CD, data are laid out on each surface as a collection of *tracks*. Each track is divided into the basic storage unit, the *sector.* Many systems will have the sector be the same size as the memory page.

Data are read and written to a disk using a *read / write* head that is positioned over a track as the disk spins. In order to read from or write to a disk, the read/write head must be moved to the right track, and then the disk must spin until the requested sector appears beneath the head, at which time the referenced location is accessed. As opposed to caches and main memory, which are electronic devices, the disk requires mechanical action before a memory location is referenced; this adds significantly to the cost of accessing data at this level in the hierarchy.

The time it takes to access the disk is a sum of the time needed to perform a number of actions. The movement of the read/write head is called a *seek,* and the time for the read/write head to move to the right track is referred to as the *seek time.* The time for the disk to rotate until the right sector appears beneath the head, once the read/write head has been positioned over the right track, is called the *disk latency.* As soon as the sector is found, the amount of time to transfer the data between the disk and the I/O bus is called the *transfer time.* The time for a disk access is the sum of the seek time, the disk latency, and the transfer time.

Other processors

In a multiple processor system, there may be interaction between the different processors when cooperative operations are performed. Because of this, we can view the data provided at different sites in the multiple processor system as being a level in the memory hierarchy (Fig. 2.5). Data are communicated using *messages,* which are packaged into same-size chunks and pushed into a network, from where the packages are plucked and unbundled, then restored to the original message.

> **Example** The Intel P6 Memory Hierarchy The Intel P6 architecture's memory hierarchy includes an on-chip cache subsystem consisting of a primary cache (called the L1 cache), an off-chip secondary cache (called the L2 cache), and an off-chip main memory system. Main memory is accessed via a 64-bit transaction-oriented bus. (In a transaction-oriented bus, each access is treated as a separate transaction.)
>
> The L2 cache is accessed via a separate 64-bit cache bus, which can process four concurrent cache accesses. The L1 cache is accessed through internal buses. A miss in the L1 cache is automatically forwarded to the L2 cache, and if the reference misses in the L2 cache, the miss is then forwarded directly to main memory.

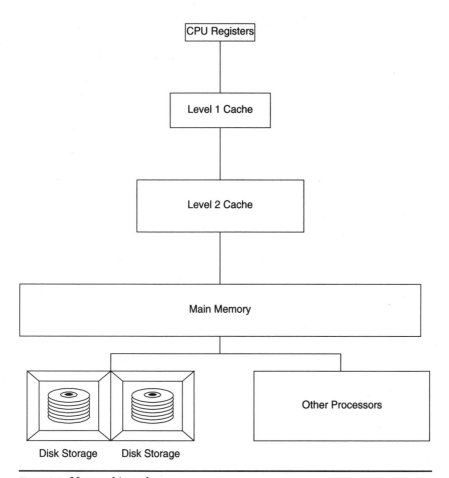

Figure 2.5 Memory hierarchy.

Summary

In this chapter, we introduced the memory hierarchy, looking at the common attributes of a level in the hierarchy: price, size, and performance. Also, we described how the levels are ranked by these attributes and how during execution, multilevel inclusion of data takes place. Since each higher level of memory is smaller, data are blocked into smaller chunks when propagated to a higher level of memory. We characterize the performance cost of hitting or missing at a level of the hierarchy by the hit rate, miss rate, hit time, and miss time.

Locality of reference, indicating nearness of computation, is the driving notion behind memory hierarchy management. Temporal locality refers to nearness in time, such as the reuse of instructions during the execution of a loop. Spatial locality refers to nearness in space, such as the manipulation of sequential elements in an array.

Optimizing compilers help with managing the memory hierarchy. We looked at some levels of a typical memory hierarchy: registers, cache, main memory, virtual memory, and disks.

3

The Cache

What Is a Cache?

As defined in *Webster's New Collegiate Dictionary*, a cache is a "hiding place especially for concealing and preserving provisions or implements," and "a secure place of storage." In the context of computers, the same meaning can be applied. A hardware cache is a small buffer built from fast memory that is used to store data elements that are to be used by the CPU. As used in a computer, a cache is an auxiliary storage location that "hides" both data (since caches are typically non-addressable) and latency (i.e., the time to load data from memory into the CPU).

While the notion of caches has been around for many years, the use of caches did not become general until the early 1980s. Early references in the mid-1960s referred to buffers and caches, and the latter word stuck as the generic name for a fast associative memory used to hold frequently used addresses. Many of the ideas relating to the design of caches are based on research done on virtual memory; we will see in Chapter 4 how some of the same notions apply to virtual memory systems in use today.

Before we can discuss how to write code that is cache-efficient, it is important to understand the basic architecture of a cache, and the different policies that affect cache operation. A programmer who has gained that basic understanding will be able to open a microprocessor's *Programmer Reference Manual*, read a two-line description of its cache systems, and know how to structure a program.

This chapter will first review the notion driving the need for a cache: locality of reference. We will then look into different kinds of caches.

This is followed by a discussion of the hardware design details of a cache, and how addresses are mapped into the cache. The processor bus is then introduced.

Set associativity describes how addresses are collectively mapped, and control bits that indicate cache line status are then discussed. We follow with an exposition of how the cache operates when the CPU reads and writes to memory. This includes investigating how data are brought into the cache, how items are kept up to date, and the protocols and policies for writing data back from the cache. We will discuss some simple code examples that demonstrate traps and pitfalls for cache usage. Finally, we look at performance issues, as well as some advanced topics. The chapter concludes with an overview of the Intel P6 cache system.

Locality of Reference

Caches are meant to address the issue of *locality of reference*. As introduced in Chapter 2, *locality* refers to the "neighborhood" of a piece of data, either in space or in time. With respect to *temporal locality*, the idea is that a memory address that has been referenced by a program will likely be referenced again at some close time in the future. With respect to *spatial locality*, the notion is that a data item that lives near a referenced item is likely to be referenced at some close time in the future.

A cache is designed with both these issues in mind. When the address of a data item is referenced, the contents of that memory address are brought into the cache, and reside there temporarily in the expectation that a subsequent reference by the CPU will access the copy in the cache, instead of accessing main memory. This expectation is the nature of temporal locality. Also, when one particular data item is brought into the cache, a collection of other data items that are nearby in the main memory location is also brought into the cache with the expectation that those items will also be referenced soon. This addresses the spatial locality.

Consider this code:

```
a[i] = 0.0;
for (j = 0; j < k; j++) {
    a[i] = a[i] + j;
}
```

This shows an example of taking advantage of temporal locality. The variable a[i] is referenced twice through each iteration of the loop, both being fetched and being stored. The expectation is that since the variable was referenced during one iteration, it is probable that the variable will be referred to again in a subsequent iteration.

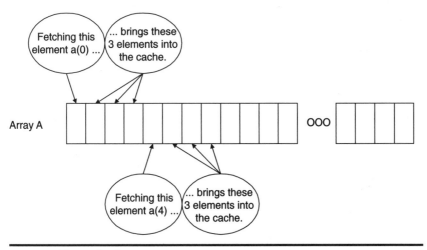

Figure 3.1 Types of cache.

The code below is a different kind of example that demonstrates a good example of spatial locality:

```
sum=0.0;
for (j = 0; j < k; j++) {
    sum = sum+A[j];
}
```

The loop is very similar to the previous example, except that each loop iteration references an array location. Note that all elements of the array A between element 0 and element k are referenced in ascending order. When the first element of the array is read from main memory, a block of elements of the array that follow the first element would be brought into the cache under the assumption that accessing one array element would potentially precede accesses to the following elements in the array. In this case, since the entire range is referenced, this assumption, based on spatial locality, would have been correct, and the subsequent references would have been found in the cache, instead of having to reference main memory (see Fig. 3.1).

As discussed in Chapter 1, the normal pipelined execution of instructions involves different kinds of memory activity. The most prevalent activity is instruction fetching, since memory is accessed for each fetched instruction. The actual execution stage of the instruction pipeline may require additional memory activity: data reads, which consist of fetching operands, and data writes, which consist of storing results of instruction execution.

Cache Types

Cache types may be distinguished by the kind of data that they hold. Cache architectures fall into four categories: *instruction* cache, *data* cache, *unified* cache, and *split* cache. An instruction cache holds only instructions, while a data cache holds only data. A unified cache holds both instructions and data, and a split cache makes use of two separate caches, one for instructions and one for data. The instruction cache is often separated from the data cache because the memory access patterns for instructions require only reading, and the memory does not need to be written back. As has been discussed, during pipelined execution, an instruction is fetched, decoded, and then executed. Because of the spatial locality of instruction issue, a special cache can be used that does not need hardware for writing. On the other hand, the accesses specific to a data cache require both reading and writing. A unified cache combines the two caches together; a split cache (known as the *Harvard architecture*) uses one set of cache hardware for the data cache and a simpler cache architecture for a separate instruction cache.

Sometimes, instead of an instruction cache there is an *instruction queue* (or an instruction prefetcher). Unlike a cache, which is indexed on the basis of the referenced memory address, an instruction queue holds onto the last few instructions executed, and prefetches the next instructions in the linear instruction stream. An instruction queue takes advantage of the spatial locality in the instruction stream. Instruction prefetchers must coordinate with branch prediction hardware.

Cache Hardware Design

In the memory hierarchy, a cache lies between the CPU/registers and the main memory modules. The cache holds quickly accessed copies of read and written memory addresses, and as we will see, is indexed through a mapping of the memory addresses referenced. The cache acts as an *associative memory,* which uses a key value to index into a set of data items. You may recall a data structure called a *hash table* from your computer science classes; a *hash table* is an example of an associative memory, and a cache works a lot like a hash table. A hash table is a data structure that stores values indexed by keys. A hash table is often implemented as an array, and an element is inserted into the hash table along with a key. A function is applied to the key to yield an index into the hash table array. A nice feature of a hash table is that the access time for a value is constant. The predictability and the speed of the access time makes the concept of the hash table ideal for a cache. With a cache, part of the referenced memory address is used as the key value, and if the cache is divided into more than one set, another part of the memory address is used to index into the right set.

When a memory address is referenced, the cache is first checked for the address. If the address has been loaded into the cache, the data are retrieved from the cache. If the address is not resident in the cache, the address must be fetched in the main memory and brought into the cache. The amount of data brought into the cache on each cache fill depends on a set of parameters. In general, these parameters can be used to classify and describe a cache:

- The size of the *addressable unit.*
- The *block,* or *line,* size.
- The *sector* size.
- The *degree of associativity.*
- The number of *sets.*

The *addressable unit* is the smallest addressable item that can be brought into the cache. Today, the size of the addressable unit is typically defined in terms of how the processor can address memory. For example, in many systems, the addressable unit is defined in terms of 4-byte words.

The *cache block,* or *cache line,* contains the smallest collection of addressable units that are brought into the cache as a group. A block with size A will contain A addressable units. Associated with each cache block is a set of bits that are used for control. For example, a valid bit will indicate that the data in the cache that corresponds to a particular address is usable, and does not need to be loaded from main memory into the cache.

The *sector* contains a number of cache blocks along with a tag. The tag is the key used to locate the address. When a memory address is referenced, the part of the address that is used as the key is compared to tags that are stored in the cache. If one of the sector's tag fields contains the address's tag value, that indicates that the memory address *resides* in the cache. If the sector size is B, then there are B cache blocks in a sector. Figure 3.2 shows an example setup for a cache.

Address Translation and Cache Mapping

The number of locations in the cache is much smaller than the number of memory locations that can be addressed, and because of this, multiple memory addresses will map into the same location in the cache (see Fig. 3.3). The cache may be broken up into collections of locations, known as *sets.* For each set in which an address may occur, the address tag is used as a key to index into a block within that set.

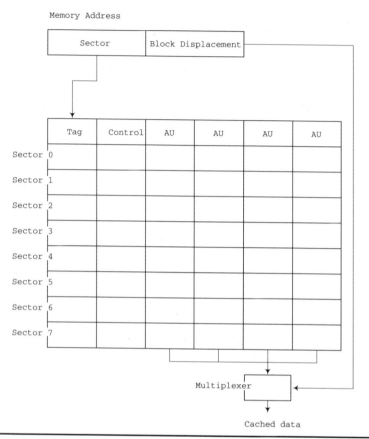

Figure 3.2   Setup of a cache.

Typically, a memory address maps into the cache via a division of the memory address into three parts. One part is used to distinguish the set that may hold the referenced address. A second part is used as the key. That key is also called a tag, and is compared to the tags that are stored with each sector. The third part is the block offset. Once a tag has been found in the cache, the block offset is used to index into the block to grab the desired addressable unit. Figure 3.4 shows how a memory address is broken up into its parts for cache mapping.

The Bus: Roadway between Cache and Memory

A *bus* is a connection path or interface between functional modules in a computer. The bus is a shared communication link between different parts of the machine. Buses are defined as a standard interface (such as the NuBus or the FutureBus), so as to allow new components to be added to the system without having to create a new intercommunication system.

A *CPU-memory* bus is a small high-speed wire connecting the CPU to main memory. The CPU-memory bus is tuned to the speed of the memory system to allow the maximization of data delivery and bus bandwidth. Communication over a bus is referred to as *bus transactions*. The first part of a bus transaction consists of sending an address as a prelude to reading or writing; the second part of a bus transaction, depending on whether it is a read or a write, respectively, receives or sends data to the sent address. A CPU executes a read transaction by sending the address to be read to the main memory, then waiting for

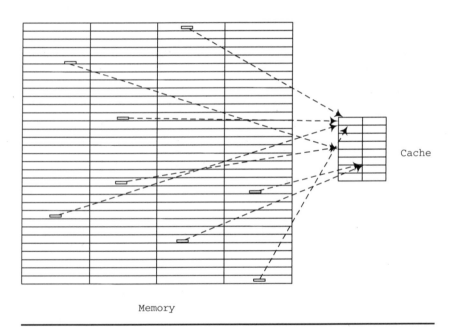

Memory

Figure 3.3 Many addresses map into same cache location.

Tag	Set Index	Displacement

Processor Address

Figure 3.4 The composition of the memory address.

the requested address's data to be sent. A write transaction on behalf of the CPU consists of sending the address to be written to the main memory, then following it up with the data to be written to that address.

When many modules are connected to the same bus, it is possible that multiple transactions are initiated at the same time. For example, a dual-processor system may have the two processors share the same main memory and, subsequently, the same bus. When the possibility of simultaneous bus requests is present, there must be some way to arbitrate between the requests to determine which request is serviced first. Because the bus transactions must be ordered, there is an incurred delay to one of the two simultaneous requests. The more bus transactions requested, the greater the bus traffic, which implies a greater possibility of bus collisions. This will result in a bottleneck, with greater possibilities for delays.

Buses may be *synchronous* or *asynchronous*. A synchronous bus executes its transactions using a clock for control, while an asynchronous bus uses *handshaking protocols* to initiate and transact communication. A handshaking protocol is a sequence of communications between devices, where the corresponding device speeds, bandwidths, etc., are exchanged in order to facilitate a common mode of data transfer.

Synchronous buses are easy to implement, but modules connected to one must all run at the same clock speed. Asynchronous buses are less efficient, but there are no same clock speed restrictions on the modules that may be integrated.

With a *split transaction* bus, instead of a module's holding the bus for the entire duration of the full transaction, the requests and replies are broken into packets, which are tagged with the transaction information. By splitting the transactions, multiple units may make use of the bus while the requested information is being accessed. Because the transaction is broken up, extra tag information (including who the requester and replier are and which transaction is in flight), must be added so that the CPU and memory know which packets are meant for which transactions. So, while split transactions increase the bus bandwidth by allowing more transactions to take place, the latency of a single transaction increases as a result of decoding all the tag information.

A goal of using a cache is not just to speed up access to variables, but also to reduce the strain on the resources. By cutting down on the need to access the main memory, cache hits will lower the number of bus transactions, thereby easing the bottleneck. This becomes even more important in multiple processor systems that share both memory and buses.

Caches and Memory: Control of the Cache

Caches may be described on the basis of the number of sets, the number of tag comparison units, the number of blocks per tag, and the number of addressable units per block. Most modern caches have one block per tag, and we will only discuss that model. We will refer again to our accountant to help illustrate the different kinds of caches.

Set associativity

The *degree of associativity* defines the way that addresses are collectively mapped into a cache. If there is only one set of sectors, there are no constraints as to the specific association of an address's tag with any sector or set of sectors. This means that any address may have a tag associated with any sector in the cache, and this flexibility allows any address to be mapped to any sector in the cache. This kind of cache mapping is referred to as *full associativity,* and a cache like that is called a *fully associative* cache. In this case, there is no need to use part of the memory address as an index into a set; this type of cache only has one set. Figure 3.5 shows an example of an eight-sector cache configured as a fully associative cache.

For our accountant, let us assume that instead of just a side table, there is a small file cabinet that holds copies of files that are currently being worked on. To keep track of which files have copies in the side cabinet, the accountant maintains a directory that indicates if a copy of a file exists, and in which slot the copy has been placed. If any file copy may be placed into any slot in the cabinet, it corresponds to a fully associative cache.

All tags in a set of the cache are compared in parallel, and the greater the number of tags to search, the more complicated the hardware design. One way to alleviate this complication is to reduce the number of tag comparison circuits by dividing the cache into more than one set. Part of the address is used as an index into one of the sets, and all the tags in that set are checked against the address tag. While the number of sectors is not decreased, the number of required tag comparison units is decreased to the number of sectors in each set. Because part of the address is used to index into a particular set, there is now a constraint on the location that any address can take in a cache. This means that a particular address is restricted to be mapped into one out of n sets simplifying the cache structure at the expense of flexibility. This kind of cache is referred to as a *set-associative* cache. The *degree of associativity* is equal to the number of tag comparison units.

In our accountant analogy, presume that the side cabinet has four drawers, each of which can hold 26 file slots. Each slot will correspond to a letter of the alphabet. Each time the accountant searches for a

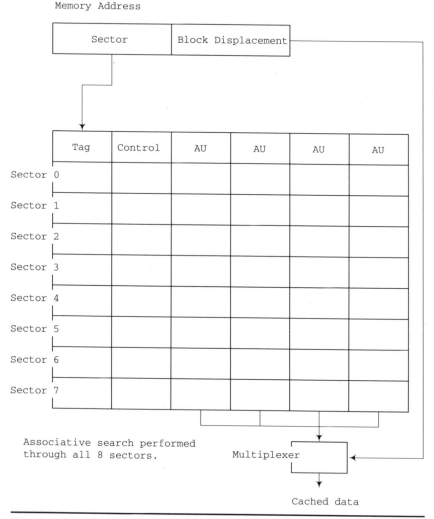

Figure 3.5   An eight-sector fully associative cache.

client's file, the first letter of the client's last name selects down into one out of 26 sets of four slots in which the file copy may be found. At that point, the accountant need only check the four slots, comparing the copies to the name of the client. This allows the accountant to limit the time spent looking for a particular file copy; it will appear only in one of the four file slots associated with each letter. This eliminates the need for an all-encompassing directory.

As an example, consider a cache with 16 available sectors. In a fully associative cache, there would be one set, with 16 tag comparison units.

If we were to divide the same 16 sectors into four sets of four sectors each, then we would need only four tag comparison units; after indexing into one of the four sets, only four tags need checking. This cache would be a *four-way associative* cache. Figure 3.6 shows a cache configured as described in this example.

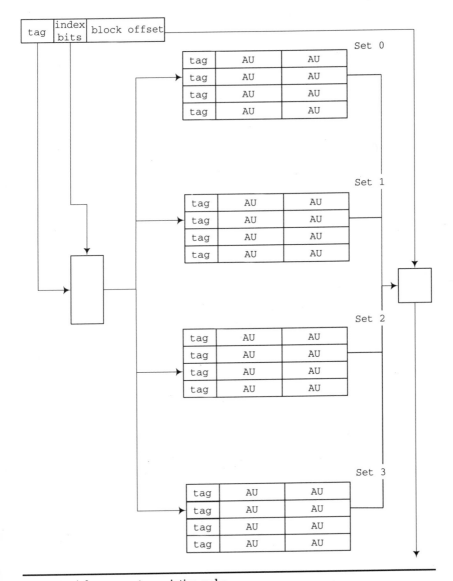

Figure 3.6 A four-way set associative cache.

At the far extreme, the cache may be constructed with only one tag comparison unit, further simplifying the design at the expense of additional mapping constraints. In this scenario, each address maps into one and only one sector, whose tag is compared for tag equality. If an address can only be mapped to a specific block in a specific sector in the cache, then the cache is referred to as a *direct-mapped cache.*

In our accountant analogy, if there were only 26 slots in the side cabinet, the accountant might choose to have each of the slots correspond to a letter of the alphabet. File copies would now only be placed in the slot corresponding to the first letter of the client's last name. This allows the accountant to limit the time spent looking for a particular file copy; it will appear only in one of the file slots.

Control: Reading and Writing Memory

How does the computer know if a memory address is resident in the cache? There are *control bits* that are used to indicate the status of a cache line. If an address's tag is found in the cache, a flag called the *valid bit* is tested to see if the data associated with that tag is usable. If the valid bit is set, the data is resident in the cache and may be immediately returned to the CPU. If the valid bit is not set (either because random bits are set in the cache or because the cache line is currently being loaded and not all the words in the line have been delivered into the cache), the CPU is notified that the data in the cache line are not available. In addition, some processor instruction sets allow the user some degree of control over cache lines; a user may have executed an instruction to invalidate a cache line.

Another important control bit is the *dirty bit.* When data are written to a memory address that resides in the cache, in some cache configurations, main memory is not written immediately. In these configurations, the dirty bit is used to indicate that the representation of the address in cache holds a more recently written copy than the actual main memory location.

In a shared memory multiprocessor system, often shared variables are loaded into different processors' caches. To maintain cache *coherency,* a flag called the *shared bit* indicates that the memory address is shared.

The last important control flag in the cache is embedded in the *least recently used (LRU)* bits. The LRU bits are used in determining which block to evict from the cache when a specific cache line is needed for a newly accessed memory address.

Reading and Writing the Cache

What happens on a memory read? When an address is referenced, the following operations take place:

- The tag part is extracted from the memory address.
- The set index is computed using the set index bits.
- The tags in the cache sectors in the set are compared against the tag.
- If the tag is found in the set, then the valid bit is checked.
- If the valid bit is set, then the block offset part of the address is extracted to index into the cache line, and the desired location is retrieved directly from the cache. This is known as a *cache hit*.
- If the tag is not found in any of the sectors, or the tag is found and the valid bit is not set, then the memory address is not present in the cache. This is called a *cache miss*.

The cache miss

There are a number of different reasons that a memory address may not be resident in the cache. One set of cache misses, called *transient* misses, results from the initial loading of a program and its data, context switches, or other operating system events, such as interrupts and system calls. Another set of cache misses, called *steady-state* misses, includes *compulsory* misses, which happen when data that were not initially loaded are referenced for the first time, *capacity* misses, which occur when there are more memory addresses referenced than will fit into the cache, and *set conflict* misses, which occur when many references to different memory addresses map into the same set.

A cache miss requires handling in order to bring the requested address into the cache. There are two possibilities in bringing data into the cache. The first case happens when there is a location in the cache into which a cache line may be loaded. The second case happens when there are no longer any locations into which the line may be loaded. This case requires a cache line to be *replaced,* and possibly *evicted*; that is, a cache line is chosen to be overwritten by the cache line holding the requested memory address.

Bringing data into the cache

The way that data are brought into the cache depends on the type of cache. In the case of a direct-mapped cache, there is only one location in the cache to hold any specific memory address; if that location is empty, a request is issued to main memory to load the cache line that holds the desired address and place it in the appropriate cache line. When the line load completes, the valid bit is set. Should a valid line be resident, that line is evicted, and the load request proceeds.

In an associative cache, there are multiple cache sectors that can hold a cache line holding a particular address. If there is an empty cache sector (i.e., one without a valid tag), that sector is reserved for the requested address's cache line, and a request is made to main memory. In addition to filling the cache line, it is necessary to fill in the sector's tag, and, when the load is completed, to set the valid bit. If no free lines are available, a line is chosen for replacement (and possibly eviction), and a request is made to main memory to fill the newly open cache line.

Write policies

What happens on a write to memory? Either the memory address written is found in the cache (a *write-hit*), or the address is not resident in the cache (a *write-miss*). Depending on the write policy of the cache, two different things may happen on a write-hit. The first cache write policy, called *write-through,* always writes the data back both to the cache line and to main memory. The second policy, called *write-back,* writes the new value into the cache line, but does not write into main memory. In the write-back scheme, if the line is ever replaced, the dirty bits must be checked to see if there are new values in the cache line. If so, then the cache line must be written to memory before the new cache line is read.

There are different issues regarding the choice of write policy. For example, the write-through policy guarantees that the image of memory in the cache is consistent with the image in main memory. Of course, each write out to memory requires a bus transaction. Also, multiple writes to the same address will invoke multiple bus transactions, which in turn causes greater bus activity, further clogging the bottleneck between memory and the cache. As an example, consider this code fragment:

```
for (j = 1; j < MAX_ARRAY; j++) {
    A[0] = A[0] + A[j];
}
```

In this code, the array location A[0] is written each time through the loop. Yet, because the intermediate values are overwritten many times, the final value that sits in the location is the only value that really *needed* to be written to memory. Therefore, the excess writes through to main memory are wasted bus cycles, and this code fragment might be better suited to a write-back cache.

The write-back policy also has its issues. While the write-back policy yields lower bus activity, there is an issue of *cache-coherence*. In shared-memory multiple processor systems, more than one processor will share memory address space as well as bus bandwidth. If processor A has loaded a memory address into its cache, and has modified the line, unless the data are written back to main memory the other processors that share the address space will have an inconsistent view of memory. In addition, the same memory address may have been loaded into processor B's cache also! In this case, there may be three different values seen for the same address: the cache line for processor A, the cache line for processor B, and the original value in main memory (see Fig. 3.7). Cache coherence algorithms make sure that each processor sees the same value in their respective caches. Another issue with write-back is that even if one address in the cache line is modified, the entire line must be written back. This also causes an increase in bus activity, particularly if the cache lines are large.

But what if the written line is *not* in the cache? As with write-hits, there are different policies for dealing with write-misses. One policy, called *write-allocate,* will read the written line into the cache, and then modify the line. The other option, called *no-write-allocate,* will write

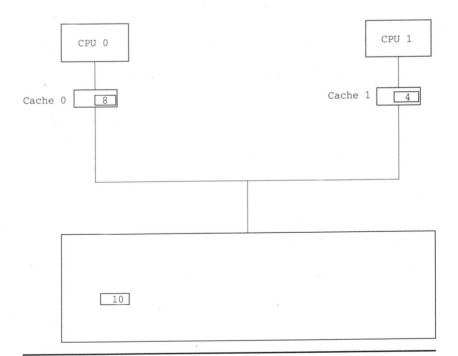

Figure 3.7 Different values in the same variable in different caches.

directly through to memory. These options may be combined with the write-hit policies, and depending on the combination there are different behaviors on writes. For example, consider a write-through, no-write-allocate cache. On a hit, the data are written both to cache and to main memory, and on a miss the data are written to memory bypassing the cache.

Eviction and replacement strategies

When a cache miss occurs, and there are no available slots in the cache, one line is chosen for replacement. If a write-back policy is in place, the replaced line may be a candidate for eviction. Since in the write-back scheme a write to a memory address resident in the cache incurs only a write to cache, the cache line is said to be *dirty,* and the dirty bit is set to indicate that the line will need to be written back to memory. When a cache line is chosen to be replaced, the dirty bit is queried. If the flag is set, the dirty line must be written back to main memory before it is overwritten by the requested memory address's cache line. If the dirty bit is not set, then the line may be directly overwritten. A subsequent reference to the replaced cache line will cause a cache miss, which will force that line to be brought back into the cache.

The choice of a line for replacement depends on the type of cache being used. In a direct-mapped cache, every memory address maps into a specific cache address; therefore, it is obvious which cache line is to be replaced. In an associative cache, most replacement strategies are based on use. An algorithm that keeps track of the usage of different cache lines is used to determine which cache line to replace.

There are a number of use-based cache replacement strategies; we will look at three. The first, called *random,* randomly selects a cache line for replacement. This algorithm is moderately easy to implement: the replaced line is chosen at random.

Another algorithm is the *LRU,* or the *least recently used*, algorithm. The choice for a replacement using LRU is the least recently used block in the cache, under the theory that the least recently touched block is the least likely to be referenced in the future. An example of code that responds nicely to this kind of algorithm is initialization code in an application. The initialization code that is executed at the beginning of a program will be brought into the cache early in the execution, but because it is only executed once, will stay in the cache unreferenced until a cache line is needed. Since the code is no longer needed, the cache space that this code occupies is a good candidate for replacement.

The third algorithm we will look at is the *first-in, first-out (FIFO)* algorithm. The block chosen for replacement is the block that has been in the cache the longest, under the assumption that it is the least likely to be referenced. Again, an example of code that works well with this algorithm is an application's initialization code.

Some Cache Traps and Pitfalls

To get a better idea about how the structure of a cache affects the execution of a program, let's look at some ways that the cache's effectiveness is affected by the way code is written.

Trap 1: Cache thrashing in a direct-mapped cache

What is cache thrashing? When a commonly referenced location is replaced by another commonly referenced location, the cache is said to thrash. The following example shows what happens when a cache thrashes.

Given an 8-KB write-allocate, write-back cache, with a line size of 16 bytes (which is four 4-byte floats), and a main memory of size 1 MB, the memory address 0 will map into cache line 0, but memory address 8192 will also map into cache address 0, as will memory addresses 16384, 24576, and all multiples of 8192. In fact, in this configuration, the number of memory addresses that will map into each cache address is (1-MB memory addresses)/(8-KB cache addresses), or 128 memory addresses for each cache address. To see how that affects the execution of a small program, consider this code:

```
#define ONE_K 1024
#define ARRAY_SIZE 8 * ONE_K
static float a[ARRAY_SIZE], b[ARRAY_SIZE];
int i;
for (i = 0; i < ARRAY_SIZE; i++) {
    a[i] = a[i] + b[i];
}
```

In this example, the arrays a and b would be allocated in consecutive memory spaces, but note that since a and b are both the same size, and given our sample direct-mapped cache configuration, each indexed reference of array a will map to the same cache address as the corresponding indexed reference in array b. The execution of each iteration of this loop would entail two array element fetches and one array element assignment. First, array element a[i] would be referenced, which would not be resident in the cache. This will force a cache line fill, which brings the entire cache line that holds that element into the cache, after which the referenced element's value is brought into a register. Second, array element b[i] is referenced. Because the array element a[i] that had just been loaded into the cache occupies the same cache address, it must be overwritten by b[i]'s cache line, after which the value is brought into a different register. The two values are added, and the result is to be stored back into array element a[i]. But remember that the cache copy of element a[i] had been over-written by the fetch of b[i]. The write-allocate policy would force the a[i] cache line to be reloaded into the cache, and then modified; the fact that it is a write-back cache would delay the write of the new value to memory until the line is overwritten. The access to a[i++] may actually lie within the same line as a[i], and so the next iteration's access to a[i++] will actually hit in the cache, but the fetch of b[i++] will miss, forcing the eviction (and write-back) of the cache line, and another cache fill.

In fact, every subsequent iteration of this loop will incur two cache misses and one write-back. This phenomenon, known as *cache thrashing*, happens only because of the interaction between the direct-mapped cache scheme and the actual layout of the arrays a and b. By understanding this interaction, it is possible to come up with a plan to alleviate the thrashing. The simplest way is to ensure that the corresponding array elements do not map to the same cache location, and a way to do this is to offset the allocation of the arrays. One suggestion is to augment the array a by an odd number of elements greater than the size of a cache line; in this case, 5 elements would do, as shown in the listing.

```
#define ARRAY_SIZE 8 * ONE_K
static float a[ARRAY_SIZE+5], b[ARRAY_SIZE];
  int i;
  for (i = 0; i < ARRAY_SIZE; i ++ ) {{
    a[i] = a[i] + b[i];
  }
```

offset Array addresses

The allocation laid out in this code would result in one cache fill for each array for every four iterations of the loop; the fetch of array element a[i] would not be mapped to the same cache line as the corresponding element b[i], and the store into array element a[i] would go directly into the cache, instead of a reload over b[i]. Also, because the direct mapping would wrap around the addressable sectors in the cache, there would be no requirement to write the stored values back until that cache line is needed again.

Trap 2: A test of locality versus functional abstraction

We have talked about how spatial locality is crucial to the smooth usage of the cache. The knowledge that the instruction sequence is res-ident in the cache is important when evaluating program performance.

In the following, we have an example of a loop that does not yield good spatial locality:

```
double d_add(double x, double y) {
    return (x+y);
}
...
double A[ARR_SIZE+5], B[ARR_SIZE];
...
    for (j = 0; j < ARR_SIZE; j++) {
        /* Some code here */
        A[j] = d_add(A[j], B[j]);
        /* more code here */
    }
```

remove Abstraction

method Call can force reload of the cache

In this example, the user has attempted to abstract the operation of the addition of two double precision numbers by placing the operation in a separate function. Without knowing how the code will be laid out in memory, it is possible that the function's code will be in an area of memory that is far away from the code for the loop. Therefore, even though in every iteration through the loop the same instructions are executed, there is a control hazard that branches control to a different portion of memory, causing a break in the spatial locality. If the code inside the loop fills the instruction cache, a jump out of the loop will force an instruction cache miss on both the destination and the return.

A better way to code this is to inline the function inside the loop. That way there is a better chance that all of the instructions inside the loop will fit inside the instruction cache:

```
double A[ARR_SIZE+5], B[ARR_SIZE];
...
    for (j = 0; j < ARR_SIZE; j++) {
        /* Some code here */
        A[j] = A[j] + B[j];
        /* more code here */
    }
```

Trap 3: Alignment, data declarations, and the cache

Alignment refers to the way that data structures are laid out in memory. An access to a data item of size s at an address is *aligned* if (the address *mod s*) is 0. An item of size 1 byte is always aligned; an item of size 2 bytes is aligned if the address ends with a 0, 2, 4, or 6. When we talk of allocating a data item on a 16-byte alignment, we imply that the address of that data item is evenly divisible by 16. While some processor programming models require that all memory references be aligned, others do not have this requirement.

In systems that do not have the alignment requirement, misaligned data can cause big cache problems. Because misaligned data items may fall across cache line boundaries, loading a misaligned data item into the cache may indicate that multiple cache lines must be loaded. While some processors may handle this load in a single slot, this is not done without some time penalty for detecting what is called a *cache unit split*. Either way, cache splitting causes delays in processing. (See Fig. 3.8.)

As an example, consider the layout of this data in the following code:

```
char    a[15];  // One byte long
int     b[15];  // four bytes long
```

In this layout, the reference to the first element of array b causes a cache split (see Fig. 3.9). A better way to lay this out would be

```
int     b[15];  // four bytes long
char    a[15];  // One byte long
```

In this layout (see Fig. 3.9), the reference to the first element of array b no longer causes a cache split. We learn from this two things. First, always lay out your arrays with largest element size first, and second, if you can, pad out your data structures to avoid misaligned data.

Trap 4: Layouts of data structures

Data structure layout should follow the same rule as above. That is, lay out the larger data items first, and try to make sure that the mem-

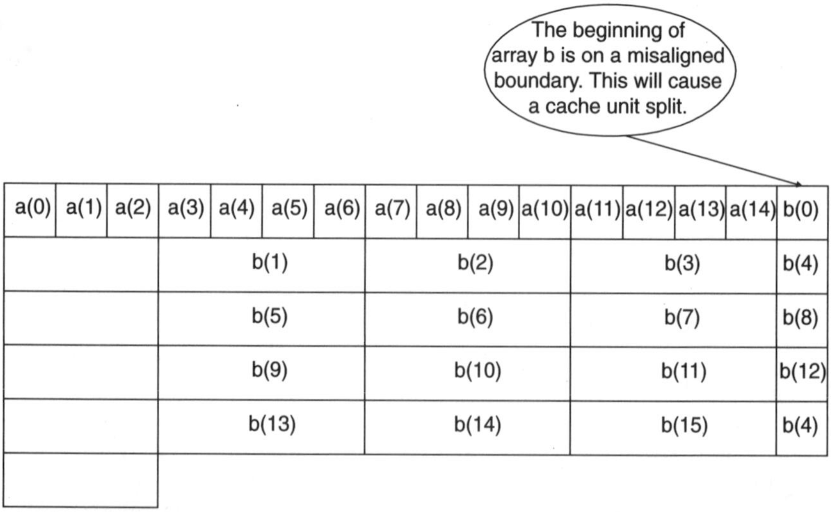

The beginning of array b is on a misaligned boundary. This will cause a cache unit split.

a(0)	a(1)	a(2)	a(3)	a(4)	a(5)	a(6)	a(7)	a(8)	a(9)	a(10)	a(11)	a(12)	a(13)	a(14)	b(0)
			b(1)			b(2)			b(3)			b(4)			
			b(5)			b(6)			b(7)			b(8)			
			b(9)			b(10)			b(11)			b(12)			
			b(13)			b(14)			b(15)			b(4)			

Figure 3.8 The cache unit split.

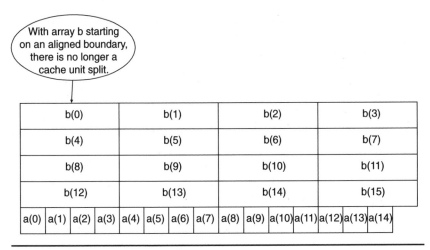

Figure 3.9 Avoiding a cache unit split.

ber elements of a class or a structure are not misaligned. When declaring data structures, always place data items that are accessed at the same time together. For example, depending on how two arrays in a single data structure are to be used, there are two different ways to declare them in the data structure. If the arrays are to be accessed separately in a sequential manner, declare the arrays as separate items:

```
struct {
        double a[1024];
        double b[1024];
} foo;
```

When the array elements are to be referenced in a corresponding manner, it would make more sense to declare the structure as a compound array:

```
struct {
        double a;
        double b;
} foo[1024];
```

This way, a reference to the ith element of array a will bring both the ith element of array a and the ith element of array b into the cache at the same time.

Cost and Performance

In determining the performance of a program with respect to the cache, it is important to come up with a way to model the time it takes to access a data item. That time, called the *effective addressing time,* is based on the probability of hitting or missing in the cache, and the time it takes to access data from both the cache and from main memory.

The time for a cache hit on a read is the time it takes to transfer that data item from the cache. For most modern microprocessors, that time is one CPU cycle. A cache miss on a read requires a main memory access, a cache fill, plus the time it takes to load the data from the cache, although that time may be folded into the cache fill time. The cache fill time is computed as the time it takes to access the first address in the block to be loaded, plus the time it takes to load the subsequent addresses into the cache.

A standard *block load* will load the cache line starting at the first address in the cache line. In some caches, the way that a cache line is loaded depends on which address in the cache line was requested. For example, if the cache line consists of four words, A, B, C, and D, and the CPU requested the address B, then the cache would load B first, then C, followed by D, with A being loaded last. This way the CPU request can be serviced as soon as the first data are brought into the cache. This is called a *wraparound load.*

If a cache line needs to be evicted, the time is multiplied by two, since the dirty line must be written out to memory before the read line is brought into the cache. This time is called *transport time.*

If *P(hit)* is the probability that a reference hits in the cache, and *P(miss)* is the probability that a reference misses, the effective address time is

(P(hit) * the cache access time) + (P(miss) * the transport time)

The transport time is computed as

Transport time = first_access + (next_access * (num_addresses/width) − 1)

where   *first_access*=the time it takes to access the first address in
                        the cache block
         next_access=the time it takes to access the next address in
                        the block
       num_addresses=the number of addresses in each cache block
               width=the number of addresses in each word

As an example, consider a system where the time to access the first address is 10 clock cycles, the time to access each following address is 2 cycles, there are 64 addresses per block, and there are 8 addresses per word. In this case, the transport time is (10 + (2 * (64/8) − 1)), or 10 + (2 * 7), which equals 24 clock cycles.

Cache performance analysis, then, becomes a question of determining how many memory accesses in an application will hit in the cache, and how many memory accesses will miss in the cache. Once that ratio is determined, and the design characteristics of the cache have been understood, a programmer should be able to make a good educated guess about the runtime of an application.

Advanced Topics

Explicit control of the cache

Caches have been designed and implemented to be transparent from the user. As programmers become more aware of the cache, the requirement that the cache be transparent is disappearing. Especially when it comes to system software designers and compiler writers, explicit control of the cache may be beneficial to better performance. Software control of the cache is concentrated on two areas. The first is establishing the cache operation mode, and the other is the preemption of cache operation.

There are different reasons for wanting to modify the cache operation for particular areas of memory. Some examples of processor control of the cache include turning off cacheable mode on specific areas of memory, or changing the write policy of some areas of memory.

A programmer who knows that a certain area of memory will be referenced many times throughout the program may want that area of memory to always reside in the cache. In order to do this, the programmer might specify that all other areas of memory be uncacheable. That would imply that any references outside the special area would go directly to memory. This feature can be used by compilers to allocate areas of the cache as vector registers, allowing inner loops that operate on arrays to execute without cache misses.

Another reason to turn off cacheable mode occurs when a process shares an area of memory with another process. To prevent the cache coherency problem of the shared area, the mode can be changed to uncacheable so that no extra copies sit in processor caches.

Changing the write-policy of an area of memory can help when the cache is used as a scratchpad. If the cache is usually write-through, it would be inefficient to use the cache for temporary variables that are used only for local computations. The reason for this is that using the temporary variables does not need allocated memory, and writing them to memory each time a modification is made would cost cycles in cache operations and bus transactions.

The other processor control of the cache is preemption of cache operation. Usually when certain instructions are executed, such as fetches and stores, there are side effects that modify the cache's contents. Often it is desirable to generate the side effects without having the explicit instruction that causes that side effect. For example, if the cache is write-back, and certain cache lines are dirty, the programmer may not want to wait until those lines are needed inside an inner loop before they get evicted. Instead, the programmer may want the write-back to occur when there is no other strain on the bus resource.

Another opportunity to preempt the cache operations is when multiple processes are using the same memory. Instead of turning off the cache operations, the programmer may desire that local copies of memory be kept in the cache. When one process modifies a shared variable, a notification is sent to other processes, which will then invalidate the cache line holding the local copy of the shared variable. Many new processors have instructions for cache operations. For example, the PowerPC has explicit instructions to evict a cache block, invalidate a cache block, and set the cache block to zero, among others.

Hiding the latency via prefetching

A new development for programming cache-based systems is that of the explicit software prefetch instructions. A *software prefetch* instruction is a machine instruction that preloads data (in a nonblocking way) into the cache, ahead of the time when the data are actually needed. That way, when the actual fetch occurs, the data will already be resident in the cache.

A programmer who has knowledge about the application's memory reference access patterns can insert cache prefetch instructions into the application in an attempt to anticipate the data need. Also, a smart compiler that can do memory reference pattern analysis should be able to also insert prefetch instructions into compiled code to reduce fetch latencies in code areas that require fast execution, such as inner loops.

Obviously, this is a powerful instruction when used. What are some of the issues with prefetch? The first thing to point out is that the success of the prefetch instruction is based on how well the prefetch anticipated the data requirements as well as how much the prefetch interfered with the execution of the program. In other words, the prefetch is useful only when it reduces the number of cache misses over the entire program execution. Why is this a problem? For one thing, inserting additional prefetch instructions lengthens the instruction stream, which, aside from increasing the number of instructions that need to be executed, may also lead to more instruction fetch misses. Also, a prefetch instruction may not be accurate; data that do not reduce the number of cache misses may be loaded into the cache. Another item to take under consideration is the overall effect on the cache population; prefetching data may evict cache lines that are currently needed, which will cause an overall deterioration of execution speed, because of increased misses. And lastly, in blocking caches, a prefetch instruction is more likely to degrade performance than result in improvement because of increased pressure on cache operation.

In using a prefetch, items that need to be addressed are the maximum number of prefetch instructions that may be added before the performance is negatively affected, and the *prefetch distance,* which is the time interval needed between when the prefetch instruction is executed and when the data are available for accessing from the cache.

Example The Intel P6 Cache System   As described in Section 2 of the *Intel Architecture Optimization Manual,* in the Pentium processors with MMX technology and the Pentium II architecture, the cache system consists of two 16-KB caches that are four-way set associative. The cache uses a pseudo-LRU replacement strategy, and the write policy is write-back. The cache is built as eight banks of memory interleaved on 4-byte boundaries.

As there are two instruction pipelines in the P6 system, the cache can be accessed at the same time by instructions from both pipelines. The cache can handle a simultaneous load and store, as long as the two instructions are in separate cache memory banks.

The P6 processors have an instruction prefetcher, which has four 32-byte buffers. Two pairs of buffers operate together with the branch prediction system, so that when a branch is fetched, if the branch is predicted to be not taken, the prefetcher continues to fetch instructions linearly. If the branch is predicted to be taken, the alternate instruction prefetch buffer is started up to prefetch from the target location. If the branch is incorrectly predicted, both prefetch buffers are flushed, and one is started up from the new instruction pointer locations, complete with a time delay for the misprediction.

Summary

In this chapter, we reviewed locality, and we looked at the different kinds of caches (instruction, data, unified, and split caches) and how those caches are designed. We examined the ways that an address is mapped into the cache and noted that there are different ways that caches can be organized, based on the degree of associativity. We looked at direct-mapped caches, fully associative caches, and (the most common) set-associative caches.

We also looked at the processor bus and how data flow between the cache and memory. We followed this with coverage of the read and write policies of a cache system, and what happens when data are read and written.

We looked at a number of pitfalls that can occur when a programmer's code interferes with the effectiveness of the cache, and some ways to address those coding problems. We looked at performance analysis of caches, and some advanced topics. Finally, we looked at the cache system of the Intel P6 architecture.

Virtual Memory

This chapter introduces the next level in the memory hierarchy: main memory. Just as the cache interacts with the memory hierarchy level above it (the CPU register file) and the memory hierarchy level below it (main memory), main memory also interacts with the level of the hierarchy above it (the cache) and below it (the disk system). In Chapter 2, we looked at how data move from the cache into main memory; in this chapter we will learn about the movement of data between main memory and a secondary storage system through the use of *virtual memory*.

What is virtual memory? Even though a computer may have the ability to address a large memory space, most often the amount of physical memory that is installed in a machine is much smaller than the memory space that may be addressed. As an example, a machine with a 32-bit processor word can generate 2^{32} physical addresses, or 4 GB; that is significantly more memory than is usually installed on a machine. Yet, for the most part, applications have been developed with the expectation of being able to use amounts of memory that may exceed the physical memory limit. Virtual memory is a mechanism that has evolved to expand the availability of the memory resource. In this chapter we will learn about the evolution of virtual memory, and we will look in detail at the implementation of virtual memory systems that use paging and segmentation, which are mechanisms to move data chunks between the main memory and a secondary memory system, effectively treating memory as a cache for data sitting on disk.

In this chapter we will concentrate on the aspects of virtual memory: memory addressing, the difference between physical addresses and virtual addresses, address mapping, page tables, and the translation lookaside buffer. The goal is to gain an understanding of the organization of virtual memory in order to understand the performance model. Once we have reached that point, we can analyze programs with respect to their virtual memory activity.

This chapter introduces the concept of "memory as cache" in analyzing programs for performance. In particular, we will look at the similarities and differences between the cache-memory interface and the memory-disk interface. The same issues of "hits" and "misses" come into play in virtual memory, and this chapter will cover hitting and missing memory references in main memory, hitting and missing in both the page table and the TLB, and what happens when a miss occurs at any of these locations. What will become clear is that the notion of locality, both spatial and temporal, will come into play when it comes to writing code that performs well with virtual memory.

Memory as Part of the Hierarchy

In the memory hierarchy described in the Introduction, main memory occupies the level between the caches and the secondary storage units. Since disks are the usual medium for the secondary level, we will use disks as the default secondary storage device. Execution of the application can only take place when the code and data are resident in memory, so when an application is about to be executed, both its code and its data are loaded from the disk into main memory. In Chapter 1, we discussed the expectation that required code and data be resident in the cache, but that referenced memory is moved between the main memory and the cache. A virtual memory system allows data and code to be moved back and forth between the main memory and the disk, but instead of being controlled by hardware only, the control is potentially performed as a combination of hardware and software. The memory hierarchy (Fig. 4.1) spans the cache, memory, and the disk.

DRAM architecture and organization

Memory latency time is calculated as the sum of two distinct costs. The first cost is the *access time,* which is the time it takes between a request for a reference and its delivery. The second cost is the *cycle time,* which is the minimum time required between allowed requests from memory. The access time is a factor of the amount of time it takes for the full address to be sent over the memory bus to the RAM chip, for the reference to be accessed at the RAM chip, and for the requested word to be returned. The cycle time is determined by the constraints of the resources; for example, a new address reference cannot be sent out on the same bus that is currently delivering the previous request.

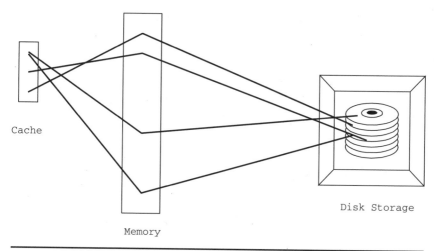

Cache

Disk Storage

Memory

Figure 4.1 The memory hierarchy.

RAM chips are constructed as a matrix of elements, indexed by rows and columns, similar to a two-dimensional array. A memory address actually is represented at the RAM level as an index into a rectangular matrix, and is specified by using a row and column index. When an address is referenced, the address is converted into its row and column indexes, and they are sent over the bus to the RAM chip. A result of the increase in size and capacity in RAM chips made the cost of separate inputs for both the row and the column too expensive; to cut the cost of addressing, the row and column indexes are multiplexed over the same set of address inputs. Therefore, memory is addressed as a sequence of *strobes,* the first being the top half (or the row portion) and the second being the bottom half (or the column portion).

Virtually all commodity computer systems have a main memory that is constructed using DRAM modules. A *Dynamic RAM (DRAM)* is a RAM chip that must be continually refreshed, or else the data contained in the DRAM will be lost. This means that every few milliseconds, the DRAM is not available because the addresses are being refreshed. A different type of RAM chip called static RAM (SRAM) does not need to be refreshed. SRAMs are designed both to be reliably fast and to have large capacity, and are typically used for caches.

One specific kind of DRAM that is widely used, called *page-mode DRAM,* has an internal buffer. When a memory address is referenced, a DRAM page is loaded into the internal buffer, and the request is settled from this internal buffer. If another requested address hits inside the DRAM page already loaded into the buffer (spatial locality!), the request may be fulfilled quicker than if the buffer required filling. But because of the refresh requirements of the DRAM, if a reference is not within a small time window, the information inside the buffer disappears, and a subsequent reference, even to the same location, will force the reload of the buffer. Therefore, a sequence of references to the same DRAM page made within *a small time threshold* may prove to be more efficient.

Interleaved memory

Our insight into spatial locality would indicate that because close areas of memory are read and written, it would make sense to optimize the reading and writing of sequential memory chunks. As we have seen with moving data from memory to the cache, data are moved in sequential blocks. Yet, if sequential data are stored on the same device, a bottleneck would occur. That is, while the first word in the sequence is being accessed, the resources to access the subsequent words are unavailable, forcing those subsequent accesses to wait.

A way to optimize these sequential accesses is to separate them from living on the same device. This organization, known as *interleaving,* uses banks of memory across which the sequential elements are striped. When a block of sequential data are requested, the same address offset is sent to each memory bank, and the sequential elements, which will live at the same relative offset within each bank, can be fetched in parallel.

The number of banks will dictate the way that addresses are mapped into memory. Typically, the addressing is mapped by means of via a modulo function of the number of banks. This is referred to as the *interleaving factor.* Figure 4.2 shows an example of a four-bank interleaved memory system.

Relative performance

To get an understanding for the kinds of performance penalties involved in the movement of data, we can look at the relative speeds of some different memory hierarchy levels. As an example, consider a system using the Intel Pentium chip. The Pentium has a small level 1 cache, and most implementations will include a secondary (level 2) off-chip cache, along with main memory and disks. The time to move a chunk of data between the primary cache and the CPU is 1 cycle. It will take 7 cycles to move the same-sized chunk of data between the level 2 cache and the primary cache. Typically, the cost of moving the 32 bytes from main memory will be about 17 cycles, or more, as we will see. And while the stream rate of the hard disk may move the same-sized chunk of data into memory in about 40 cycles, a typical

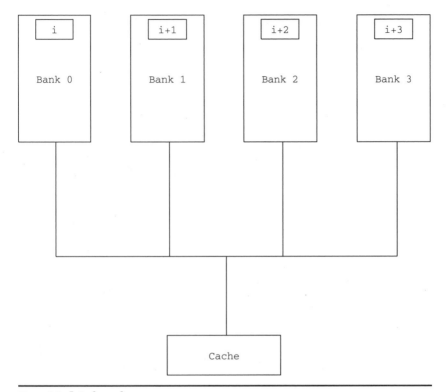

Figure 4.2 Interleaved memory.

random access to disk may take on the order of tens to hundreds of thousands of cycles.

Memory as a cache for the disk

Virtual memory essentially turns main memory into a cache for the disk. Both the cache and virtual memory use levels in the memory hierarchy as an illusion to the user, although the basics of that illusion differ in a very distinct way. A cache provides the illusion of a faster way to access main memory; virtual memory provides the illusion of a large address space that is extended by disks. In both cases, the notion of multilevel inclusion holds. Also, the way addresses are mapped into specific locations and the movement of data between levels in the hierarchy are governed by similar protocols. Some of the similarities between the cache and virtual memory are enumerated in Table 4.1.

However, recognizing that the design of virtual memory and the design of a cache derive from different requirements, there are some organizational differences. Some of those differences are enumerated in Table 4.2.

TABLE 4.1   Some Similarities between the Cache and Virtual Memory

	Cache	Memory
Size	Cache is smaller than memory in the hierarchy level below it	Physical memory space is smaller than virtual address space, and holds subset of data in virtual address space held on disk
Speed	Cache is faster than memory	Memory is faster than disk
Locality	Residence in the cache exploits locality	Residence in physical memory exploits locality
Miss handling	Details of hits and misses are similar	Details of hits and misses are similiar

TABLE 4.2   Differences between Cache and Memory

	Cache	Memory
Size	The size of the cache is determined independently of the design of the processor address	The size of virtual memory is determined by the size of the address capability of the processor
Replacement	Replacement of cache lines is executed by hardware	Replacement of virtual memory pages is executed by the operating system
Lower level	The backup level to the cache (memory) is used solely for program execution	The backup level for memory (disk) is used both for execution and for other purposes (such as the file system)
Primary use	The cache is used primarily to take advantage of locality by reducing access latency	Virtual memory is often used to expand the available space for program execution at the expense of an increase in access latency

Virtual Memory

The evolution of virtual memory

In early computer systems, the amount of actual memory installed in a machine established the limit of memory space available for an application. The memory was divided into two partitions: one partition for operating system code, called the *resident monitor,* and the other partition available to the user. Programmers spent many hours laboring over their codes to make sure that both the code and the data would fit into the available memory.

Often users were unable to make the code fit into memory. In this situation, the user would divide the program into modules, and then determine which modules did not need to be resident in memory at the same time. For example, an initialization module is no longer needed past the beginning of a program; it does not need to stay resident throughout the entire execution. Therefore, the area of memory occupied by the initialization module may be reclaimed at a later point in the execution and used to hold another module. Each of these mutually exclusive modules, called *overlays,* would be loaded and unloaded into memory during the application's execution as required and specified by the user. The overlays were loaded into memory from the disk on demand; when the time came for the code to be executed, the code was found on the disk and copied from the disk into memory. When the transfer was complete, execution would restart.

Partitioned allocation

A different pressure also led to memory contention problems: the invention of multiprogramming, where multiple processes share the CPU to execute in an interleaved fashion. Each process requires its own memory space, and that led to the development of partitioned allocation. Memory is broken up into different-sized chunks, and a job is allocated into one of these chunks on the basis of its size. For example, a 64-KB memory may be divided into one 32-KB partition, one 16-KB partition, three 4-KB partitions, and two 2-KB partitions. An entering job of size 6 KB would have to be placed into either the 32-KB partition or the 16-KB partition, which would be the only partitions large enough to fit it. Because the job is smaller than the partition into which it has been allocated, there is an amount of memory that is allocated but unused. The wasted portion of the partition is referred to as *internal fragmentation.*

When using partitioned allocation, a job may be loaded into memory at any particular starting point. Therefore, the addresses referred to in a particular job must not be bound to exact real memory addresses. Instead, addresses are offset from the beginning of the job's memory (an *offset address*), and the physical memory addresses would be computed at execution time. One way to do this is to keep track of the base address of the partition in a special register, and each memory reference in the program effects an address computation by adding the offset address to the base address register to yield the absolute address.

Another by-product of using partitions is that, because the addresses in the blocks are offset relative to the beginning of the block, the block can be placed in *any* large enough partition, and the offset addresses can still be resolved using the base address of the chosen partition. Therefore, as operating systems developed that were able to manage the partitions, jobs could be moved from one partition to another without disrupting the memory addressing capability of the job. This notion of seamlessly moving the jobs from one partition to another is called *relocatable partitioned allocation.* The development of the ability to move chunks of an application around physical memory was a significant step leading to today's virtual memory systems.

The use of overlays loosened the restriction of the physical size of memory. Partitioned allocation allowed more than one user to use memory in a relocatable way. The extra burden placed on programmers with the added techniques of relocatable addressing led system designers to invent *virtual memory,* which would automatically manage the movement of program pieces back and forth between the memory and the secondary storage level.

Virtual memory

Virtual memory is a way to provide the image of a large linear address space that is mapped onto a small physical address space. Having learned from the difficulties of programming with overlays, it is clear that the management must remain transparent to the programmer. This management may be done using hardware, software, or a combination. The goal is to provide a system that allows each user to have a large address space, to allow jobs to not be bound to any particular address location in memory. This system should allow the program's data structures to grow without having to force a relocation and compaction *(relocatability),* should *not* allow other user's code to interfere *(protection),* yet should allow two jobs to share a section of memory when required *(sharing).*

In summary, these are the features a virtual memory system must provide:

- *Large address space.* A program needs an address space that is large enough to support all the memory requirements such that all the data locations are assigned unique names.

- *Sharing.* Data items that are shared between computations should be referred to by the same name.

- *Protection.* Data items that are not shared between computations should be protected from unauthorized access.

We will see how these requirements are provided in today's virtual memory systems. But before analyzing the fulfillment of these requirements, the basics of virtual memory must be understood: address mapping, paging and segmentation, and address translation.

Addressing, Paging, and Segmentation

Symbolic names are the names that are used by the programmer to refer to specific memory locations. An example is the use of a variable name in a program written in any programming language. At all times throughout the computation, if the variable has been allocated to memory[1], any time the user refers to a variable, that variable's name represents a particular memory location. During execution of the program, this symbolic name must be mapped into a physical memory location; this mapping is the job of the virtual memory system.

The transformation of a symbolic address to a physical address is performed via a sequence of mappings from an *effective address,* which is the system's equivalent to a symbolic name, to a *virtual address,* which is an address in the expanded virtual address space. A virtual address is then translated into a *physical address,* which is also referred to as a *real address,* or a *main memory address.* The physical address is made up of a reference to a chunk of memory and an offset into that chunk. The chunk is found in main memory through a translation table, and when that chunk is found, the offset is used to index into the chunk to find the absolute address. That chunk may be either physically determined (by using *pages*), or logically determined (by using *segments*).

Virtual memory organization

There are three types of virtual memory organizations used today, and each is based on how the memory of an application is divided into chunks. These are:

Paged

Segmented

Paged-segmented

A paged virtual memory system divides physical memory into fixed-size slots called *page frames,* and a program's memory needs are divided into blocks of the same size, called *pages.* Pages are the block size of the data transferred between main memory and the disk, and the memory covered by one page does not overlap with the memory

---

[1]During program compilation with optimization, variables are either assigned to memory or not. A variable whose address is never taken (e.g., is never passed as a reference parameter) and that can live in a register throughout the entire execution may be assigned to a register. In that case, there is a variable that is not assigned a memory location, and so there is no requirement for name translation or indexing into main memory.

covered by another page. A table called the *page table* keeps track of which pages are loaded into frames. A *page miss* occurs when there is a reference to a memory location whose page is not resident in physical memory. Paging represents a physical division of data that is unrelated to the type of data being divided.

In a segmented virtual memory system, the program's memory requirements are divided into variable-length chunks called *segments*. Segments must have their variable-sized chunks made available at run-time, and they are addressed using a base register. One segment may overlap with another. As in paging systems, there is a *segment table,* or a set of *segment registers,* used to indicate which segments are currently available in memory. Typically, segments are divided based on the content of the memory being stored. For example, in a single application, there may be a code segment for the application's instructions, a text segment, which holds the constant values used in the application, and one or more data segments to hold the application's variables.

Because segments are of variable length, two registers must be used in a pure segmentation system. A base register is used to indicate the base address in memory where the segment is loaded. A second register holds the length of the register so that the system will not attempt to access a memory location that exceeds the boundary of the segment. Another way to attack this problem is to use a combination of segmentation and paging, called *paged segmentation.* In a paged segmentation system, there is a segment table that keeps track of the base address and the extent of the segment. In addition, the segments are divided into pages, and those pages are managed by using a set of page tables.

The memory effects seen in paged systems and segmented systems are similar. For convenience, we will concentrate on paged systems in our further discussions.

Virtual address space and memory mapping

Understanding the mapping of an effective address involves learning how virtual addresses are constructed. Since virtual addresses are mapped into pages, the page offset of the address is stripped and later reused to offset into the page; therefore, the bits that are used to offset into a page are reserved, and cannot map into page identifiers. Given a 32-bit processor with a 32-bit address register, if a page is 1 KB, 10 of the 32 bits must be used for the offset, leaving only 22 bits for page IDs, or 2^{22} pages.

To allow for a larger virtual address space, there must be some way to extend the number of bits available to make an address. Two ways to do this are by using *register extensions* or by using a *table of extensions.*

A register extension is an extra register that is prepended to the effective address. Some widely used systems, most notably the 386, 486, and Pentium-based machines, employ extension registers to construct a virtual address.

In a table of extensions, some of the bits in the effective address are used as an index into a special table that holds segments or address extensions. The entries in that table will have additional bits that are prepended to the effective address. The number of segments or address extensions in this table is the number of active "windows" or "views" into virtual memory. That is, any effective address that indexes into the table will yield a virtual address that lies within a bounded region of virtual memory.

As an example, consider a virtual memory system having an address width of 32 bits, a page size of 1 KB, and an address extension table with 16 entries, each extension giving an additional 22 bits. The 10 least significant bits of an address are used to offset into a page, and the 4 most significant bits of an address are used to index into the address extension table. When the 22 bits from the table are prepended to the 32 bits of the effective address, a virtual address of length 50 bits is generated. Subtracting the 10 bits used for the page offset leaves a virtual memory system with 2^{40} virtual pages. Figure 4.3 shows an example of a table of extensions.

Whether the extension register or the address extension table is used, by extending the effective address additional bits, the virtual address may map into a much larger address space than implied by the width of the processor word. Using address extension tables may limit the number of actively addressable segments to the number of entries in the table. If the extension register or the address extension table is loadable under program control, the number of available virtual pages is limited by the number of bits in the virtual address.

Address translation

Once a virtual address is generated, it must be transformed into a real address. A virtual address can be viewed as a combination of two parts: a page number and a displacement in that page. We can refer to the address as a pair (n, d), where n is the virtual page number and d is the displacement. The translation process maps the virtual page number into a real page, effectively applying a mapping function $f()$ to the virtual page n.

The mapping function $f()$ is usually implemented through a set of translation tables which collectively make up what is called a page table. It is through this mapping that the virtual page is transformed into a physical page address, $f(n)$; the displacement d is then added

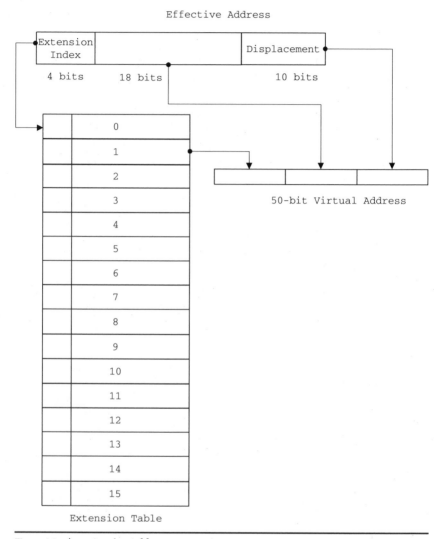

Figure 4.3   An extension table.

to the physical page address to yield the equivalent physical address. We will concentrate on a type of page table called a direct page table; later we will look at a cachelike page table called a *translation look-aside buffer.*

Virtual addressing and the cache

In a system with virtual addressing, the cache can be located either before the virtual address translation (i.e., on the CPU side of the addressing) or after the address translation (i.e., on the main memory side of the addressing). If the cache is located on the CPU side, addresses referenced are virtual addresses, and the cache is called a *logical cache.* If it is on the memory side, the referenced addresses are physical addresses, making it a *physical cache.*

A problem that occurs with a logical cache is that of *aliasing.* Since in a virtual memory system more than one logical address may correspond to the same physical address, multiple copies of the same physical address may reside in the cache under different virtual tags. A write to one of these copies, therefore, would require that all copies be found and updated. This problem, called the *coherency problem,* is not limited to virtual caches; it also appears, as we will see in Chapter 12, in multiple processor systems with shared memory.

Paging

As described above, the virtual address space is divided into same-sized blocks called *pages,* while physical memory is divided into slots called *page frames.* Pages and page frames are the same size, and pages are loaded into page frames. Since virtual address space is larger than physical memory, not all pages will be present in memory at all times. The page table is used not only to yield the actual addresses of virtual pages, but also to indicate whether the physical page is present in memory at all.

Two conflicting requirements for a page table exist. The first requirement is that a page table must be allowed to be very large. With virtual addresses of lengths of 32, 40, or 52 bits (as in the PowerPC microprocessor) and specific page sizes of 1 KB to 4 KB, the number of virtual pages is extremely large. As an example, given a 32-bit virtual address and a 4-KB page size, the 12 low-order bits must be taken for the displacement, and the high-order 20 bits are used to index into 2^{20} pages, or 1,048,576 pages, for a total address space of 4,294,967,296 bytes, or 4 GB. If we use the 4 high-order bits to index into a segment table that yields an additional 12 bits which would be prepended to the low-order 28 bits, this gives us a virtual address of 40 bits. Dropping the 12 least significant bits for the page displacement gives 28 bits for addressing 268,435,456 virtual pages, or 1 terabyte (TB).

The second requirement is that the virtual-to-physical address mapping must be fast. With each instruction requiring one or more memory references, any out-of-cache fetches will slow execution. A reference to memory needs to be as fast as possible, and therefore, the action of mapping a virtual address through a page table should not add significantly to the delay. Unfortunately, this translation often *will* add to the delay; this is incorporated into the performance model discussed ahead.

The implementation of a page table

One simple implementation is to keep a *direct-indexed* page table with an entry for every page in virtual memory. In a direct-indexed page table, mapping the virtual address to the physical address is a matter of indexing the virtual page number in a table, yielding the physical page number. In a system with a small virtual address space, this implementation is reasonable, but when the virtual address space gets to be very large, (as in our 1-TB example above), the number of virtual page entries could take up more memory space than is available! For example, a system with a 64-bit virtual address and a 4-KB page size would require 2^{52} entries! Figure 4.4 shows an example of a direct-indexed page table for a virtual memory with 8 pages and a physical memory with 4 pages.

There are other methods for implementing a page table:

- Inverted page table
- Multilevel page table
- Cache-based/associative memory

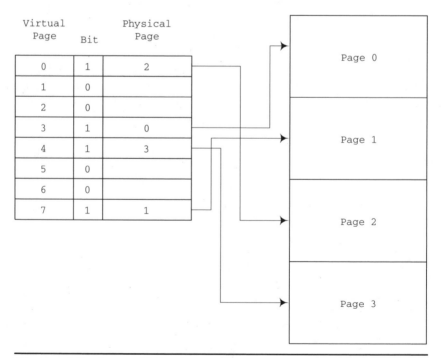

Figure 4.4 A direct-mapped indexed page table.

In an inverted page table, the table has an entry for every page resident in memory. That is, entry i contains the information about the page occupying frame i. An inverted page table is indexed like a cache, using a hash function.

In a multilevel page table, a direct-indexed page table is implemented in a hierarchy, with a tree structure imposed on the table. That is, the page address is divided into multiple pieces; the first piece indexes into the first level of the table, yielding the first part of the page table entry. The second half of the page address indexes into the second level of the page table.

The associative memory, or cached page table, is often implemented as a supplement to the page table in the form of a special page table entry cache called *the translation lookaside buffer (TLB)*. Because the interaction between the cache, memory page tables, and the TLB is critical to the performance characteristics of virtual memory, the details of the TLB are discussed in a separate section below.

Control information in the page table

Just as in the entries referring to memory addresses stored in the cache, there needs to be control information in the page table entry (see Fig. 4.5). These are the flags required for control:

- *Present bit,* used to indicate that the associated page is present in memory.

- *Reference bit,* used to indicate that the page has been referenced (critical during the page replacement algorithm).

- *Modified bit,* indicates that the page has been written.

- *Protection bits,* used to guarantee protection with respect to the access rights allocated to the different processes in execution.

These control bits are consulted during the normal operation of virtual memory references.

Page placement

Where can a page live in virtual memory? In many caches, there is a strict protocol as to where data may be placed. In using virtual memory, the penalty for missing involves going out to disk, which can be extremely costly. Therefore it is worthwhile to minimize the miss rate. This is helped by making the virtual memory fully associative, allowing a page to be placed anywhere in memory.

Virtual page #	P	R	M	Protection	Physical page #

Figure 4.5   The composition of a page table entry.

Page faults

On a memory reference that misses in the cache, an attempt is made to access the referenced address in main memory. The virtual page number is extracted from the virtual address, and that virtual page is looked up in the page table. If the page table entry for that page has the present bit set, the associated page is in memory; the mapping of the virtual address to the physical address is completed. The physical page is accessed and is offset by the page offset. If the action was a fetch, the referenced memory location is brought into the cache, and if the action was a store, the store completes, the interaction with the cache being in accordance with the specific write-allocation policy.

If the page table entry's present bit is not set, the referenced page is not present in memory. This is called a *page fault*. When a page fault happens, the page holding the requested address must be brought into memory.

On a page fault, the page with the requested address must be brought into memory. This can be done only if there is an available page frame. If so, the disk is accessed, and the page is brought into memory. The page table entry for that page is updated to reflect the page's residence in main memory.

If there are no free frames, however, a resident page must be chosen for eviction. That page is chosen by using a *page replacement algorithm*. There are a number of different page replacement algorithms; this is a list of some of the more commonly used ones:

NRU, or not recently used

FIFO, or first-in, first-out

LRU, or least recently used

The *NRU* algorithm involves keeping track of how often each page is referenced and modified. Occasionally, the operating system will clear the bits for all the pages; as each page is read or written, the referenced and modified bits are set. The NRU algorithm chooses a page randomly from the pages whose modified and referenced bits are not set. This choice implies that the page chosen to be evicted is one that has not been used in a while. In using this algorithm, since the OS resets the modified bit, there must be an additional way to know whether the page has been written.

The *FIFO* algorithm implements a queue of the pages that have been brought into memory. When a page fault occurs, the page at the head of the queue (which has been in memory the longest) is the one that is chosen to be evicted. One problem with this algorithm is that it does not take locality into consideration when the choice of eviction is made. Just because a memory reference was made early in the execution of the program does not mean that the same page is not referenced later in the execution. The FIFO algorithm, when used, is often used in conjunction with other algorithms.

The *LRU* algorithm uses special hardware counters that keeps track of how recently the page has been referenced. The page to be evicted is the page that has been referenced furthest in the past. The hardware to implement LRU is relatively expensive; often an implementation is done that simulates the LRU algorithm.

If the page chosen for eviction has been modified (i.e., the modified bit has been set because the page has been written), the page must be written out to disk before the referenced page may be brought into memory. When the evicted page has been copied, the page table entry for the evicted page is updated to reflect that the page is no longer resident. At that point, the newly referenced page may be read from the disk. As soon as the page has been completely loaded, the page table entry for the referenced page is updated, and the access continues as described before.

In summary, here is the sequence of events during a page fault:

- Save the process state
- Choose a page for eviction
- If the page is dirty, write the evicted page back to disk
- Allocate a new page in real memory
- Determine the location of the referenced page on the disk
- Read the page from disk to the allocated page frame
- Update the page table entry
- Update the TLB entry
- Restore the process state, and resume execution

Choosing the page size

There are a number of issues regarding the choice of the page size in a paged memory system. In a paged system, a user's memory requirements do not always fit into an exact number of pages. Given a page size, the number of pages required by an application is the ceiling of the application's size divided by the page size. The last page needed by the application will usually be only partially full. Since a page is allocated as a unit, there is some memory that is inside the page but is not used by the application. Like the excess unused memory in a partitioned allocation system, the unused portion of memory is called a *fragment,* and because it is internal to a page, the effect is called *internal fragmentation.* Internal fragmentation is bad because it creates unusable memory, and reduces the available memory resource in a way that cannot be fulfilled until the application has completed its execution.

As the page size increases, the opportunity for loss of memory resources due to internal fragmentation increases as well. Therefore, the choice of page size is dependent on the amount of internal fragmentation the system is willing to tolerate.

The page table size

The choice of smaller pages will decrease the internal fragmentation, but it has an effect on the size of the page table. As page size decreases, the number of pages increases, thereby increasing the need for page table entries. This means not only increased overhead in supporting more page table entries, but also increased memory space to hold the page table. At some point, the benefit of using small pages is countered by the increased memory needs to hold the page table entries!

The Translation Lookaside Buffer

The time to perform the address translation can take many memory cycles. As a panacea, a hardware cache meant only for page table entries is included to take advantage of locality. Frequently accessed page table entries are stored in a *translation lookaside buffer (TLB).* The TLB takes advantage of temporal locality; when an address in one page is referenced, the principle of temporal locality indicates that once something is referenced, it is likely to be referenced again. The TLB acts like a cache, being indexed by a tag derived from the virtual address. The action of the TLB is similar to the cache, although the nomenclature and the operations on the TLB differ from the cache.

The hierarchical nature of address translation

The inclusion of a TLB in a hardware system adds to the hierarchical level of address translation: The protocol for translation begins with the TLB; if the referenced page's entry is not in the TLB, the stored page table needs to be checked. Because the area of memory holding the page table may be resident in the processor cache, the cache becomes the second level in that hierarchy. If the requested entry is not in the cache, the page table in memory needs to be accessed.

TLB organization

The TLB is an associative memory, indexed by the virtual address. Instead of storing data, a TLB holds the page table entry. A TLB may be organized as a fully associative cache or a set-associative cache, or it may be accessed through a hashing function. TLBs are described in terms of the number of entries, instead of in terms of sectors or the number of sets.

The operations on a TLB are

- Lookup entry
- Add entry
- Delete entry
- Replace entry

It is important to note that, because the TLB mirrors the page table resident in memory, modifications to the entry in the TLB must be reflected back to the page table. While the same coherency issue existed for caches and memory, that situation is covered by the hardware. However, while the TLB is handled by hardware, the page table is software-controlled. Because of this, modifications to the TLB must be coordinated with software updates to the page table; this requires locking and unlocking of the page table.

The address lookup is done via the standard cache lookup operation. A tag is derived from the virtual address, and that tag is used to search in the table for a corresponding entry. If the entry is in the TLB, the page table entry information is returned.

If the entry is not in the TLB, then the entry must be added to the TLB. If there is a vacant entry in the TLB, the requested entry may just be added into the TLB. When the entry is inserted into the TLB, a corresponding entry must also be inserted into the software page table in memory. This involves locking the page table, adding the new entry, then unlocking the page table.

If there is no free slot, an entry is chosen to be evicted. If that chosen entry is not consistent with the copy in the page table, the page table must be locked and entry invalidated, then updated, and marked valid, then the page table is unlocked.

Performance Issues

There are two main issues regarding performance in a virtual memory system. The first has to do with the name translation time, and the second has to do with the time associated with a page fault.

Name translation

The name translation time is the average time it takes to translate a virtual address into a physical address. Having looked at different ways that a page table is maintained, we can see that there is a difference in times required depending on the form of the page table. The time to access the page table entry in a direct-indexed table completely held in memory will be different from the time to access a page table entry in a TLB, and they will both be different from the time needed to walk through a multilevel page table. In each way, though, some time is required to access the page table, and some amount of computation is required to determine the status of the page referenced.

Name translation is a good example of the mechanism of the memory hierarchy, because there are many levels through which a request for name translation must travel. It is possible to characterize the name translation time by looking at an example system. The UltraSparc memory management unit (MMU) contains a TLB and a page table called a *software translation table*. The software translation table is an operating system (OS) data structure that lives in memory. In order to facilitate the fast refill of TLB entries, a direct-mapped cache called a translation storage buffer (TSB) interfaces between the TLB and the software translation table. The TSB is a software-managed table of translation table entries.

When a virtual address is presented to the MMU for translation, the TLB is consulted. If the translation table entry is resident in the TLB, the translation continues. If, instead, there is a TLB miss, the hardware checks if the appropriate entry is in the TSB. If so, the entry is loaded into the TLB, and then the translation is restarted.

If the entry is not in the TSB, the TLB miss handler must jump to a more sophisticated handler that will check the OS software translation table. This table lives in memory, and reading the table takes the same path as a regular memory read. That means that it is possible that the requested translation table entry is resident in the first-level cache. If so, the entry is returned, and then forwarded to the TSB, then back to the TLB, whereupon the translation sequence is restarted. A miss in the first-level cache may be resolved at the second-level cache; the memory reference is loaded into the first-level cache, then forwarded to the TSB, then back to the TLB, whereupon the translation is restarted. A second-level cache miss will initiate a fetch from memory, with all the multiple levels being backfilled, whereupon the translation is restarted.

In summary, the worst case possible for a TLB miss on the Ultra-Sparc requires passing through the TLB, the TSB, the first- and second-level caches, and main memory before the name translation begins!

Page fault

The cost of a page fault is determined by the amount of time it takes to allocate an empty page frame, access the page from the disk, and read the newly accessed page from the disk. If there is not a free frame, one of the pages must be chosen for eviction. One of the pages must be selected to be replaced. If the dirty bit indicates that the page has been modified, the page must be written out to disk. The page table entry for that page is updated to indicate that the page is no longer resident in memory.

Therefore, the maximum time it takes for a page fault is equal to the amount of time it takes to copy a page from memory to a random location on the disk plus the amount of time it takes to reposition the disk head and read in a page from the disk.

Access Control

Protection is an issue of making sure that a process does not interfere with memory areas that should not be modified or accessed. For example, certain areas of memory are assigned to resident OS routines. This area of memory should be restricted from access by user programs; otherwise, rogue programs could interfere with the proper execution of other jobs.

Another issue is that of allowing accesses at different levels of protection. For example, one process may allow read access to its memory, but not write access. Some methods of access control include the use of bounds registers, access tables, and distinct address spaces. Bounds registers are used to indicate the start address and length of a process's memory. Any reference outside of those bounds would be an improper access and would be trapped. Access tables are used to keep track of which processes have which set of rights to access other processes' memory. Using distinct address spaces will definitely protect one process's memory from another's; if a process cannot construct an address into another process's memory, it will not be able to read or modify it either.

TLB Pitfalls

Pitfall: Accessing data along the wrong dimension

The best kind of example of how virtual memory works is one that has predictable paging behavior. Let us assume a system that has 1-KB pages, and 8 MB of memory. If the system uses a 32-bit processor word, the simplest configuration for virtual memory would allow at least 4 GB of addressable space. Let us also presume that the system has a TLB that can hold 64 page table entries.

Our example consists of a simple two-dimensional matrix transposition. We are given 2 two-dimensional matrices, A and B. These matrices contain double precision values, and are of size 1024 by 1024. In the code in the listing below, there is a doubly nested loop that fetches the elements of matrix B and assigns them into the transposed positions in matrix A.

In the runtime model for the C and C++ programming languages, multiple-dimensioned matrices are stored in row-major order. That means that all the elements of each row of the array are stored sequentially, followed by the elements of the next row. In our example, the element A[0][0] is followed by the element A[0][1]; the last element in the first row, A[0][1023], is followed by the first element in the next row, A[1][0].

```
#define ROWSIZE 1024
#define COLSIZE 1024
double A[ROWSIZE][COLSIZE];
double B[ROWSIZE][COLSIZE]
      for (i = 0; i < ROWSIZE; i++) {
            for (j = 0; j < COLSIZE; j++) {
                  A[i][j] = B[j][i];
            }
      }
```

Each of the arrays contains 1024*1024 elements. Each element is a double, which takes up 8 bytes. Therefore, the size in bytes of each array is 8 MB, each enough to take up all of the physical memory! If this code sample exhibited good spatial locality, there would be no performance issue, but instead, this short loop is a good example of code that will tax the virtual memory system.

Let's examine the behavior of this loop. The references to the stored matrix A are performed in an order that does exhibit good spatial locality; the elements are assigned directly in their storage order (A[0][0] is assigned before A[0][1], etc., and these elements are sequentially stored). But the references to matrix B are not performed in the storage order. In fact, each subsequent reference to matrix B lives on a different memory page. The first fetched element of matrix B is $B[0][0]$; the second fetched element of B is $B[1][0]$, which is 8096 bytes, or 8 pages, away.

The access pattern for matrix B indicates that, on each iteration of the inner loop, a different memory page is referenced. Each iteration will check the TLB and see that the page table entry for that page is not there. That will initiate a memory page table lookup, which will indicate that the page is not currently in memory. That page will be loaded from the disk, and the memory page table entry will be updated, as will the TLB entry. Since the TLB can only hold 64 entries, at best, after 64 iterations, the TLB will be full, and every subsequent B reference will cause a TLB miss.

In fact, after the first 512 iterations of the inner loop, main memory should be holding half of the elements of matrix A and half of the elements of matrix B. At that point, the physical pages of main memory are full; any reference to a page that is not in memory will cause a page fault. Since each iteration refers to a different page of B, *every* subsequent reference to that array will cause a page fault. Even when the inner loop has completed, the outer loop iterates for the first time, and an element of B is referenced that lives in a page that has been seen before, any remnant of that page will have been evicted from main memory, and that will also cause a page fault.

So in this simple code fragment, every iteration of the inner loop will cause both a TLB miss and a page fault. That amounts to 1024*1024 TLB misses and page faults—quite a performance penalty! There are ways to attempt to examine code fragments of this type and determine that in fact there is some degree of locality for the fetched matrix, which would lead the programmer to write the code in a more efficient manner. This kind of examination will be the subject of the later chapters.

Pitfall: Choice of algorithm can affect TLB performance

Most efficient methods for locating a single data item in a large set assume that the data elements have been sorted into a predefined order. A sorting algorithm is an algorithm that takes as input a set of elements and a comparison routine that defines a partial ordering relation between two elements, and permutes the data elements such that the partial ordering relation holds between any two consecutive elements i and $i + 1$.

A well-known sorting algorithm is quicksort. In quicksort, a data set is sorted by partitioning the set into two parts, then recursively sorting each partition separately. A simple view of the partitioning process is to find (or create) a location i in the array a such that the ith element is in its final place, all the elements to the left of a[i] are less than or equal to a[i], and all elements to the right of a[i] are greater than or equal to a[i]. This partitioning step usually involves scanning through the array from both the left and the right, swapping values until the scans cross each other or meet. Quicksort is then called recursively on both partitions. Here is the code:

```
void quicksort(int a[]; int left; int right) {
        int i, j;
        int item;
        item = a[right];
        i = left - 1;
        j = right;
        if (right > left) {
                for (;;) {
                        while (a[++i] < v)
                                ;
                        while (a[j-] < v)
                                ;
                        if (i >= j) break;
                        swap(a, i, j);
                }
                swap(a, i, right);
                quicksort(a, left, i - 1);
                quicksort(a, i + 1, right);
        }
}
```

If the array to be sorted is a very large array (on the order of 1 million or more elements, assuming the same system as in the previous example), we see that the memory accesses do not behave as well as we might like. Because the scans move from both the left and right sides, during the early instances of the process, many of the references will cause page faults, since the entire array will not fit in memory. Only as the partitions decrease in size will there be a greater degree of locality that doesn't cause TLB and page misses.

A solution to this pitfall is to combine sorting methods. Mergesort is a sort that recursively sorts and combines the sorted partitions of an array. Since quicksort exhibits good runtime behavior on the smaller partitions, it makes sense to block the array to be sorted into smaller chunks, perform quicksort on the smaller chunks, and then use mergesort to combine the sorted chunks.

Summary

In this chapter, we looked at the interaction between program execution and the main memory, and how virtual memory was developed to expand the available addressing space to an application. We looked at some of the organizational aspects of memory, and how memory acts as a cache for the disk. This was followed by a history of virtual memory and a look into memory addressing, paging, and segmentation.

In our investigation of paging, we looked at how pages are maintained in memory, and how the system keeps track of which pages are currently loaded into memory through a page table. The details of the page table include the control information that is stored with each page table entry, the page fault mechanism, and the policies and algorithms for page replacement. We focused on the translation lookaside buffer (TLB), which holds part of the page table in a cachelike memory.

We then looked at some examples that showed how unblocked data references can cause havoc not only with the cache but also with the TLB. Suggestions were given to address the data reference blocking question.

Disks and
File Systems

The importance of the relationship between the CPU, registers, cache, and main memory, as levels in the memory hierarchy, is made clear throughout the literature. However, the concentration on the existence of other layers in that hierarchy somehow begins to fog at the bottom boundary of main memory. Yet, in many ways, the speed of data movement through the levels below main memory may have a greater effect on the performance of an application than the speed through the higher levels of the hierarchy. The dependence of an application on the arrival of data from a slow disk or slow network will drag down the application's performance quite noticeably.

It is comforting, though, to realize that despite the existence of the different "flavors" of lower levels of the hierarchy, the optimization of the movement of data from the disk to memory, or the movement of data over a network, is similar to that of the levels about which we have already elaborated. Understanding the details of data movement across *any* levels of the memory hierarchy will provide enlightenment on how to optimize the movement of data between alternate layers in the hierarchy for better performance.

As an illustration, we can use our accountant from Chapter 2. Remember that we were concerned about the movement of files between the accountant's side table and the desktop, and, similarly, the movement of files from the file cabinet to the side table. Accordingly, the method of accessing files from the accountant's long-term storage in the warehouse across the street and bringing them into the office and into the file cabinet "shadows" the way that files move between different stations in the office. Given a certain schedule of a week's work on Monday, the accountant can go to the warehouse, pick up the boxes containing the folders he will need for the week, and put them into the file cabinet in the office, thereby providing some potential for locality.

What are the different lower levels in the hierarchy? We have already looked at one during our discussion of virtual memory: the disk. Disks not only act as a secondary storage for virtual memory, but also for data stored in files on disks. In this chapter, we will look at the structure of disks, the limits of disks, and methods for enabling greater performance using current disk technology.

Disks

To get an understanding of the place of the disk in the memory hierarchy, we will use a set of characteristics to describe the architectural and organizational details. These characteristics include:

- Storage capacity
- Bandwidth
- Throughput
- Response time
- Cost

The *storage capacity* refers to the amount of data that may be stored on the device. The actual capacity of a system reflects the performance requirements of the system. For example, early personal computers did not need a large amount of storage; the applications available at the time did not act on large data sets. Today, large databases and graphics files are used on PCs, and the storage requirements and capacity have increased. (See Fig. 5.1.) As another example, server systems that provide file system service to a network of computers have high capacity requirements.

The *bandwidth* of a disk system describes the rate of bytes transferred per time unit. Depending on the type of application, the bandwidth requirements of a system will change. For example, scientific applications may require less bandwidth than commercial applications.

Throughput represents the amount of requests that can be satisfied per unit of time. The throughput, related to the *response time,* represents the amount of requests that can be satisfied per unit of time. With multiprogrammed computer systems, multiple processes have

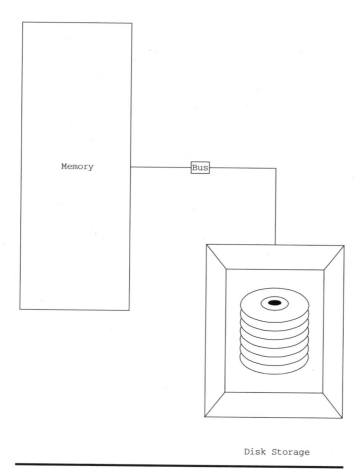

Disk Storage

Figure 5.1 Secondary storage.

their requests serviced in an interleaved manner. Because of this, average throughput may be increased despite a slowdown in average response time.

Lastly, the *cost* of secondary disk storage has a great effect on the other characteristics. Over time, the cost of mass storage has decreased by a tremendous amount. At the time of this writing, commodity hard disk drives were selling at the cost of approximately $0.10 per megabyte, while 10 years ago, the cost was approximately 100 times as much.

Disk taxonomy

Just like virtual memory, disk systems are organized as a hierarchy of storage areas. The smallest unit of storage is the *sector*, which usually contains a small number of bytes (ranging from 32 to 4000). Each *track* on a disk consists of 4000 to 8000 sectors, and there are on the order of thousands of tracks on a *disk surface*. Often, both surfaces (the top and the bottom) of a disk are used; this is referred to as a *platter*. A collection of platters together form a *disk unit*.

Disks are read and written using a *read/write* (r/w) head mounted on a movable arm. The different arms in a disk unit can move independently or as a single unit (see Fig. 5.2). When the arms move together, the tracks located beneath the r/w head are referred to collectively as a *cylinder*.

A *disk controller* is a software/hardware interface that controls the activity to and from the disk unit. The controller receives requests from the CPU for disk I/O, and satisfies these requests. As processes request I/O events, the CPU marshalls the requests and sends them to the device controller. The controller internally maintains the list of requested device transactions and schedules those actions on the available resources. A single disk controller can control more than one device. In a multiprocessor system, more than one processor may be connected to the same controller. Because of this multiple connectivity, the actual waiting time for a process request may be increased both by bandwidth restrictions and by queuing time at the controller interface.

To read or write a disk sector, the controller must move the arm to a position over the track that contains that sector. This is referred

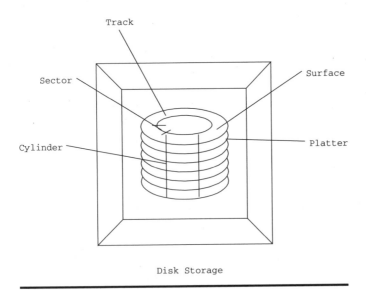

Figure 5.2 The anatomy of a disk.

to as a *seek*. Once that track is found, the disk must rotate until the requested sector is positioned beneath the read/write head. As soon as the sector rotates beneath the head, the data may be transferred.

Access time

All disk accesses incur a certain delay in an application's execution. Through the evolution of the notion of *multiprogramming* in modern operating systems, the possibility for an application to be evicted and prevented from executing on the CPU during an I/O transaction to the disk has allowed for some of the *access time* to be overlapped with the execution of other processes. As processes require accesses to the I/O device, they are removed from executing on the CPU, their requests are put on an I/O request queue, and the process is suspended until the I/O is completed. When the I/O is completed, the process in inserted back into the system scheduler's ready queue. While the process is suspended, other processes may be swapped into the CPU. This is a classic example of overlapping one computation with the latency of another application's memory accesses.

The disk access time is a sum of the times of each step of the disk access protocol. First, the time for the arm to seek to the correct track is called the *seek time*. Disk manufacturers often report a set of seek times: the minimum seek time (which is the minimum amount of time to perform a seek, usually involving the shortest distance of arm movement), the maximum seek time (which is the maximum amount of time to perform a seek, or the longest distance the arm moves) and the average seek time. The reported average seek time is often an average of a large collection of seeks that travel approximately one-third the distance across a disk.

We should be wary of the seek times that manufacturers advertise, since during the average execution of applications, there are many issues that affect the seek time. Seek time is a function of more than just the distance to the next requested track. To move the arm to the next location, it must be accelerated in the appropriate direction, either from a static position (a "cold start") or after just having moved in the opposite direction. Also, as the arm reaches the destination track, the arm must decelerate as well, then stop and wait until it stops vibrating before the next access can proceed. Because seeks are usually not random, but are affected by the neighborhood of track references made by the applications executing at any one time, the average seek time could be said to be a function of the seek locality.

Once the "seeked" track is found, the time for the right sector to appear beneath the read/write head is called the *rotational latency,* or just the *latency.* As soon as the sector is found, the transfer of data may begin. The time to actually transfer the data are called the *transfer time,* which usually ranges from 1 to 4 MB (or more) per second.

Also associated with each request is the overhead required for the controller to attend to the aspects of the request, including the time to insert the request into a queue, and for determining the order of the currently queued requests. In addition, because there may be requests to access a device that is shared among a number of controllers, the controller overhead may include the time waiting for the requested device to become available. Therefore, the total time to fetch data from the disk to memory is computed as a sum of the time spent waiting for the disk controller, the seek time, the rotational delay, and the time to transfer the data.

File Systems

Layered on top of the physical disk system is the facility to handle files. A file management system is a software layer above the I/O hardware to provide for the creation, deletion, and modification of files. Basic file systems are layered on top of the device drivers, and provide the placement of blocks of data on the I/O device.

Above the basic file system are layers that deal with I/O initiation and termination, scheduling, and buffering between the CPU and the disk. Access methods provide the interface for different ways to access information from files. Files may be organized for sequential access, indexed access, and random access, among other organizations. The way that users create and modify files can affect the performance characteristics of the applications that access those files.

File Organization and Allocation

Files are organized according to a blocking strategy that makes best use of the available space on the disk. Disk block allocation for files is meant to provide rapid access of data, provide a simple maintenance mechanism, provide economy of usage, and ease the way files are created and updated. Clearly, some of these goals are contradictory. For example, to increase the speed of accessing a specific location in a file, one may use additional index files, which themselves will take up significant amounts of storage space.

These issues aside, what concerns our discussion of the memory hierarchy is the way that files are allocated on the disk. As mentioned before, disks are divided into blocks onto which file data are mapped. Most files are too big to fit into a single block. Obviously, some method is required to allocate multiple blocks for the storage of a file.

Different allocation schemes have been developed, and we will look at a few of these schemes and how they affect the time to move data from the disk to the process. Let's assume that a disk has been subdivided into B blocks, each of size P.

Contiguous allocation

For a file of size N, a collection of T contiguous blocks is allocated to store the file, where $T = \text{ceiling}(N/P)$. To access the ith address in the file, that address is divided by the block size P, to yield the index of the block holding the reference. The remainder after this division is the offset in the block. (See Fig. 5.3.)

Accessing data in this scheme is relatively quick; finding the disk location only requires performing some arithmetic. But contiguous allocation has its pitfalls as well. As more files are added to the disk system, the number of contiguous blocks that can fit new files dwindles, while external fragmentation increases. Eventually, the files on the disk need to be *compacted,* or copied to new locations and shifted together to free up larger blocks of contiguous space. Appending data to a file is not trivial, since either the file must be preallocated with room to grow, leaving a potential for internal fragmentation, or the file must be reallocated, since another file may be directly adjacent on the disk, leaving no room for expansion.

Contiguous allocated files are well suited for spatial locality. Because all the data are laid out sequentially in disk memory, sequential accesses do not require wide movements of the disk hardware to scan through any sequence of data. If the file is not being used for random accesses, contiguous allocation will perform well, except if the file needs to expand, or if there is a high enough level of multiprogramming that the I/O requests are separated from each other.

Chained allocation

In a chained allocation scheme, blocks are individually allocated when a file needs more space. Each block in the file contains a pointer to the next block in the file. An example of this is shown in Fig. 5.4. With chained allocation, external fragmentation is not a problem, since

Figure 5.3 Contiguous allocation.

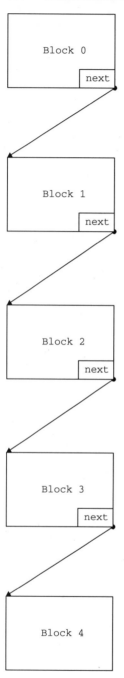

Figure 5.4 Chained allocation.

blocks are only allocated when needed. There is no limitation on the placement of file data on the disk. To find a specific address, the chain of blocks must be traversed until the block with the reference is found.

In terms of locality, chained allocation is a disaster. Since the search for any address requires traipsing through a large portion of the file, any kind of accesses that are not increasingly sequential accesses will cause a significant hit in performance. Additionally, since the blocks may be spread out all over the disk, walking through the chain may be costly in terms of the increased number of seeks to find each successive block.

Indexed allocation

In an indexed allocation scheme (Fig. 5.5), one block contains a list of pointers to the blocks actually holding the data. This indexing alleviates the chaining problem, but will still have some affect on the locality characteristics of the file. As in chained allocation, there is no constraint as to the placement of blocks, so references that logically appear to be contiguous may physically be far away from each other on the disk.

With an indexed scheme, there is a new factor dealing with the memory access time: the multiple address reference. Because the blocks in the file are indexed in the first block, to find the ith location, one must first read the index block to find the address of the block holding the ith address, then seek to that block. Indexed accesses are slower than accesses to contiguously allocated files.

When building your application, be sure to find out what kind of disk allocation strategy is being used. If it is a contiguous allocation, it may make sense to try to determine exactly how big the files will be before allocation, and to grab enough space so that reallocation will never be needed. For an indexed allocation, it may be worthwhile to rebuild the file once its construction has been completed; the potential to actually allocate contiguous space may be increased upon reallocation.

Disks and Efficiency

The rate of increase of speed of disk systems is not as fast as the rate of increase of speed of both processors or memory. While the cost of disks has decreased, the speed has not kept up with other system components, and therefore new ideas are needed to bridge what is called the *access time gap* between SRAM or DRAM chips and magnetic disks.

There have been a number of new ideas that have been implemented both in supercomputer systems and in desktop systems. We will discuss three ideas that have been brought to some degree of maturity: the *solid-state disk* (SSD), *RAID* (or redundant arrays of inexpensive disks), and the *disk cache*.

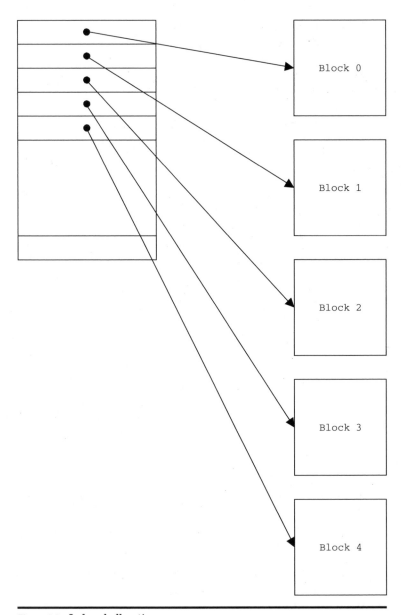

Figure 5.5 Indexed allocation.

Solid-state disks

A solid-state disk is not really a disk at all; it is a collection of semi-conductor memory chips (such as DRAM chips) along with some kind of backup mechanism. This backup usually includes a battery, and often a magnetic disk as well. Solid-state disks are interconnected to the computer system using the same interfaces as a regular magnetic disk.

Because there are no moving parts, a solid-state disk does not incur any seek time nor any rotational latency. Solid-state disks are good for systems that run applications that require short-burst I/O operations, since these I/O operations are dominated by the seek time and the latency. As the size of the I/O transfers grows, the lower the benefit of the SSD, since the memory access time becomes dominated by the transfer time.

Disk arrays

As mentioned earlier, while the cost of disks is dropping and available capacity rises, the rate of increase of speed of the disk is not keeping pace with that of processors and memory. One way to address this is to create a virtual disk drive out of a collection of individual physical disk drives, and use parallel access as a lever to higher overall performance.

More formally, a *disk array* is a set of physical disks grouped together to form a single logical disk drive. Having multiple independent disks allows data to be allocated across the disk drives in a distributed way, thereby increasing bandwidth and reducing the overall access latency. Multiple read/write heads allows for greater transfer bandwidth since data may be transferred simultaneously from many disks.

In a manner similar to interleaved memory, data can be interleaved on a disk array. A *stripe unit* of data is the size of data that can be allocated to a single disk. A *data stripe* consists of a set of consecutive stripe units interleaved across the set of disks. The *degree of interleaving* is the number of disks over which a stripe can be allocated. (See Fig. 5.6.)

For example, consider a disk array system with a stripe unit of a quadword and n disks. In this system, a data stripe would consist of n quadwords. A file with $(4*n)+2$ bytes would be broken up into five data stripes, allocated across the n disks. All but two of the disks would hold four stripe units, while the last two would hold five stripe units. The access time for the whole file is equal to the seek time and rotational latency, plus the time to transfer five stripe units (i.e., the maximum number of stripe units on any of the disks).

RAID

Despite the benefit of gaining bandwidth by using multiple disks, there are drawbacks as well. Most pointed is the issue of hardware failure. A single disk can be expected to fail at some point in its lifetime; what PC user has not been bitten by this? A disk drive has a

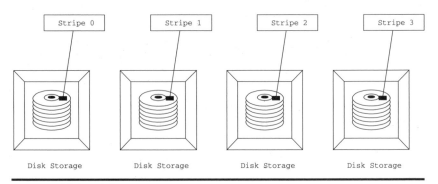

Figure 5.6   Disk striping.

mean time between failure or (MTBF) which, loosely, is the average time it takes for a disk drive of that sort to fail. In a system with a single disk drive, a disk failure will disable the system, but the MTBF may be long enough to sustain a certain amount of work before the system failure.

In a disk array, however, because the data are striped across all the disks in the array, the failure of a single disk causes the failure of the entire array, even if all the other disks are operating correctly. Additionally, as more disks are added to the array, the probability that one of the disks in the array will fail increases. Therefore, some measures must be taken to address fault-tolerance in terms of both failure detection and error correction.

One answer to this problem is to provide some degree of redundancy in the system. The term coined for a configuration of this sort is *RAID,* or redundant array of inexpensive disks. Originally, there were five degrees of RAID systems described, and today there is an extra level that can be described. Each of these RAID levels is designed to provide some degree of reliability in the presence of a disk failure.

RAID 1.   The redundancy at the RAID 1 level involves complete redundancy. Called *shadowing* or *mirroring,* each read and write to the disk array is also made to an identical set of disks. All files are striped equivalently across each set of disks. The RAID 1 system is shown in Fig. 5.7.

The benefit of a RAID 1 system is that the increased bandwidth of the disk array is not compromised, with the full advantage of having data accesses performed in parallel. The major disadvantage, though, is that the cost of the system is twice that of a nonredundant disk array.

For error checking, a read to a RAID 1 system involves two data reads, one from each set of disks. The two values are compared, and if the values agree, the read is considered to be successful and correct. If the values do not agree, a failure has been detected, and some arbitration must be performed by the operating system to determine which of the two values is correct.

RAID 2. As in a regular disk array, data in a RAID 2 system (Fig. 5.8) is striped across the set of disks. Instead of imposing a complete copy of the data as was done in RAID 1, though, the redundancy is provided by a set of error-correcting codes (ECC) for each stripe, which are stored on a separate set of disks.

The ability to detect errors as well as correct errors requires different numbers of additional bits for each correcting code; for example, to be able to detect two errors and correct one error, the system requires on the order of $\log_2(m)$ extra bits, where m is the number of disks in the disk array. The error-correcting codes themselves must be striped across the ECC disks, in case of a failure in one of the ECC disks.

In a RAID 2 system, each write requires a read of all the disks that share the data stripe holding the element to be written. The reason for this is that the error-correcting codes for that stripe must be recomputed if the data on the disk are changed. If this seems

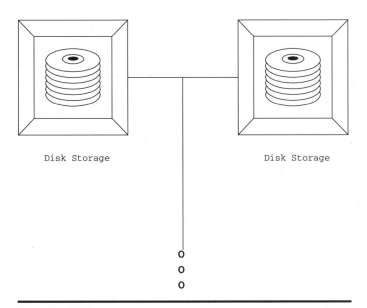

Disk Storage   Disk Storage

Figure 5.7   RAID 1.

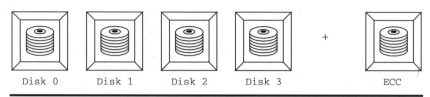

Figure 5.8 RAID 2.

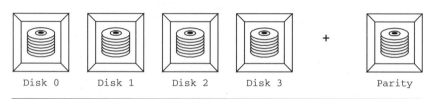

Figure 5.9 RAID 3.

familiar, recall the read-modify-write protocol used for a write-back cache. This requirement will reduce the overall bandwidth of the disk array, since each write to a single location requires a full stripe read and write.

RAID 3. RAID 3 (Fig. 5.9) is similar to RAID 2 except that the stripe unit may be either a bit or a byte, and because there is significant checking assigned to each disk, there is no requirement for full error-correcting codes. It turns out that simple parity is sufficient for error recovery; that is because if any of the disks fail, the individual disk checking will signal the disk's failure to the system. A separate parity disk is used, and the parity values stored on that disk can be used to infer the correct value from the failed disk. If the parity disk fails, the rest of the bits are known to still be good, so the remaining data values are still correct.

RAID 3 still requires a read-modify-write scheme when writing. It should be clear that because a specific disk resource is allocated to be the parity disk and parity must be rewritten for every data write, the parity disk may become a bottleneck. The increased load to the parity disk may also increase the potential for a failure as well.

RAID 4. A RAID 4 system is similar to a RAID 3 system, but the stripe unit is increased to the size of a sector, and data interleaving is no longer performed. That means that while files are distributed across the machine, there is no increased bandwidth due to parallelism. If the disk array has independently moving read/write heads, disk transactions for different files may be performed simultaneously, but there will be no increase in speed in reading from a single file. As with RAID 3, the disks have independent checking for failure.

Parity is maintained at the byte level. As with RAID 2 and RAID 3, the read-modify-write protocol is used for data writes. As with RAID 3 the parity disk needs to be written on every write, which may cause a bottleneck.

RAID 5.   RAID 5 (Fig. 5.10) is like RAID 3 and 4, except that the parity data are distributed across the disks in the array. Not only will this decrease the strain on a specific parity disk, but it will also contribute to breaking the performance bottleneck at the parity disk.

With RAID 5, there are two failure modes. The first occurs if a disk not holding parity data for an accessed stripe fails. In this case, the configuration is the same as RAID 3. The second failure mode occurs when a disk holding parity data fails. In this case, because the rest of the stripe is known, the parity data can be reconstructed.

RAID 6.   RAID 6 is the first "new" level of RAID described after the original description in 1987. RAID 6 expands the idea of distributed parity by extending an additional dimension to the array of disks. By configuring the disk array as a two-dimensional system, parity can be maintained across both the rows and the columns of the disk system. A RAID 6 configuration will allow continued operation in the presence of two disk failures.

Disk caches

Just as the notion of locality holds for data brought from memory to the CPU, data referenced on disks are also subject to locality of reference. A way to take advantage of disk locality is to cache data read

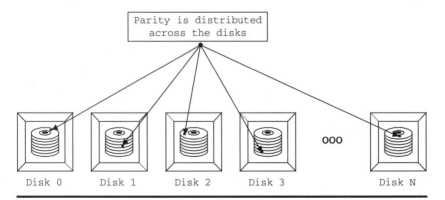

Figure 5.10   RAID 5.

from disk in memory. A dedicated buffer or set of buffers in memory, called a *disk cache,* is used to hold a copy of some of the sectors on the disk. When a request is made for I/O, the disk cache is first checked to see if the requested data are in memory. If so, the data are read from memory; if not, the disk cache is filled with the data read from the disk.

Disk caches work similarly to hardware caches in behavior. Disk caches are limited in size and there needs to be a replacement strategy when new data are read. Also, when a disk cache block needs to be replaced, if the block is dirty the data needs to be written back out to the data file.

Alternately, disk caches are different than hardware caches in that disk caches are software-controlled, and there is some flexibility in the implementation. Additionally, an issue with disk caches is that reading from the disk cache may result in copying data from one location in memory to another. One implementation of the replacement strategy is the Least Recently Used (LRU) strategy, implemented as a stack in memory. As a block is read, it is placed on the top of the stack. When the cache is full and a new block is to be brought in, the block that is on the bottom of the stack is chosen as the replacement victim.

Other replacement strategies involve a Least Frequently Used (LFU) scheme, or some modification to either LRU or LFU. In an LFU strategy, a counter is assigned to each block. When a block is brought into memory, its counter is set to 0. At each reference, the counter is incremented. When a victim needs to be chosen, the block with the lowest counter is picked as the victim.

A problem with the LFU algorithm is that locality may actually work against efficiency. One block may be referenced many times in a short time span, bumping up the reference counter. At some later point in the execution, the block may no longer be referenced, yet because of the high reference count, the block would not be evicted from memory.

Other considerations have to do with write-back strategies. One idea is to group together blocks to be written, and order the writes to the disk to minimize the seek time. Another issue is a sharing problem; as with multiprocessor caches, if more than one CPU uses the same file system, there may be a cache consistency problem.

As long as the cache hit ratio is relatively high, disk caches can be good for performance. Keeping the hit ratio high is a function of the size of the disk cache, the replacement strategy, and whether the disk cache is kept in addressable virtual memory or is subject to being swapped out of memory back to disk, which would defeat the purpose of having a disk cache!

Efficiency in Disk-Oriented Applications

The definitions described above become meaningful when we put them in the context of applications. The applications that most frequently rely on efficient disk usage are database applications. We will look at three operations that rely on efficient usage of the disk: searching, sorting, and indexing.

Searching

When querying a database, a user typically phrases the query in some query language (such as SQL). The query typically requests that all records that satisfy some set of criteria be accessed and presented to the user. In the worst case, all records of a database must be searched for records matching the criteria. Therefore, a sequential scan of the database needs to perform well.

If a database file is stored using a contiguous allocation scheme, a sequential search will perform moderately efficiently, because the disk head can move in one direction, accessing the data and streaming them into main memory. Also, as the CPU scans through data that have already been brought into memory, the disk controller can be streaming data into another area of memory. If the file is stored using a chained allocation scheme, a sequential scan will be less efficient, because the disk arm will have to move to different areas of the disk to access the data.

Another aspect of searching revolves around the amount of database operations to be performed (such as selections, projections, joins, etc.) and the size of the data space that needs to be searched. In particular, in relational database systems, because the data are stored as a set of database tables related to each other, in order to look for information with attributes that cross tables, joins must be performed, which expand the search space. Frequently, there are different alternatives in the order of performing these operations. Processing called *query optimization* is performed to examine the different ways that a query can be executed and to identify a plan that is the most efficient way to perform the query.

Sorting

One way to increase the efficiency of searches is to sort the data according to a primary key used for queries. Sorting is critical to database applications. As we saw in the previous chapter, the performance of different sorting algorithms is affected by the memory hierarchy.

Since sorting records in a file requires that all the data are brought into memory, a goal of a file sorting algorithm would be to limit the amount of time spent moving data between the disk and main memory. As opposed to the standard sorting methods for in-memory data, external sorting can be made more efficient by blocking the data from the disk that is to be sorted, and making sure that the size of the data block does not force memory page misses!

The file can be broken into blocks that can be read, sorted, and written back to the disk. On a subsequent pass through the file, two sorted blocks are loaded, merged, and written back. This process is iterated until the entire file is sorted.

A way to increase the efficiency of this process is to provide a way for the sorting computation to overlap the movement of data back and forth to the disk. This can be done by using multiple buffers in main memory. With a dual-ported, dual-head I/O system, a three-buffer scheme would make use of one buffer for loading data, one buffer for sorting, and one buffer for writing. During the ith iteration of this process, buffer (i mod 3) would be used for loading, buffer (i mod 3)+1 would be used for sorting, and buffer (i mod 3)+2 would be used for writing. This sets up a multibuffered pipelined system that overlaps computation with communication.

Indexing and sorting

Since users typically expect that database records are returned in a certain order, databases are frequently indexed to provide the image of a sorted order. An index file presents a mapping between the records of the database file, and their proper sorted order. So while two database records may appear to be consecutive in the presentation of the data to the user, the two records may actually live in completely different sectors in the file. From our discussion of disk drives, we know that accessing sectors that are not nearby on the disk drive can incur extremely large miss-time penalties. In addition, since accessed data from the disk is buffered in memory, loading blocks of many records just to access a single record in the block is wasteful of both the mapped memory space and the disk transfer latency.

Our understanding of the notion of spatial locality implies that it would be desirable to place records that would be displayed at the same time close together in their memory hierarchy level. The database records are stored in a file on disk, and the order of the records in the database may shadow the order in which the records were originally input. Presorting the records in the file into a sorted permutation of the database will ensure that consecutive records in the order are close together in the sorted file. Creating an index based on the sorted file should increase the record loading speed, since each loaded block will contain more desired records, and the miss latency will be reduced.

The importance of sorting with respect to databases appears during bulk updates to databases. Essentially, the information in the update needs to be merged with the current database. This merging relies on the records being sorted to minimize the number of scans through the data.

Indexing

An index is a directory that keeps track of where records with particular keys are stored in the file. Obviously, if we only maintain the file as a sorted sequential file, we would still have to scan through almost the entire file to find records with keys starting with X. Using an index file, the application can look up the key in the index and know where in the file the records with that key sit.

Another indexing scheme is using balanced B-trees. In this scheme, a tree hierarchy is imposed throughout the index file. While we don't elaborate on this algorithm here, we will look at a problem that occurs when building what is called an *ordered index.*

In an ordered index, not only are the records indexed by a key, but the records themselves are stored on the disk in their ordered sequence. For data searching and data access, an ordered index exhibits great locality of reference! When creating an ordered index, each file block must contain some amount of empty storage space so that newly inserted records can be written directly into the file.

When there is no longer enough space on the disk, new space must be made in the right spot. Unfortunately, this means that all the data subsequent to that location must be moved. This incurs a huge performance penalty on inserting records into an ordered index.

The problem becomes much more acute if the index key is not unique. In this case, many insertions will be repeatedly made to the same place in the file, forcing many instances of data copying. A solution to this problem is to avoid the nonunique index problem altogether. If the index key is not unique, the ordered index key can be composed from multiple fields to form a unique key. This way, repeated insertions into the same location will not occur!

Summary

In this chapter we looked at the capacity, bandwidth, throughput, and costs of disks. We investigated access time, made up of latency and transfer time. This was followed by a discussion of file systems, and file organizations, including the different ways that files are allocated across the disk system. We then looked at different ways that disk systems are made efficient, including solid-state disks, disk arrays, and organizing arrays of disks for increased fault tolerance in RAID systems, as well as disk caches.

The last part of this chapter focused on applications that require efficiency in the disk system. The database operations include searching, sorting, and indexing. We finally looked at ordered indexes and ways to avoid the pitfall of nonunique keys in an ordered index.

Performance

6

Optimization Basics

Optimization

Our goal is better performance, and while our focus has been on memory hierarchy performance, we will take a short detour to discuss traditional optimizations and optimizing compilers. The motivation for this is that, in order to understand how to improve an application's speed, we should know what to expect from an optimizing compiler, as well as what to do when the compiler cannot or will not perform the optimization that the programmer expects.

An important note to remember is that a compiler will optimize code only if it knows that it is safe to do so. This means that the compiler guarantees that the program will compute the results the programmer wants, even if it is done in a different way. Therefore, the correctness-preserving transformations performed by a compiler are done only when the optimization algorithms can verify the noninterference of the modification.

All the optimizations that we discuss here should be performed by the compiler. This can be checked by compiling using switches that will generate assembly code, and by "eyeballing" the generated code. In this chapter we will look at the notion of simple transformations and the way execution flows through a program, and then enumerate some optimizations that are expected from an optimizing compiler.

Simple Transformations

Traditionally, code optimizations were classified on the basis of the context through which the code transformation took place. Because in the past the runtime bottleneck was at the CPU, traditionally, most optimizations were performed to cut down on the computation time. For this reason, most of the traditional optimizations are designed to reduce computation. While our concern is enhancing locality of reference by examining the memory reference activity of a program, there may be a lot of "junky" code that clutters up a program and hides opportunities for memory optimizations. For this reason, it is important to learn about simpler transformations that make the more complex transformations easier to apply.

Before discussing the different classes of optimization, it is worthwhile to give an overview of a program's control flow structure. The control flow graph of a program is its road map; the control flow graph shows the sequence of execution of code throughout the lifetime of a process executing the program.

Control Flow

Control flow is the term used to describe the way that execution flows through an application. Nodes in a control flow graph represent straight-line sections of code called *basic blocks*. A basic block is a sequence of executable statements where the execution can begin only at the top of the sequence, and is not interrupted by branching of any kind until the end of a sequence. In a programming language, control structures such as IF-THEN, WHILE, DO, dictate how control moves from one basic block to another. Ultimately, the entire program can be mapped into a control flow graph. The constructs of the code determine how the basic blocks are attached to each other. In other words, a program can be described as a control flow graph where each vertex in the graph is a basic block, and the directed edges of the graph represent the way that the control in the program moves from one basic block to another.

Assignment statements do not affect a change in the control flow, while any conditional statements, looping statements, and GOTO statements will. A control flow graph is built by determining where basic blocks begin and end, and how they are attached to each other. For example, in the following set of statements:

```
x = z;
if (x > 10) {
    y = x * 2;
}
```

there are three basic blocks. The basic block structure is shown in Fig. 6.1.

Local versus global optimization

An optimization is referred to as a *global* optimization if the transformation affects execution across more than one basic block. An

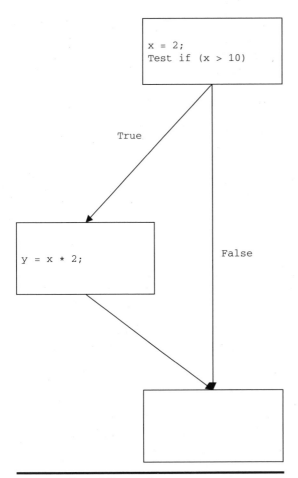

Figure 6.1   Control flow graph.

optimization is said to be a *local* optimization if the transformation affects the execution within a single basic block. Local optimizations are those that modify code on a *local* level, such as on operations within the same statement, or within a sequence of adjacent statements. Global optimizations may modify more than one statement in different basic blocks.

Kinds of Optimizations

All optimizations are meant to enhance an application's performance, whether by improving the time performance or the space performance. Optimizations can be loosely grouped into these categories:

- Reduction of computation
- Reduction of space consumption
- Reduction of code size
- Reduction of complexity
- Reduction of latency
- Distribution of work

It is worthwhile to point out that sometimes these goals interfere with each other. It can happen that in order to reduce latency, code size and complexity will increase. We will see examples of this later in the book.

Reduction of Computation

The simplest area of optimization is that of reducing runtime computation. These opportunities happen because of two reasons. The first is that a value may be precomputable at compile time, and the second is that the compiler algorithms can determine at compiler time that a value needed at runtime had previously been computed and can be reused. Let's look at ways this can be analyzed.

Constant propagation

Most programming languages provide a way to define named constants that can be referenced later in the program. Between named constants and explicit constants, whenever a constant is assigned to a variable, the compiler can tell that until that variable is reassigned, it holds the constant value. In later uses, these variables may appear combined with constants. When they occur, these constant-valued variables may be replaced by the values they had been assigned. This replacement, called constant propagation, is illustrated by this example:

```
PI = 3.14159;
...
area = 2 * PI * radius;
```

This can be replaced by:

```
PI = 3.14159;
...
area = 2 * 3.14159 * radius;
```

Constant folding

The compiler can also identify all operations that involve only constant operands. Since those values will not change at runtime, the operations may be precomputed, and the result may replace the expression. This optimization, called constant folding, can be performed on a local or a global level. In the example from above, the code could now be changed to:

```
PI = 3.14159;
...
area = 6.28318 * radius;
```

The compiler applies these two optimizations iteratively. As constants are propagated, opportunities for precomputation appear. As new values are precomputed, new opportunities for constant propagation appear.

Copy propagation

Just as the compiler can determine when variables hold constant values, the compiler can identify when two variables hold the same value. When a variable is directly assigned the value of another variable, as long as there are no other intervening assignments to either variable, any references to the assigned variable may be replaced by the variable whose value was taken. As an example:

```
x = y;              // Statement S1
...                 // no intervening changes to x̄
z = x + 10;  // Statement S2
```

can be changed to

```
x = y;          // Statement S1
z = y + 10;   // Statement S2
```

Common subexpression elimination

Just as it can identify precomputable constant expressions, the compiler can identify when two expressions compute the same value at runtime (even if the exact value cannot be precomputed). The optimization called *common subexpression elimination* deals with trying to determine if values have already been computed, and if so, to reuse the computed values. For example, consider this code:

```
a = x + y;  // Statement S1
b = x + y;  // Statement S2
```

In this code segment, the two variables x and y are added together in Statement S1, and again in Statement S2. Common subexpression elimination is performed to determine that the value of the sum of x and y in S1 is the same as the value of the sum of x and y in S2, and the result can therefore be reused. In essence, a compiler would assign the value of x + y into a temporary and use that temporary twice:

```
t = x + y;
a = t;
b = t;
```

Note that this optimization can be performed because there are no intermediate changes to the values of x and y between the two statements. If there were, we would no longer be able to assume that the sum of the two variables is the same. By iteratively applying copy propagation and common subexpression elimination, the amount of computation will be reduced.

Common subexpression elimination can help alleviate some stress on the memory system by reducing the need to access variable values in memory, and instead holding intermediate values in registers. If there are enough registers to hold onto the intermediate values, this is a good use of the top level of the memory hierarchy. On the other hand, if there are a lot of common subexpressions being stored in registers, this may induce a strain on the registers, requiring register spilling into the cache (and main memory).

Partial redundancy analysis

Programming languages allow the programmer to specify the control flow in a program using constructs such as IF-THEN-ELSE and WHILE. Global common subexpression elimination can be combined with another set of optimizations that are performed globally, which involve combining computations along different paths in the control flow graph. Frequently, after some constant and copy propagation have been applied, expressions appear along a branch of control more than once. This is called a redundancy, and if the compiler identifies redundant computation, the code will be moved to avoid computing the value more than once. By evaluating which expressions are computed along different paths into and out of different basic blocks in the flow graph, there can be some reduction in computation.

Often, certain computations are executed along different paths in the execution sequence. As an example, the following code segment contains an *if* statement:

```
v = x * y;
if (x == y) {
    z = x * y;
}
```

This code segment produces the flow graph contained in Fig. 6.2. Note that the value of (x * y) is computed both before the *if* statement, as well as inside the *if* statement. This recomputation of a value along a specific path of the flow graph is an example of *partial redundancy*. In other words, the value is computed once along one pathway in the flow graph, but is computed twice along a different path.

The optimization for this partial redundancy is to eliminate the recomputation along the pathway where it occurs twice. The value of (x * y) can be hoisted out of the *if* statement, above the assignment to the variable *v*, and stored into a temporary, which can then be referenced for both the assignment to *v* and the assignment to *z*:

```
temp = x * y;
v = temp;
if (x == y) {
   z = temp;
}
```

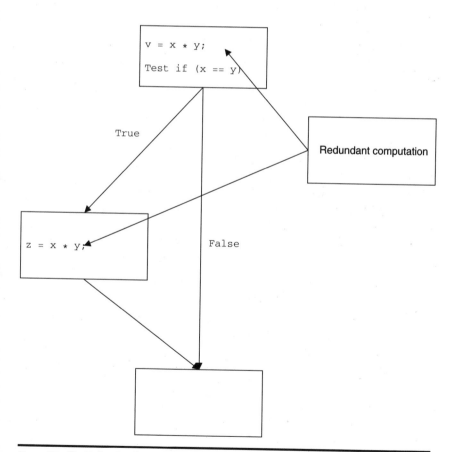

Figure 6.2 Partial redundancy.

Removing loop invariant code

The notion of common subexpression elimination can be applied to computations within the body of a loop. If a subexpression is computed each time through the loop, but the operands' values remain the same, we would like to remove that computation from each iteration and perform it only once. Consider this loop segment:

```
for (i = 0; i < N; i++) {
  A[i] = x + y;
}
```

We can see that the values of the variables x and y do not change inside the body of the loop, and therefore the value of $(x + y)$ will not change from iteration i to iteration $i + 1$. For this reason, the sum of $x + y$ should be moved outside of the loop, to be computed only once, instead of $N + 1$ times:

```
t = x + y;
for (i = 0; i < N; i++) {
  A[i] = t;
}
```

Code that does not change from one iteration to the next is called loop invariant code. When loop invariant code has been found, it can be moved to a location in the execution that preserves the correctness. This is an example of an optimization that is performed in preparation for more advanced loop optimizations.

Reduction of space

Most compilers do not have many explicit space reduction optimizations, but there are algorithms that analyze the use of space, and they can bring about a small reduction in memory usage.

Elimination of local temps

A local temporary is a variable used within a well-defined functional scope whose lifetime exists only throughout that scope. If that local variable is never used in a context where an address is needed (e.g., used as a function argument passed by reference, or its address assigned to a pointer), then it does not need to be assigned to memory. In other words, there is no need to allocate space for the variable. Instead, it can be placed in a register.

Useless variable elimination

If, after the previously discussed optimizations, a variable is seen to have been assigned, yet never accessed, the variable is said to be useless.

Because other optimizations have been performed, there is no longer any need for the variable in the program. Useless variables may be removed from the application.

Reduction of Code Size

Since machine instructions are stored in memory, they are subject to all the same memory hierarchy issues as variables. Hardware optimizations for instruction prefetching, branch prediction, and out-of-order execution help on the temporal locality front, but large code chunks or programs with many branches will have an effect on the spatial locality aspect. It is therefore beneficial to reduce code size when possible, especially inside loops.

Dead code elimination

In each program's control flow, it is possible that some branches of flow are never taken. In building code with diagnostics statements, or debugging statements, this will happen frequently. Any code along a path that is never traversed is called dead code. Since those computations are never reached, the code will never be executed, and can therefore be removed. An optimization called dead code elimination is applied to identify and remove code that is never executed.

The analysis for this optimization involves evaluating the values that are output to the user when the program is run and determining the computations involved in producing those outputs. All computations that are not pertinent to the output are not required. Often, code segments are bounded by *if* conditions whose values are known ahead of time. If the condition is known to be false, then the body of the *if* statement will not be executed. Since there is no way for that code to be reached during the program's execution, it is called dead code. A common example is debugging code, which is often bounded by an *if* statement checking if a debugging variable is set:

```
if (debug) {
   cerr << "The value is " << x << endl;
}
```

In code such as this, often the variable debug is assigned a 0 if there is no reason to be dumping out diagnostic messages, and is assigned the value 1 if the diagnostics are required. In this case, if debug is assigned a 0, the code inside the *if* statement is dead code; dead-code analysis would help to determine this.

Useless code elimination

All programs take input and compute some output. Any computations that are not directly associated with the output results are not necessary for the successful completion of the program. These computations that are not needed are called useless code, and they may be eliminated.

Useless code usually involves some computation whose effect is overruled without there being any use of the computation. Most often, useless code consists of an assignment to a variable followed by an assignment to the same variable without an intervening use. The first assignment's effect is nullified by the second assignment, so the first assignment is therefore useless.

As a simple illustration, consider this code segment:

```
x = y;    // Statement S1
x = z;    // Statement S2
```

Obviously, this contrived example shows how the assignment to the variable x in Statement S1 is useless, because immediately there is an assignment to the same variable in Statement S2 without there being an intervening read. This kind of pathological example does not occur often in programs as such, but will often appear as other optimizations are applied. For example, consider this code segment:

```
x = y + 2;    // Statement S1
z = x;        // Statement S2
x = y * 3;    // Statement S3
```

In this example, there is an assignment to the variable x in Statement S1. That value is used at Statement S2, and x is reassigned in Statement S3. We can see that the value assigned in Statement S1 need not be stored into x; instead, it can be stored directly into the variable z at Statement S2. By changing S2 to reflect this assignment, we get the following code:

```
x = y + 2;    // Statement S1
z = y + 2;    // Statement S2
x = y * 3;    // Statement S3
```

As a result of having made this change, the assignment to x in Statement S1 has become useless and can therefore be removed. Local useless code elimination can take place only on the basic block level, which does limit the amount of opportunities for applying this optimization.

Combination of optimization creates dead code

Most programmers do not write programs with dead or useless code. Both appear as a consequence of applying other optimizations. Once other optimizations have been performed, the usefulness of some pieces of code is diminished, sometimes to the point where the code can be eliminated. Consider this example:

```
x = 10;              // Statement S1
y = 20;              // Statement S2
z = x * y;           // Statement S3
if (x == y) {        // Statement S4
  z = z + x * y;     // Statement S5
}
cout << "The value of z is " << z << endl; // Statement S6
```

If we look at the variable output in Statement S6, we see that only the value of variable z is needed. There is an assignment to z at Statement S3 and at Statement S5. But we see that the value of x is 10, while the value of y is 20, so the test of (x == y) at Statement S3 is known ahead of time to evaluate to false. This makes the body of the *if* statement dead code, since there is no way that the code can be reached. Having eliminated that statement as dead code, the *if* statement now has an empty body; this makes the *if* statement itself useless, and then it can be eliminated. Also, knowing the values of the variables x and y (respectively 10 and 20), we can propagate the constants into statement S3, and fold the values into the expression assigned into z. Having performed these two optimizations, the assignments to x and y at Statements S1 and S2, respectively, have now become useless, and they can be eliminated. Finally, the value assigned into the variable z is known ahead of time, and can be propagated into its use at Statement S6. This propagation eliminates the need for the assignment to z at Statement S3, which can then be removed. The result of the combination of other optimizations and dead/useless code elimination is the following code:

```
cout << "The value of z is " << 200 << endl;
```

Peephole optimizations

Another code reduction technique is performed after code generation takes place. Frequently, instruction sequences that are close may be transformed into simpler (or shorter) sequences. Opportunities for these peephole optimizations were more frequent in CISC machines, but they still occur in RISC systems. For example, when an operand that appears as the result of one instruction is used as the source operand in the following instruction, with no further use, the instructions may be combined:

```
mov   8, r4
add   r3, r4, r5
```

If there is no further use of r4 before it is modified, this sequence may be changed to:

```
add   8, r3, r5
```

Reduction of Complexity

A set of optimizations deals with reducing the complexity of the computations that take place, since it is assumed that more complicated computations will require more execution time.

Strength reduction

Arithmetic operations can be classified by their "strength" in terms of how much computing power is needed to complete the operation. For example, exponentiation requires more computation than division, division requires more computation than multiplication, multiplication requires more computation than addition, etc. Strength reduction is the process of identifying code that can be transformed into functionally equivalent code of lower strength. For example, here is an opportunity to transform division into multiplication:

$$x = y/6$$

can be restated as multiplication by changing the division by 6 to a multiplication by $\frac{1}{6}$, (which, of course, will be precomputed at compiler time):

$$x = y * \frac{1}{6}$$

Another common example is that of the transformation of indexing expressions for arrays referenced inside loops. Consider this loop:

```
double a[ARRSIZE], b[ARRSIZE];
for (i = 0; i < ARRSIZE; i++) {
  a[i] = b[i];
}
```

The computation for the index expression for both arrays involves determining how far into the array to reference. For example, if i is

5 (i.e., the 6th iteration), then the address of a[5] is computed by multiplying the value of i by the size of each element of a, or 5 * 8, which is 40. The address to be stored during the 6th iteration is the address of a plus (5 * 8). This multiplication can be replaced by an addition when we recognize that since the induction variable is increasing by 1 each time through the loop, the address is incrementing by 8 bytes each time through the loop. Instead of computing the address by multiplying, we can compute the address by adding 8 to the address used in the previous iteration.

Algebraic simplification

Often a user may program expressions whose values can be calculated with a formula that is mathematically equivalent but computationally simpler. Simple examples reflect algebraic identity relations, such as addition of 0 to x being equivalent to (x), or multiplication of x by 1 being equivalent to (x). These equivalences may seem obvious, but are often only uncovered once other optimizations have taken place.

The table below lists some common algebraic simplifications.

Expression	Equivalent expression
$x + 0$	x
$x * 0$	0
$x * 1$	x
$x \wedge 2$	$x * x$
$x * 2$	$x + x$
$x / 1$	x

Reduction of Latency and Distribution of Work

Latency is the time spent waiting for data to be ready and available. We have already looked at some ways to reduce latency, such as instruction prefetching and branch prediction (i.e., reduction of instruction delivery latency) and out-of-order execution (i.e., reduction of operand latency). We have also talked about distribution of work in our discussion of pipelining and superscalar architectures.

The discussion of code optimizations for reduction of latency and for distribution of work is relevant enough to the memory hierarchy that it warrants its own chapter. We will look at these optimizations in the next few chapters.

Summary

In this chapter, we talked about some compiler optimizations, and what we can expect when code is written in a way that enables the compiler to do its work. We talked about the different kinds of reasons for optimizations, and then followed that with an enumeration of the different classes of optimizations. These include reduction of computation, reduction of space consumption, reduction of code size, and reduction of complexity. We covered a number of examples of these kinds of optimizations.

Some more complex optimizations regarding reduction of latency and the distribution of work are to be covered in later chapters.

7

Program Analysis

In this chapter, we will look at tools and techniques to help with performance analysis. First, we will put together a framework for comparing performance across different platforms, including ways to get a solid basis for analysis. The next section discusses timers and timing, which leads to a section on program profiling. We then discuss a few tools that can be used to do profiling. Once we show those tools, we will discuss what to do with the results: finding the best opportunities to optimize. This will lead to a section on techniques for analysis, including some examples.

Performance

Now that we have some insight into the organization of the memory hierarchy, how do we go about isolating the locations in a program that are performance problems? Recognizing sections of code that touch many hierarchy levels is a start, but when a user sits and waits for his program to finish, what do you do?

One suggestion is to wait for the update to the operating system, with all its optimizations, or to just purchase a faster upgrade to the hardware. Obviously, a Pentium running at 200 MHz is twice as fast as one running at 100 MHz, right? On the other hand, the processing requirements will always expand to the available resources—remember when personal computers sported only 64 KB of RAM? And we know that, despite the fact that a processor may be running faster, if the same bottlenecks exist, the doubled speed will not provide the expected kick.

Realize that, whatever the hardware level, a performance bottleneck rarely goes away; in fact it may even become magnified! Twenty years ago, machine instructions took many cycles, and the push in the world of code optimization was to cut the number of cycles of operations no matter how many instructions were used. An anecdote tells about how the floating-point division instruction on a particular machine was so slow that a bright programmer used approximation techniques (such as the Newton-Raphson method) to perform division. He replaced the single divide instruction with a sequence of 20 instructions, yet the approximation method gave the same result in 20 fewer cycles. Today, many of the same instructions take one cycle; doubling a processor clock speed will halve the execution time of those instructions, but the operands *still* need to be fetched from memory. If the speeds of the memory devices are not increased at the same rate, you cannot expect the execution time of all applications to decrease at the same rate.

Timers and Timing

The simplest way to measure the performance of an application is to time it. The range of granularity with which a program may be timed ranges from checking the clock to fine-grained timings kept track of inside the code. While wall-clock time is a discrete measure of an application's speed (i.e., how long the user sits and waits for the code to finish running), it does not give any kind of picture of the performance of individual sections of code.

Coarse-grained timing

Many systems provide a shell-level utility that can be used to time the execution of a program. As an example, the UNIX system facility called time, when invoked at the commandline along with the program to be timed, will print out a gross summary of the time spent during the program's execution. There are a number of results reported on the result line of the time facility, most of which are pertinent to the identification of performance bottlenecks, including:

- User time, in seconds. This is the amount of time the program executed in user code.

- System time, in seconds. This is the amount of time the program executed in system code.

- Total elapsed time. This is the total time, in seconds.

- Average amount of shared memory used. This is the memory space used to store the program code.

- Average amount of unshared memory. This is the amount of memory used to store variables and data structures.

- The number of page faults that occurred.

These measurements yield a gross approximation to key aspects of an application's performance. For example, the distinction between user time and system time indicates to the programmer whether the bulk of the execution time is spent in user-programmed code or in system code. If it is in the programmer's code, there may be opportunities to optimize, but if it is in system code, there may not be that much the programmer can improve (other than making sure that the application doesn't rely too much on the operating system).

Knowing the number of a program's page faults gives the programmer an idea about the virtual memory performance, and can help give some intuition as to where to look to improve the performance. The memory usage statistics are useful as well. If a large amount of unshared memory is used, and there are many page faults, perhaps the programmer was not so careful in data structure design and management. If there are a lot of page faults and the shared memory is large, it could be rectified by reducing the volume of code in the application.

Fine-grained timing

The operating system time utility is good for a very rough idea as to the performance characteristics of code. For a finer-grained analysis, a *timer* routine can be used to keep track of the amount of time spent in a particular piece of code. A timer is a function call that instantiates a ticking clock, usually calibrated to the machine's internal clock. For example, a timer may "tick" every 500,000 clock cycles. A timer will have a small number of functions, including *clearing, starting, stopping,* and *reporting.*

Clearing the timer means setting the clock to 0. Starting will begin the clock counting, and stopping will halt the counting. A timer can be queried to report the current accumulated time.

Timer functions are provided by the operating system for the use inside a program, although often the API for these timer routines do not specify a timer as we just described. For example, in HP/UX, there is a system call called `getclock`, which fills in a data structure with the number of seconds and nanoseconds since the system was booted. Figure 7.1 shows a C++ object definition for a timer.

In this object, there are private members that invoke the system call and log the time when the timer is started (in both seconds and nanoseconds). When the `clear_timer()` method is invoked, the private members `cumulative_seconds` and `cumulative_nanoseconds` are set to 0. The `stop_timer()` method will invoke the system call again, and subtract out the difference between the current time and the logged starting time to compute the cumulative time since the timer was last

```
#ifndef _SYS_TIMERS_INCLUDED
#include <sys/timers.h>
#endif
class my_timer {
  int cumulative_seconds;
  int cumulative_nanoseconds;
  int current_start_seconds;
  int current_start_nanoseconds;
  struct timespec i_time;
public:
  My_timer() {
    cumulative_seconds = 0;
    cumulative_nanoseconds = 0;
    current_start_seconds = 0;
    current_start_nanoseconds = 0;
  };
  void start_timer();
  void stop_timer();
  void clear_timer();
  void timer_gettime(int *, int *);
};
void My_timer::start_timer() {
  getclock(TIMEOFDAY, &i_time);
  current_start_seconds = i_time.tv_sec;
  current_start_nanoseconds = i_time.tv_nsec;
}
void My_timer::stop_timer() {
  int ns_i, s_i;
  getclock(TIMEOFDAY, &i_time);
  s_i = i_time.tv_sec - current_start_seconds;
  ns_i = i_time.tv_nsec - current_start_nanoseconds;
  if (ns_i < 0) {
    // We overstepped the nanosecond cycle
    s_i--;
    //since ns_i is negative, cum nsecs is 10**9+ns_i
    cumulative_nanoseconds = 1000000000+ns_i;
  } else {
    cumulative_nanoseconds += ns_i;
    if (cumulative_nanoseconds >= 1000000000) {
      cumulative_nanoseconds -= 1000000000;
      s_i++;
    }
  }
    cumulative_seconds += s_i;

}
void My_timer::clear_timer() {
  cumulative_seconds = 0;
  cumulative_nanoseconds = 0;
  current_start_seconds = 0;
  current_start_nanoseconds = 0;
}
void My_timer::gettime(int *secs, int *nsecs) {
  *secs = cumulative_seconds;
  *nsecs = cumulative_nanoseconds;
}
```

Figure 7.1   A C++ object definition for a timer.

started. This cumulative time is added into the members for cumulative time. With this object, a timer may be cleared, then started and stopped a number of times, with the cumulative time between start and stop always being added. The user, when finished timing the code, can invoke the `gettime()` method, which will report the accumulated seconds and nanoseconds. An example of the use of this timer object is shown in Fig. 7.2.

In the Microsoft Windows 3.1 API, there are two function calls that return the number of milliseconds since the system was booted. Those functions, `GetCurrentTime()` or `GetTickCount()` can be used to implement a code timer like the UNIX timer shown in Fig. 7.1.

The Precision and Accuracy of Timers

While system timing routines are calibrated to the machine clock, the precision and accuracy of the timers is implementation-dependent. For example, consider a machine with a 200-MHz processor clock. An internal timer interrupt may be configured to tick on every 200,000 cycles, or every 2000 cycles. If it is the former, each tick represents 200,000/200,000,000 seconds, or 1/1000 of a second. If it is the latter, the tick represents 2000/200,000,000 seconds, or 1/100,000 of a second.

In the first case, the timer ticks occur less frequently, so the timer interrupts interfere less with the application being timed. In the second case, the timer interrupts occur frequently, and there may be some interference with the application, possibly increasing the application's overall execution time. Our conclusion is that while the first timer may be less precise than the second timer (because its granularity is fairly large), it may be more accurate overall (because it is less intrusive to the applications). Conversely, the second timer is more precise (because of the fine granularity), but may be less accurate.

Timing and Optimization

One frequent stumbling block that appears when timing for performance improvement is the interference of optimizations the compiler may perform with timing. What happens is that unexpected transformations modify the code under investigation to the point that what the user thinks is being timed is very different than what really is timed.

Example   Compiler and timer interference   We can use the compiler optimization called useless code elimination as an example. Consider the following program:

```
main() {
int i,s,f;
double d;
My_timer * t1, * t2, * t3;
t1 = new My_timer;
t2 = new My_timer;
t3 = new My_timer;
t1->start_timer();
t2->start_timer();
for(i = 0; i < 1000000; i++)
  d = (double)i* (double)i;
for(i = 0; i < 1000000; i++)
  d = (double)i* (double)i;
for(i = 0; i < 1000000; i++)
  d = (double)i* (double)i;
for(i = 0; i < 1000000; i++)
  d = (double)i* (double)i;
for(i = 0; i < 1000000; i++)
  d = (double)i* (double)i;
for(i = 0; i < 1000000; i++)
  d = (double)i* (double)i;
t2->stop_timer();
t3->start_timer();
for(i = 0; i < 1000000; i++)
  d = (double)i* (double)i;
for(i = 0; i <> 1000000; i++)
  d = (double)i* (double)i;
for(i = 0; i < 1000000; i++)
  d = (double)i* (double)i;
for(i = 0; i < 1000000; i++)
  d = (double)i* (double)i;
for(i = 0; i < 1000000; i++)
  d = (double)i* (double)i;
for(i = 0; i < 1000000; i++)
  d = (double)i* (double)i;
for(i = 0; i < 1000000; i++)
  d = (double)i* (double)i;
for(i = 0; i < 1000000; i++)
  d = (double)i* (double)i;for(i=0; i < 1000000; i++)
  d = (double)i* (double)i;
for(i = 0; i < 1000000; i++)
  d = (double)i* (double)i;
t3->stop_timer();
t1->stop_timer();
int secs, nsecs;
t1->gettime(&secs, &nsecs);
cout << "It took " << secs <<" seconds and " << nsecs << "
nanoseconds\n";
t2->gettime(&secs, &nsecs);
cout << "T2 took " << secs <<" seconds and " << nsecs << "
nanoseconds\n";
t3->gettime(&secs, &nsecs);
cout << "T3 took " << secs <<" seconds and " << nsecs << "
nanoseconds\n";
}
```

Figure 7.2 The use of a timer object.

```
const MAXCOUNT = 1024 * 1024;
main() {
    double     a[MAXCOUNT], b[MAXCOUNT], c[MAXCOUNT];
    My_timer   *t;
    int        i;
    int        nsecs, secs;
    t=new My_timer;
    (*t). clear();
    for (i = 0; i < MAXCOUNT; i++) {
      b[i] = 0;
      c[i] = 0;
    }
    (*t). start_timer();
    for (i = 0; i < MAXCOUNT; i++) {
      a[i] = b[i]+c[i];
    }
    (*t). stop_timer();
    (*t). gettime(&secs, &nsecs);
    cout << "It took " << secs <<<" seconds and " << nsecs << "
nanoseconds\n";
}
```

When this code is compiled with high degrees of optimization, the user, in executing the timing statements, will find that the code runs significantly faster than expected. Why is this? The reason is that the compiler identifies all the code that is relevant to any output statements. That code is "useful," and any other code is "useless." Since useless code has no effect on the output, the optimizer eliminates it to speed up the execution.

In our example, the timed loop modifies the induction variable i and the array a. But no reference to either variable is made in the output statement, making the entire loop useless. The optimizer will eliminate the loop, effectively leaving this program:

```
const MAXCOUNT = 1024 * 1024;
main() {
    double     a[MAXCOUNT], b[MAXCOUNT], c[MAXCOUNT];
    My_timer   *t;
    int        i;
    int        nsecs, secs;
    t = new My_timer;
    (*t). clear();
    (*t). start_timer();
    (*t). stop_timer();
    (*t). gettime(&secs, &nsecs);
    cout << "It took " << secs <<" seconds and " << nsecs <<"
nanoseconds\n";
}
```

No wonder the program ran so quickly!

Fixing the timing interference problem

To fix this, the programmer must make sure that the timed code is not useless. This can be done in a few ways. One way is to add a call at the end of the program that uses the stored array a:

```
const MAXCOUNT = 1024 * 1024;
double get_max(double *ar);
main() {
    double    a[MAXCOUNT], b[MAXCOUNT], c[MAXCOUNT];
    My_timer  *t;
    int       i;
    int       nsecs, secs;
    double    foo;
    t = new My_timer;
    (*t). clear();
    for (i = 0; i < MAXCOUNT; i++) {
      b[i] = 0;
      c[i] = 0;
    }
    (*t). start_timer();
    for (i = 0; i < MAXCOUNT; i++) {
      a[i] = b[i] + c[i];
    }
    (*t). stop_timer();
    (*t). gettime(&secs, &nsecs);
    foo = get_max(a);
    cout << "It took " << secs <<" seconds and " << nsecs << "
nanoseconds to compute" << foo << endl;
}
```

This fix is useful for timing small loops that completely make up a
program. Another way to fix this timing issue, particularly useful
when there are many loops being timed in a large program, is to add a
dummy function call in the middle of the loop. Adding a function call
in the middle of a loop is a bit hazardous when it comes to timing, since
it may involve some saving of context and memory switching that will
affect the tested code, so use this method with care. Also, if the function call is completely empty and is contained within the same code
file, some sophisticated compilers may be able to inline the function,
then eliminate it:

```
const MAXCOUNT = 1024 * 1024;
void foo(double *a);
main() {
    double    a[MAXCOUNT], b[MAXCOUNT], c[MAXCOUNT];
    My_timer  *t;
    int       i;
    int       nsecs, secs;
    t = new My_timer;
    (*t). clear();
    for (i = 0; i < MAXCOUNT; i++) {
      b[i] = 0;
      c[i] = 0;
    }
    (*t). start_timer();
    for (i = 0; i < MAXCOUNT; i++) {
      a[i] = b[i] + c[i];
      foo(a);
    }
```

```
(*t). stop_timer();
(*t). gettime(&secs, &nsecs);
cout << "It took " << secs <<" seconds and " << nsecs << "
nanoseconds\n";
}
```

Profiling

While timing a program or a function will give you some insight into the performance characteristics of a piece of code, it is better to be able to see the relative performance of different pieces of an application. The context in which a sequence of routines is called may have an effect on the execution time.

In timing a specific segment of code by wrapping timer calls around it, the runtime computed is the total time of that function, along with all its descendants. To get a better feel for the component times, programmers will use a *profiler*, which is a program that analyzes the profile of an application; it comprises details about the runtime of each individual function in the application.

A profiler will build a collection of runtime statistics about each routine in the application. For example, a standard UNIX profiler called prof will produce a table with an entry for each routine specifying the percentage of time spent in the routine, the number of times the routine was called, and the average number of milliseconds for each call to that routine. Figure 7.3 shows a simple program that we'll use to demonstrate the output of prof. Note that there are three functions, each of which should execute in different amounts of time due to the nesting of the loops. The inner loop in the first function, func1, iterates 100,000 times. The inner loop in the second function, func2, executes 100,000,000 times: 1000 times more than the loop in func1. The inner loop in func3 executes 1,000,000,000; that is 10,000 more times than the loop in func1, and 10 times more than the inner loop in func2.

When this code is compiled with profiling information (consult the manual pages for your compiler's profiler switches), the generated executable has embedded code that will generate profiling information that can be understood by prof. First the program is run, and then the profiler is run, generating a file containing the information shown in Fig. 7.4.

Note that, as we expect, the program spends significantly more time in functions func2 and func3 than in function func1. Yet, even though the inner loop of function func2 executes fewer times than the loop in func3, function func2 took much longer than func3. This would point out to the programmer than function func2 might be a good candidate for investigation! The other entry points are also tagged with their profile information.

```
int func1() {
   int i;
   int h = 0;
   for (i = 0; i < 100000; i++)
      h = h + i;
   return(h);
}
int func2() {
   int i, j;
   int h = 0;
for (i = 0; i < 10000; i++)
   for (j = 0; j < 10000; j++)
      h = h + i + j;
   return(h);
}
int func3() {
   int i, j, k;
   int h = 0;
   for (i = 0; i < 100; i++)
   for (j = 0; j < 1000; j++)
   for (k = 0; k < 10000; k++)
      h = h + i + j + k;
   return(h);
}
main() {
   int i;
   for (i = 0; i < 100; i++) {
   printf("%d\n", func1());
   printf("%d\n", func2());
   printf("%d\n", func3());
   }
}
```

Figure 7.3 Sample code for profiling.

Call graphs

A way to add to the profile information is to build a *call graph,* which will indicate the nesting of function calls within the execution of a program. The timing that is counted is tallied for both the amount of time executed within a single function and the amount of time executed within a function and all its descendants. This way the user can get an idea of the time spent along a specific call sequence.

A commonly used call graph generator is called `gprof`, which is distributed as part of the GNU tools. This tool will perform an analysis similar to that done by `prof`, but a call graph is generated. An example of some of the output of `gprof` is shown in Fig. 7.5.

Keeping a clean machine

It is important to realize that, in timing or profiling an application, there should not be any other applications running that might interfere with the timing of the application under investigation. The reason for this is that, in a multiprogrammed environment, other processes are swapped in and out of memory and the CPU at different times. Not only does this affect the timing of the processor performance, because of the context switching time, it also affects memory performance.

As processes are swapped off the CPU, both their cache contents and memory pages are disrupted. It would not be surprising if data references that were in the cache before the swap might cause not only cache misses, but page misses and TLB misses as well after the swap. Therefore, it is worthwhile to run benchmarks and timing tests only on a clean system. The fewer running processes, the more accurate the timings will be.

Time	Seconds	Cumsecs	#Calls	msec/call	Name
88.0	19.38	19.38	5	3875.83	func2
11.8	2.61	21.99	5	521.98	func3
0.1	0.03	22.02	5	6.00	func1
0.0	0.00	22.02	1	2.50	_ioctl
0.0	0.00	22.02	16	0.00	_doprnt
0.0	0.00	22.02	16	0.00	_write_sys
0.0	0.00	22.02	16	0.00	write
0.0	0.00	22.02	15	0.00	_memchr
0.0	0.00	22.02	15	0.00	_printf
0.0	0.00	22.02	15	0.00	_wrtchk
0.0	0.00	22.02	15	0.00	_xflsbuf
0.0	0.00	22.02	1	0.00	__findbuf
0.0	0.00	22.02	1	0.00	_creat
0.0	0.00	22.02	1	0.00	_creat_sys
0.0	0.00	22.02	1	0.00	_getpid
0.0	0.00	22.02	1	0.00	_ioctl_sys
0.0	0.00	22.02	1	0.00	_monitor
0.0	0.00	22.02	1	0.00	_sigsetreturn
0.0	0.00	22.02	1	0.00	_sprintf
0.0	0.00	22.02	1	0.00	_start
0.0	0.00	22.02	1	0.00	atexit
0.0	0.00	22.02	1	0.00	exit
0.0	0.00	22.02	1	0.00	isatty
0.0	0.00	22.02	1	0.00	main
0.0	0.00	22.02	1	0.00	profil

Figure 7.4 Information file from prof.

% time	self	children	called	name
	0.00	22.12	1/1	_start [3]
[1] 100.0	0.00	22.12	1	main [1]
	19.44	0.00	5/5	func2 [4]
	2.65	0.00	5/5	func3 [5]
	0.03	0.00	5/5	func1 [6]
	0.00	0.00	15/15	_printf [394]

Figure 7.5 Output of gprof.

Low-Hanging Fruit

Aside from timers, profilers, and call-graph generators, the true measure of an application's performance is gauged against the user's time requirements. An application's performance is measured by its ability to complete the job within the allotted time constraints. To attain this performance, it is best to analyze a program to determine the best opportunities for improvement.

There is, however, a practical limit to how much a program may be improved. Consider a program with five functions: A(), B(), C(), D(), and E(). Let's say that 50 percent of the execution time is spent in function A(), 20 percent in function B(), and 10 percent each in function C(), D(), and E(). Let's say that we were able to improve the performance of function A() by a factor of 2. The runtime of the entire program would now be 75 percent of the original time, showing a 25 percent increase in speed. Now, if the performance of function B() were to be improved by a factor of 2, the time spent in function B() is 10 percent of the original program, and the runtime of the program will be 65 percent of the original runtime. This is about a 13 percent improvement over the last improvement, and an additional 10 percent improvement over the original time.

The other functions can be improved as well, but as we can see, we choose to grab for the "low-hanging fruit" first, trying to get the best improvements early. The process of performance improvement continues until each of the functions has been sped up as much as possible, but each improvement yields a lower increase in performance. Eventually, the runtime is dominated by the code that cannot be further improved.

Amdahl's law

This is an instance of the application of Amdahl's law, which, loosely, says that the execution time of a program will be dominated by the parts that cannot be improved. Amdahl's law gives us a practical limit on the improvements that can be made to a program. Amdahl's law was originally stated regarding the speedup that can be achieved by adding hardware processing elements to a computer system. The implication of the law is much broader, though. Amdahl's law specifies that after a certain point, the benefit that can be gained by attempting to increase the resources decreases as the benefits accumulate along the way.

As applied in the hardware situation, it means that after a saturation point, adding processors, memory, or disk space can only incrementally improve performance. As applied in the software optimization case, it means that as code is improved, the opportunities for more improvement decrease, as does the degree of improvement.

Top-Down Analysis

Using the timing and profiling tools, we can concentrate on finding the hot spots in the code. When we think about the places where performance could be an issue, we can infer the locations on the basis of some simple rules of thumb and some knowledge about the application.

The most obvious rule of thumb is that the code that is to be executed most frequently is the probable target for optimization. Remember our notions of locality of reference from the earlier chapters. The code that is executed most frequently will probably touch the same variables many times, or may compute arrays of values, and the code itself is referenced frequently. We see both spatial and temporal locality, which indicates an opportunity for memory hierarchy optimization. It is worthwhile to point out that despite the fact that some pieces of the code may have the potential to contribute to the runtime, most of the time there is some specific sequence of code that covers most of the execution. A good example is our sample code from Fig. 7.3. Our expectation may have been that the function whose inner loop was executed the most would have contributed the most to the execution time; it turned out that the code with the most loop nesting proved to be the costliest. Timing and profiling are the tools that will guide you to the right spot. We can concentrate on two other basic themes for isolating the target for performance analysis: data structures and inner loops.

Objects and data structures

Data structures are the abstract tools that are used to design the implementation of an algorithm. Since well-defined data structures are used throughout the execution of a program, a programmer's data structures designed with the memory hierarchy in mind will be more efficient overall.

Designing data structures with memory in mind evokes a number of questions. Is the object statically allocated (created once at program loading time) or dynamically allocated (created during execution time)? Only global data and static local variables are created statically, so another question arises: Is the object globally accessible or only locally accessible? Either way, it may be easier to plot the memory access patterns.

If the object is dynamically allocated, is it created all at once, or are different pieces created at different times? Is it created, deleted, and then created again? Can the dynamically allocated pieces be allocated in groups? Is it allocated in small chunks or large chunks? How often are the chunks allocated? How are they accessed?

Is the data structure big or small? If it is small, perhaps it will fit into a register, or a cache line. If it is big, will it fit into a memory page? If the way that the structure is accessed involves many memory references, is it possible to allocate the components so that they cause the least number of page faults? These are all questions to take into consideration in building a data structure.

Inner loops

The loop is a basic operation in computer programs; iteration is a good way to abstract an operation over a data structure, and the loop construct is used for most program implementations. When it comes to performance, one thing is clear: The code within a loop is executed many times. Make the code inside a loop perform well, and the loop itself will exhibit good performance. Analysis of the inner loop code must be done with the data structure being accessed kept in mind. The inner loop code will define the access pattern for the memory.

The workings of inner loops are prime target for performance analysis. It is important to remember, in talking about the effects of the code on the memory hierarchy, that it is not only the code *inside* the loop that must be monitored, but more important, it is the relationship between *different iterations* of the loop that must be analyzed. For example, remember the matrix addition example from Chapter 1? The code within the loop was very simple, but the fact that successive elements of the array were being accessed during each successive iteration was what affected the performance of the loop overall. We saw that for each element access, a set of array elements was brought into the cache, making the following iterations run without a fetch delay.

Example   As an example, let's look at a commonly used data structure, the hash table. Hash tables are used to index large amounts of data, and, as we discussed earlier, the notion of a hash table, or associative memory, is the basis for indexing into caches. A hash table is an array that is used to maintain an index based on a key. The data item indexed by the key is stored in the hash table along with its key as a <key, data> pair, and when the hash table holds many <key, data> pairs, it will grow very large. A *hash function* is applied to the key to yield the index into the array. As we have seen with caches, the attempt to map a large set of keys into a smaller data structure will result in a *collision* when more than one key hashes into the same index.

Handling hash table collisions

There are different ways to handle collisions: shifting the entry down in the array, rebuilding the table each time, or using buckets, which is the most common way. In a hash table, a bucket is a linked list of nodes hung off the hash table entry. Each node in the linked list holds a <key, data> pair. During a hash table lookup, the hash function maps the key into an index, and that index's bucket's linked list is walked, with each key compared to the search key along the way. If the matching key is found, the data item in the <key, data> pair is returned. Otherwise, failure is specified.

There are two stages of processing with a hash table. The first stage is building the hash table, and the second, more important, stage is the use of the table for key lookups. The construction of a hash table involves hashing each key into a hash bucket, allocating a new bucket node for the pair, and inserting the new node into the bucket. When a new bucket node is needed, it is allocated using the language's heap space allocation system. In C, and often underlying the new facility in C++, is `malloc()`, the heap space manager.

Hash tables, dynamic memory, and `malloc()`

How does `malloc()` work? The heap is configured as a set of lists of free chunks. When a request for a block or chunk of memory of a certain size is made, `malloc()` looks for the list of chunks in that size, in search of the first free chunk of that size. The first free block is assigned to be allocated, internal structures are updated, and a pointer to that block is returned to the caller. When a process frees memory, the released block is added to the list of free chunks of that block's size. When the program begins execution, the heap may be full of large chunks that are close to each other in the address space, but as the execution continues, chunks are allocated and freed, and the heap will become fragmented. When this happens, there is no guarantee of any degree of locality; each memory chunk can come from anywhere in the heap. There is a high probability that any two blocks adjacent on the free list are many pages away from each other.

Hash table access patterns

The hash table application will request many small chunks of memory for each new list node; if the hash table is large, this allocation request will happen many times. If the heap has become very fragmented, the linked lists in each of the buckets will be built as a linked list with no inherent locality.

A probe for a key into the hash table consists of hashing the key into an index into the hash array, accessing the bucket's linked list, and traversing the linked list until the key is found. What are the characteristics of the memory access patterns for this operation? Since, as we have seen, it is possible that the linked list was built from small memory chunks allocated from all over the heap, there is a sequence of memory accesses that involve no locality. Clearly, this poses a performance problem, and it can be viewed as a problem based on both the data structure itself (the way the structure is built) and the object's reference patterns (the way the structure is accessed) through its inner loops. The problem is that when a probe takes place, the walk through the buckets will probably cause not just a set of cache misses, but perhaps a set of page faults as well. If the goal of the hash table is to maintain a fast indexing system (remember, caches are like hash tables!), then a sequence of page faults on every probe will not help in attaining this goal.

Solution

How can we attack this problem? Remember that the performance focus is on optimizing probes into the hash table. If the nodes on each linked list bucket are from the same (or nearby) pages, chances are good that probes will exhibit some locality. A simple way to address this is to build the hash table the first time by inserting all the information into it, but then *rebuilding* the hash table. After the first time the table is built, all the information about the exact size of the hash array, the total number of entries, the number of buckets, etc., is known. The memory needed for the entire hash table can be reallocated as a single big block of memory. Then the data structure can have each of its pieces allocated separately through self-managed memory techniques.

Self-managed memory involves allocating one or more large chunks of memory to hold the different parts of the data structure. Each *pool* of self-managed memory is used for a different piece of the data structure; one pool for the hash array and another pool for the linked lists. When the table is rebuilt, for each bucket, only allocate nodes that share locality. This way, when a probe is performed, the loop that walks the linked list is walking along memory that comes from the same pool. Hopefully, this pool will lie in a set of memory pages that are near to each other, yielding a large degree of spatial locality when the buckets are walked. This simple trick of rebuilding the hash table will result in a more efficient hash table lookup sequence.

Summary

In this chapter, we looked at techniques for measuring the performance of an application. We focused on timers, then looked at profiling.

Having done our analysis, we then discussed the methods for choosing targets for further analysis. Since, as more optimizations are applied, there is a limiting factor to further improvement, we look at choosing "low-hanging fruit," or the code sections for whose optimization we stand to gain the most. Top-down analysis is a good method that helps focus on highly executed portions of the code.

We then looked at the example of the hash table, looking at the high executed probes into the hash table, and investigating its memory access patterns.

8

Writing Optimizable Code

Any programmer with an eye toward performance will (of necessity) use an optimizing compiler. But even optimizing compilers can become confused when accosted by unoptimizable code. In this chapter, we will look at some of the programming issues that prevent optimization or reduce performance, revolving around language and memory concerns. This will be peppered with some specifics about the performance of the Intel P6 architecture. We finish up with a discussion of how to address these optimization and performance issues in programmer source code.

What Prevents Code Optimization and Affects Performance?

In the previous chapters, we looked at what optimizing compilers will do. In this chapter, we start to look at what the compilers won't do. In the context of what we saw in the last chapter, we should be able to see what will prevent optimization.

Excessive use of registers

As we have discussed before, local uses of scalar variables are assigned to registers. In the load-store architecture, all values must be loaded into registers before operations may be performed. Therefore, when many scalar values are used at the same time, they must all be assigned to registers. But what happens when there are more scalar variables in use than available registers? To make room for the values in use, those not immediately needed are temporarily stored back to a preassigned location in memory, to be loaded back in when the value is needed. This is called *register spilling,* and the compiler inserts special code instructions called *spill code.* Spill code is bad because it might not only interrupt a streamlined execution without touching memory, it also exerts new pressure on the cache, forcing a new cache line (associated with the spill locations) to be brought into the cache, possibly displacing more important data.

Excessive use of globals

Global variables are anathema to optimizers for a few reasons. First, because globals are accessible to any module (as long as an interface has been expressed), they must be assigned to real memory locations, typically together in a segment of memory. Recall that local scalar variables, if their addresses are not taken, may be assigned to registers and have their need for storage eliminated. When scalar global variables are referenced, they must be assigned and loaded into registers, and modifications to globals will require copying back to memory. This is because at any later time the variable (or its address) may be referenced in another module.

Second, increased use of globals increases the complexity of global optimizations such as copy propagation and common subexpression elimination. More globals will increase the global register allocation pressure, thereby increasing the chances for register spill code, which causes extra context overhead in addition to taking up precious cache real estate.

Third, if globals are used in the program where local variables would suffice, the compiler will not necessarily recognize the "localness" of the computations, thereby forcing a storage requirement where it really is not needed. For example, if a global variable is used as an induction variable in a loop, the final assigned value of the variable must be stored back to memory. If a local variable is used for the loop counter and is not referenced before it is assigned again, it can be viewed as a local temp, and be assigned strictly to a register.

Most important, though, is the interaction between globals and pointers.

Function calls

In languages like C and C++, the compilation model allows for module-independent compilation. In other words, the programmer may write many functions, save them in different files, compile them separately, and link them together when completing the construction of an application. This means that while there is an interface exposure requirement for all modules, the compilation process cannot know what happens within any called functions.

Because of this, function calls are assumed by the compiler to be relatively destructive. That means that in the control flow mapping, a function represents a place where all global variables, as well as any data objects passed by reference to the function, may be assumed to be modified. Remember that even though your functions may not "kill" memory like that, the compiler cannot know this, and therefore optimization opportunities may be decreased.

Excessive use of pointers

Pointers are poison to optimizing compilers. We discussed copy propagation, the method of remembering that an assigned value is still stored in a variable, and that all copied variables share that value. When storing a new value to a variable, it is said to "kill" the previous value of the variable. Remember that a pointer can point to any region in memory accessible to the executing program, and therefore writing through a pointer kills all memory locations (including all global variables) that can be pointed to by that pointer, which cripples many optimizing opportunities.

For example, consider this function:

```
void vec_copy(double *a, double *b, int N) {
   for (int i = 0; i< N; i++)
     a[i] = b[i];
}
```

It may be clear that this is a simple function to copy one vector to another. We may not truly know, but our intuition may say that the assumption is that the function takes two nonoverlapping double vectors as arguments. But because the pointers a and b may point to any region of memory, they may point to the same or overlapping areas of memory.

Because of this, the compiler would not be able to perform any more than simple loop-oriented optimizations (e.g., strength reduction for the induction variable i), since doing so would violate unintended data hazard conditions.

Spaghetti code

As we have seen, branch prediction is a critical hardware optimization, so any code that defeats the branch prediction algorithms will affect the instruction pipeline, thereby defeating a key memory hierarchy optimization. Code that has many strands of execution (i.e., spaghetti code) will contain many conditional and unconditional branches. The more branches there are, the more the internal branch table must keep track. Spaghetti code will probably not adapt well to internal optimizations.

Not talking to the compiler

Have you ever wondered why there are so many programming languages, yet it takes a very long time for programming language standards to be defined? C++ was created in the early 1980s, but the first C++ standard was not agreed to until at least 10 years later. Programming languages are designed with certain issues in mind, depending on the kinds of work meant to be done and the kinds of machines targeted. In particular, certain language features are added to enable the compiler to do a good job.

A good example is the C++ language feature CONST. In C++, a CONST declaration defines a variable that is not to be modified. Under the best circumstances, a CONST variable is assumed never to change, so the compiler can avoid assigning memory to the variable. Therefore, using CONST can reduce the complexity of global optimizations and encourages constant and copy propagation.

More importantly, CONST variables passed into functions do not force a kill of any other variables. If all arguments passed to a function are CONST, and the function doesn't modify globals, then the function call is pure, and if the compiler is savvy enough, it can optimize through the function call.

Sometimes you can specify to the compiler some notions that override what is in the code. A good example of this would be a "-noalias" switch, which tells the compiler that even though there is use of pointers in a function, none of the pointers point to any of the same memory as any other pointer. In this case, the compiler would be safe performing certain optimizations that would not be performed otherwise. Consult the compiler documentation for available switches and options, and check to see what each option means, since many compilers may have the same switches with different meanings (e.g., the -O4 switch may mean different things to the Sun C++ compiler than it does to the GNU g++ compiler).

What Prevents Optimization: At the Processor

For elucidatory purposes, let us look at some of the kinds of code that can affect performance, and identify what the programmer needs to remember so that the compiler can do its work well. This will preserve the opportunities for performance improvement made available by any hardware improvements.

Partial register stalls

On the Pentium Pro and Pentium II processors, different-sized named registers are related. For example, two 8-bit registers are paired to form a single 16-bit register (e.g., the two 8-bit registers AL and AH together form the 16-bit register AX), and a 16-bit register is part of a 32-bit register (e.g., AX is part of EAX).

Overlapping uses of the partial portions of the register with the extended register creates a dependency between two instructions:

```
mov   8, BL
ADD   EBX, EAX
```

In this example, there is a move of 8 into the partial register BL, followed by a use of the expanded 32-bit register EBX. Since in the P6 architecture the instruction execution pipeline moves executed instructions to the retirement unit for completion, and dependent uses of values cannot be used until the store is completed, the second instruction must wait until the first instruction is retired. This is referred to as a partial register stall. Note that because of out-of-order execution, the instructions do not need to be adjacent in the code stream for this to happen.

Self-modifying code

Self-modifying code is code that modifies its own instruction stream. In cache-based architectures with instruction caches or instruction prefetching, self-modifying code can be hazardous. That is because the instructions that are being modified may have already been prefetched or loaded into the instruction cache when the modification takes place. Also, writing to the instruction stream turns the section of code into both code and data. In systems with separate instruction and data caches, this will cause a copy of the same information to sit in multiple caches—a cache coherence problem.

Obviously, if an instruction that had been prefetched is modified, the prefetched instruction is incorrect. Therefore, the instruction prefetcher needs to be stopped and reinitialized at the modified location. This incurs a significant delay, considering all prefetched instructions behind the offending instruction also need to be reloaded.

What Affects Performance: Memory

Misaligned data

What does it mean for data to be misaligned? Remember that data items are sized in terms of the number of bytes. An address is aligned on a particular byte boundary if it is evenly divisible by that number of bytes. In many processor programming models, accessing data that is not aligned on prescribed boundaries is not allowed. During execution, an attempt to access a data item whose memory is not allocated on the correct boundary will cause a runtime error (such as the mysterious, yet ubiquitous, "bus error" or "segmentation fault" messages that frequent UNIX systems). On the P6 processor, accessing misaligned data is allowed, but will cause a serious hit in latency. To understand this, we should review how data are loaded into the cache.

When a cache miss occurs, an entire cache line is brought into the cache. The data in the cache line is broken into four chunks (or blocks) of 8 bytes each (for a total of 32 bytes per cache line). The data chunks are streamed into memory using a round robin order. Let's refer to each of the four blocks as block 0, block 1, block 2, and block 3. In a round robin streaming, if the referenced address causing the cache miss is in the first 8 bytes of the cache line, the blocks are brought into the cache in the order: block 0, block 1, block 2, then block 3. If the address is in the second block, the fill order is blocks 1, 2, 3, 0. If the address is in the third block, the order is 2, 3, 0, 1, and if the address is in the fourth block, the order is 3, 0, 1, 2.

Remember that the bus is configured to transfer data in blocks of 32 bits, and the addressing mechanism for the bus will potentially require elision of low-order addressing bits (i.e., the low-end bits are dropped). This implies that if a data item is misaligned (Fig. 8.1), there is a chance that the data item might span two bus addressing locations, which in turn will force the machine to perform more than one bus access to grab the two aligned referenced 32-bit blocks. Once all the data have been brought into the cache, the referenced data item needs to be composed and loaded into a register.

Now, let's say that the data are not only misaligned on the bus boundary, but also on a cache line boundary (Fig. 8.2). A reference to the address will pull in the entire cache line, and if it is in the fourth block, the cache line is filled in the order 3, 0, 1, 2 before the second half of the data item is even brought in! There is a second cache line fill, followed by the split bus transaction and the composition of the

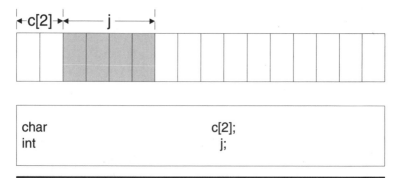

Figure 8.1 Misaligned reference.

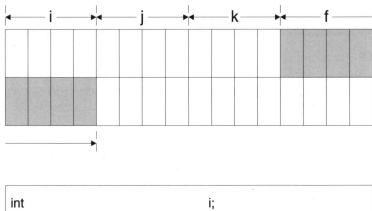

int	i;
int	j;
int	k;
double	f;

Figure 8.2 Split across a cache line boundary.

loaded data when transferred to a register. A misaligned reference that crosses a cache line boundary can incur a delay of 9 to 12 clock cycles, a significant latency hit! If an entire array is misaligned, an iterative loop access will have major performance degradation.

A programmer might say, "I have nothing to worry about—the compiler will handle data alignment for me." In simple programs, this will be true, but when programmers use more sophisticated memory management, they can get into trouble.

Let's assume that we want to manage a block of memory for generic data access. Since we don't want to limit our use of memory, we allocate the block as an array of char:

```
char  *mem = (char *) malloc(MEMSIZE);
```

We will allocate the memory as shown in Fig. 8.3.

We now manage our own array of memory, and allocate pieces out of that block. If we are not careful, it is possible that a data item as allocated (and later referenced via pointer) will be misaligned. For this reason, be careful when managing memory blocks.

Poor use of the data cache and poor data declaration

Before writing our code, it is useful to assess the cache configuration to see if it will have an effect on code performance. For example, loops

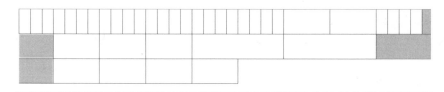

Figure 8.3   Some allocation.

similar to the vector addition example will have different performance characteristics depending on whether the cache is a write-through cache or a write-allocate cache. Recall from Chapter 3 that with a write-through cache, if the memory address that is being stored is not in the cache, the value is sent directly to memory. In a write-allocate cache, if a stored address is not in the cache, its cache line is first loaded and then the value is stored.

The wisdom behind using a write-allocate cache is twofold. First, there is a locality presumption that there will be reuse of the stored data at a future point in the execution. Second, the effect of a cache-line flush yields a "burst" write of data (i.e., the cache line is written out as a chunk of data) instead of individual writes, which thereby reduces bus traffic. But write-allocate can be disadvantageous when the memory addresses being stored are not close to each other, such as in this strided vector assignment:

```
for (i = 0; i < MAX; i = i + 9) {
  a[i] = b[i];
}
```

As we can see, in this example every 9th element of the array b is being assigned to the array a. With a cache employing a write-allocate scheme, each assignment to a[i] will load a cache line, then assign the value in the cache. Because there is no spatial locality (since no consecutive locations are being assigned), the two cache line fills (one for each array element) per iteration will slow down this loop in more ways than if the cache had a write-through organization. First, since there are two cache line loads instead of one per loop, there is twice the latency for loading data. Second, since we require loading from two different memory areas, there may be additional DRAM paging effects, as described in Chapter 4. Finally, if the architecture has multiple bus lines for reading and writing, in a write-through organization the assignments to array a can be overlapped with the cache line fetches for array b.

Another set of issues revolves around the declaration of data. The first issue is data layout. Some compilers allocate memory for variables in the same order in which those variables appear in the code.

Because of this, some layouts will cause misalignment. Misalignment and cache line splits may also occur if data structures are poorly defined. For example, if the compiler allocates memory for variables in the order in which they occur, consider the memory layout:

```
char   c;
int    a[12];
```

With this allocation, referring to elements `a[3]`, `a[7]`, and `a[11]` will cause cache line splits (see Fig. 8.4).

Another issue deals with the use of a data structure versus its declaration. A very simple example is the data structure called a compound array, which can be declared this way:

```
class compound_array {
private:
   int a[1024];
   int b[1024];
public:
   compound_array();
   ~compound_array();
   ...
};
```

This declaration implies that the component arrays are laid out in memory sequentially, first the a array followed by the b array. If the program accesses the two arrays sequentially, the performance should be fine. On the other hand, if the program always references the array elements in parallel, as in vector operations and, frequently, in graphics operations, then it may be better to declare the compound array as a collection of paired elements:

a[0]	a[1]	a[2]	a[3]
a[4]	a[5]	a[6]	a[7]
a[8]	a[9]	a[10]	a[11]
a[12]			

Figure 8.4 Allocation of memory causes cache line splits.

```
struct compund_array_element {
  int a;
  int b;
};
class compound_array {
  private:
  compound_array_element[1024];
  public:
    compound_array();
    ~compound_array();
    ...
  };
```

Poor use of instruction caches or prefetching

Remember that during pipelined instruction execution, one phase of the instruction pipeline is the fetching of instructions. In machine organizations with instruction pipelining, either instruction caches or instruction prefetch buffers are used to make sure that there are no stalls in execution due to waiting for instructions to be delivered to the CPU. Yet it is possible that some code can confound these hardware optimizations.

The most obvious instance is when control of execution jumps to many different locations. While hardware branch prediction is meant to help alleviate this by attempting to predict which branch will be taken, it is possible that the algorithms may be confounded when there are many branches that are taken in an unpredictable way.

Another way that the instruction caching can be confused is when code contains long and/or many deeply nested loops. A nice property of small loops is that they exhibit locality in both their data access patterns and their execution patterns. That is because typically the same instructions are executed over different data. If the loop is small enough, the entire set of instructions will fit in the instruction cache.

On the other hand, if the loop is large, then the chance that all the instructions will fit into the instruction cache is slimmer. If the instructions cannot all fit in the cache, the same kind of thrashing behavior will be seen as when the data access patterns indicate a blowout of the cache. That is, at some point, when the cache is filled, each subsequent instruction reference will require a cache line fill. (Note that there is no issue of a cache line flush, since instructions should not be modified during execution!)

Memory interference

The effect of accessing data elements that are not close to each other in memory, or that will not exhibit some kind of temporal locality, is that the benefits of the memory hierarchies will degrade. In other words, if the programmer is not careful about inserting apparent data dependencies inside tight loops or inside code streams that otherwise exhibit locality, the performance will be affected. We see many examples throughout the book that demonstrate this.

This may happen in some other ways as well. One simple example is the reuse of global variables for multiple purposes throughout the code. Frequently, programmers may make use of a single global variable as a test or sentinel for pursuing some action at different parts of the execution. When this happens, references to that variable may appear multiple times, even if the actual usage is not necessary at that time of the execution. Depending on the way the compiler interacts with the memory system, reuse of these kinds of variables may incur register spill and unspills, cache line fills, and TLB misses.

Another effect of interfering memory references takes place whenever significant state needs to be recomputed to access the data. Again, the DRAM paging mechanism is a good example of memory interference, where interleaved accesses to different arrays will result in downgraded performance.

Hints for Writing Performance Code

Pay attention to hardware effects

When the processor provides hardware optimizations, be aware of these optimizations and try to write code that enables them. In the P6 architecture, we have seen examples of hardware optimizations:

- Branch prediction
- Out-of-order execution
- Instruction prefetch
- Instruction scheduling

Data alignment

As we discussed regarding data alignment, many compilers will lay out data in the same order as declared in the program. Just as this can work against us, it can also be used to work for performance. Remember our biggest issue: misalignment causing cache line splits. Our goal, therefore, is to declare data in a way that avoids cache line splits. Also, we want to avoid declaring and using data structures that are not "cache-friendly." Here are some guidelines:

- Arrange your data so that the larger items are declared earlier than the smaller items.

- Declare arrays before scalars.

- If consecutive arrays' extents correspond to the cache alignment block size in a direct-mapped cache, there may be significant interference. Adjust the array sizes such that the two arrays' elements are not aligned to the same cache lines by adding some elements to the array.

- Make sure that data structures are aligned.

- Arrange data elements in a data structure such that individual elements do not cross the cache line boundary.

- Place data variables that are accessed at the same time close together.

- Place variables that are used frequently together.

- Pad arrays and data structures to make their sizes equal to multiples of the size of a cache line.

- Use static variables.

- Use `malloc()` to manage your own memory and verify alignment at runtime.

Software pipelining

Software pipelining is the method by which multiple instructions from different iterations of the same loop can be combined to be executed effectively in parallel. On a superscalar machine, if software pipelining has been performed, then iterated loops can be "folded on top of themselves." In other words, performance improvements may be found if, considering the execution of the entire loop instead of just iterations of the loop, the code can be transformed such that multiple iterations are in flight simultaneously. For example, consider this loop:

```
float X[MAX], Y[MAX], A;
for (i = 0; i < MAX; i++) {
  Y[i] = A * X[i] + Y[i]
}
```

This loop computes a constant A times a vector X plus a vector Y. Because in each iteration, the value being stored requires two loads, two floating-point arithmetic operations, and one store, each iterative assignment inside the loop must wait for the values to be loaded and for the operations to be performed before the value can be stored. This is a clear indication of a stall in processing, even though there shouldn't be any interference. Yet, if we look at the data dependence requirements of this loop, we see that there are no violating dependences. This means that the iterations may be performed in parallel. If this is true, then if we can restructure the loop so that iterations are being performed in parallel, then we can expect a gain in performance.

The way that we parallelize this loop is through software pipelining. Note that in the ith iteration of the loop, there are 5 operations: load ith element of X, load ith element of Y, multiply ith element of X by A, add to ith element of Y, and store back to ith element of Y. Yet, it is not necessary that these actually happen in the same iteration! In other words, let's instead break up the sequence of operations such that in each iteration i, pieces of the work from multiple operations are taking place:

```
T1 = X[0];   // First element of X
T2 = Y[0];   // First element of Y
R = T1 * A   // A * X[0]
T3 = T2      // Remember Y[0]
T1 = X[1]    // Second element of X
T2 = Y[1]    // Second element of Y
for (i = 2; i < MAX-2; i++) {
  Y[i - 2] = R + T3   // Store back (A * X[i - 2] + Y[i - 2])
  R = T1 * A          // A * X[i - 1]
  T3 = T2             // Remember Y[i - 1]
  T2 = Y[i]           // Get ith element of Y
  T1 = X[i]           // Get ith element of X
}
Y[MAX - 2] = R + T3   // Store back (A * X[MAX - 2] + Y[MAX - 2])
R = T1 * A            // A * X[MAX-1]
T3 = T2               // Remember Y[MAX - 1]
T2 = Y[i + 1]         // Get last element of Y
T1 = X[i + 1]         // Get last element of X
Y[MAX - 1] = R + T3   // Store back (A * X[MAX - 1] + Y[MAX - 1])
```

In this example, three iterations are taking place simultaneously. In each iteration, we are fetching the values required for two iterations ahead; we are multiplying A by the element of X for one iteration ahead, and we are adding and storing the values of Y for this iteration. Because we need to have three operations in flight at all times during the execution of the loop, there is a requirement for software pipeline "fill" code that precedes the loops and software pipeline "drain" code that pulls the last two values out of the pipeline.

Small loop bodies

Arranging iterative code using small loop bodies provides a number of benefits:

- It becomes easier for the compiler to identify opportunities for instruction scheduling.

- It becomes easier for the compiler to identify opportunities for automatic software pipelining.

- Small loop bodies have small amounts of code, which will not tax the instruction prefetch mechanism, and instead, all the instructions could sit in the cache.

- Small loops can be easily manipulated and combined.

- Small loops are better for compiler-directed cache and memory management through the use of automated loop transformations as described in Chapter 10.

In applications that make use of large array computations, it may be worthwhile to separate out the loops, optimize them, and maintain these computations as separate class libraries.

Language and compiler issues

All programming languages are designed to improve the way programmers write applications. Whether it is for performance reasons, ease of programming, or even just to optimize for a specific kind of application, different languages have different rules, syntax, and semantics. To this end, it is important to be aware of the differences when you are looking for optimization and performance.

As an example, a feature of Fortran that does not exist in C or C++ is the vector assignment. Similar in effect to the vector operation examples we have written in C++, in Fortran an array can be assigned directly to another array as long as the dimensionality and extents are the same:

```
REAL * 8 A(100), B(10, 10)
A(1:100:10) = B(2,:)
```

This means that the second row of the two-dimensional array B is assigned to every tenth element of the array A, as seen in Fig. 8.5. The same code in C++ would be:

```
for (i = 0; i < 100; i + = 10) {
  A[i] = B[1][i/10];
}
```

Because this capability is in the language, it is easier for the compiler to optimize for this code, since it is clear that there is no dependence. In C++, it might not be so clear. On the other hand, the object encapsulation capability of C++ allows the programmer some freedom in embedding the mechanisms by which operations take place.

Array A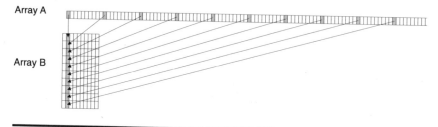

Array B

Figure 8.5 Fortran array segment assignment.

Summary

In this chapter, we first looked at what kinds of code prevented optimization. This included excessive use of registers, excessive use of
globals, too many function calls, and excessive use of pointers. We also
looked at why spaghetti code is unpleasant to a compiler, and why it is
important to understand the switches and options available at compilation time.

We then looked at some particular instances of processor-level code
and issues that prevent performance code from being executed, especially on the Intel P6. That included partial register stalls, and self-
modifying code. This was followed by a discussion of data alignment
(and misalignment), poor use of the caches, and poor data declaration.
We also discussed poor use of the instruction cache and prefetching, as
well as issues of memory interference.

The next section discussed some hints for writing optimizable code:
Pay attention to hardware effects, make sure data are aligned, be
aware of the possibilities of software pipelining, and keep loop bodies
small. We finished with a brief discussion of language issues. We will
follow up this discussion over the next few chapters, where we discuss
dependence analysis, advanced optimizations, and concurrency.

9

Data Access and Dependence Analysis

In this chapter, we will look at the ways that data are accessed during the execution of a program. In particular, we will look at an example of linked lists, which are ubiquitous in algorithmic programming. This will be followed by a discussion of data dependence, including some examples. The rest of the chapter deals with the analysis of data dependence.

Accessing for Locality

Now that we have taken a tour of the memory hierarchy, we can begin to look into the way that applications access memory. By looking for the code that exhibits poor locality characteristics, we can propose methods for optimization. In particular we will concentrate on small, tight loops of code that, because of their frequency of execution, may turn out to be the sources of many performance problems. We will look at some examples, and then investigate why certain code configurations will execute slower than others while performing the same function. In these examples we will concentrate on the locality issues that arise, and how they are addressed.

Sections of code have a certain pattern of accessing data. Memory access patterns of many code sections are relatively simple to determine, although there are complicated codes that are hard to untangle. Once a program's access patterns can be determined, the program may be evaluated for performance improvements, leading to modifications to the code as long as the correctness of the code is preserved. Different computer organizations and architectures may lend themselves to different kinds of performance improvements, but hopefully, in evaluating memory access pattern performance, the abstract memory hierarchy optimizations should be applicable across the board.

This chapter will concentrate on investigating some simple examples, discussing the access patterns, and isolating the memory hierarchy levels affected. Also in this chapter are a more formal discussion of memory access patterns and an introduction to data and control dependence, which are both important when evaluating code both for optimization and correctness. Finally, some techniques for dependence analysis will be introduced and discussed.

Linked Lists

High-performance linked-list code is important because of the frequent inclusion of linked lists in many basic data structures and applications (see Figs. 9.1 and 9.2.) Linked lists are used for list management, as well as the basis for trees, heaps, priority queues (as examples of more complex, yet still mundane data structures), and are pervasive in advanced applications such as compilers and operating systems. Linked lists are in widespread usage throughout computer science, and for this reason we use it as our first example.

There are two parts to a linked-list code: construction and traversal. The construction phase builds the data structure, and all accesses, including insertion into the tree, or searching or removal are all examples of traversal. Let's look at each of these operations in more detail.

The constructor of this class calls new() to create a new list node, and returns the node. The insertion method inserts the new node at the beginning of the list. The find() method traverses the list until the sought-after item is found, and the delete() method traverses the list until the correct item is found, but then removes the item when it is found.

As this code is written, the functionality of the linked list is implemented in a relatively naïve way when it comes to memory traversal. There are at least three issues that must be addressed in terms of memory performance, all stemming from the way that memory locations are accessed either during the creation of a list node, or during a traversal of the list.

Issue 1: Allocation

The first issue has to do with the way that the list nodes are allocated. Each time a value is to be inserted into the list, the C++ memory allocation method (new) is called to allocate a new list_node object. These list nodes are allocated from heap memory. The internal memory allocation system

```
#ifndef LINKED_LIST_INCLUDED
#define LINKED_LIST_INCLUDED
#define NULL 0
#define FALSE 0
#define TRUE 1
class list_node {
public:
  int data;
  list_node    *next;
  list_node(int datum) { data = datum; next = NULL;}
  ~list_node();
};
class linked_list {
public:
  list_node *root;
  list_node *last;
  linked_list();
  ~linked_list();
  bool insert(int datum);
  list_node    *find(int item);
  bool remove(int item);
  void dump();
};
#endif
```

Figure 9.1 Linked-list header file.

Figure 9.2 Linked-list code.

```
#include "linked_list.H"
#include <iostream.h>
list_node::~list_node(){}
linked_list::linked_list() {
  root = last = NULL;
}
linked_list::~linked_list() {
  list_node    *p, *q;
  p = q = root;
  while (q->next != NULL) {
    p = q->next;
    delete q;
    q = p;
  }
}
bool linked_list::insert(int datum) {
  list_node    *new_node;
  // Create a new list node with the data item inside
  new_node = new list_node(datum);
  // Insert the new node at the end of the list
  if (last != NULL)
    last->next = new_node;
  else
    root = new_node;
  // Reset the last node pointer
```

(Cont.)

Figure 9.2 Linked-list code (*Continued*).

```
    last = new_node;
    return(TRUE);
  }
list_node *linked_list::find(int item) {
    list_node *q;
    // Start at the beginning of the list
    q = root;
    // repeat until end of list
    while (q->next != NULL) {
      // If q holds this data item, then return it
      if (q->data == item)
        return(q);
      // Otherwise, go to the next
      q = q->next;
  }
    // Didn't find it? Return NULL
    return(NULL);
  }
bool linked_list::remove(int item) {
    list_node    *p, *q;
    // Start at the beginning of the list
    p = q = root;
    // repeat until end of list
    while (q->next != NULL) {
      // If q holds this data item, then delete it
      if (q->data == item) {
        p->next = q->next;
        delete q;
        return(TRUE);
      }
      // Otherwise, go to the next
      p = q;
      q = q->next;
    }
    // Didn't find it? Return FALSE
    return(FALSE);
  }
void linked_list::dump() {
    list_node *q;
    // Start at the beginning of the list
    q = root;
    // repeat until end of list
    while (q != NULL) {
      cout << q->data << endl;
      // go to the next
      q = q->next;
    }
  }
```

will search for a chunk of memory that is the right size for the element
requested. With the help of some insight into the way that internal memory
allocation takes place (such as that provided by malloc(), the library routine that often lies beneath new()), the free chunks of heap memory are
maintained in a linked list themselves. When a request is made for a chunk
of memory, the free list is traversed until a chunk of memory the right size

is found to hold the to-be-allocated data. Since there is no guarantee that any of the nodes on the free list are close to each other (see Fig. 9.3), the effect of traversing the free list may affect the cache behavior as well as virtual memory. The latter effect is especially true if memory requests are matched on a fine grain (meaning that the list is searched to find the best fitting chunk for the requested size), because the free list may contain many entries. Because of the size of the list, parts of the free list itself may have been paged out of physical memory. In the case of the code above, if many insertions are interspersed with many deletions, the free list may represent a relatively fragmented view of free memory chunks, exacerbating the problem.

Issue 2: Memory fragmentation

The second issue is that there is no guarantee that after allocation, any of these heap memory chunks are close to each other in physical memory. Therefore there may be a chance that there is no locality of reference for allocating memory as the linked list is being built.

Issue 3: Locality in traversal

This leads to the third issue: if memory for each list node is allocated from a different area of memory, then when the linked list is traversed, there will be no locality of reference either. That means that as the list is walked, there is potential for cache misses and page misses as well. The implementation above, even though it can be derived from any standard textbook, may exhibit poor memory behavior because of its simplicity.

In order to implement a memory-efficient mechanism for linked lists, we should address these three memory issues: memory allocation, fragmented and disparate free memory chunks, and the constructed list's traversal behavior. Our goal is to find an implementation that minimizes these effects while still providing equivalent functionality.

Instead of looking at the individual component functions applied to a linked list, let's think about the way that the data are accessed. For the most part, construction of each node of the list takes place only once, while traversal of the list may take place any number of times. Since the main function applied to the list is traversal, our object is to figure out a way to minimize the costs of walking the list. Obviously, if each node in the list lives in a different part of memory, the worst-case scenario involves a cache miss, or even a page miss on each traveled link. Instead, knowing that we would like to keep a set of nodes living in the same memory area, it would make sense to allocate them from the beginning so that they live in the same locale. Taking this idea a bit further, if we were to allocate a set of nodes from the same pool of

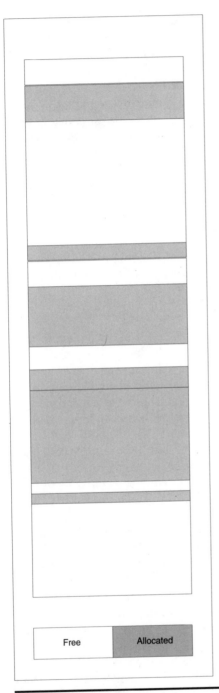

Figure 9.3 Allocated blocks from the heap do not always exhibit locality.

memory, the calls to the memory allocation routines would not cause the same kinds of problems enumerated above. On the other hand, it would be necessary for the object to handle allocation of objects from its own pool of available list nodes.

The solution is to have the linked list object allocate a collection of list nodes all at once, and manage its own free list internally. When the pool is allocated, a single large chunk of memory is allocated at one time, instead of a collection of smaller chunks at many different times. As soon as the pool is allocated, create an internal free node list as a stack from which to grab list nodes when needed. This way, when a new node is requested, it can be pulled directly from the free list, and the chances will be good that there will be locality: Presumably, the new node resides in the same memory page as many other nodes on the list. Another potential benefit is that by using a stack for the free list, there is a better chance for locality because the freed node may still have a copy in the cache. (See Figs. 9.4 and 9.5.)

```
#ifndef LINKED_LIST_INCLUDED
#define LINKED_LIST_INCLUDED
#define NULL 0
#define FALSE 0
#define TRUE 1
#define LIST_NODE_POOL_SIZE 1024 * 1024
class list_node {
public:
   int data;
   list_node    *next;
   list_node    *freenext;
   list_node(int datum) { data = datum; next = NULL; }
   ~list_node();
};
class linked_list {
   list_node    *root;
   list_node    *last;
   list_node    *pool;
   list_node    *freeptr;
   list_node    *grab_new();
   bool return_old(list_node *used_one);
public:
   linked_list();
   ~linked_list();
   bool insert(int datum);
   list_node    *find(int item);
   bool remove(int item);
   void dump();
};
#endif
```

Figure 9.4 Modified linked list: header file.

Figure 9.5 Modified linked list: code.

```
#include "linked_list.H"
#include <iostream.h>
list_node::~list_node(){}
linked_list::linked_list() {
  // allocate a pool of list_nodes
  list_node *_new_pool = (list_node *) ::new
char[LIST_NODE_POOL_SIZE *
sizeof(list_node)];
  // Allocated ok?
  if (_new_pool == 0) cerr << "Error in constructor\n";
  pool = _new_pool;
  // insert them into the free list
  // Free list links through the "next" member of list_node
  for (int i = 0; i < LIST_NODE_POOL_SIZE-1; i++) {
  _new_pool[i].freenext = (list_node *) &_new_pool[i + 1];
  }
  // The last node has a null pointer
  _new_pool[LIST_NODE_POOL_SIZE-1] = NULL;
  // Set the head of the free list to beginning of _new_pool
  freeptr = &_new_pool[0];
  // set default values
  root = last = NULL;
}
list_node *linked_list::grab_new() {
  list_node *p = freeptr;
  // Check to see if we are out of nodes?
  if (p == NULL) {
    cerr << "Out of nodes\n";
    return(NULL);
  } else {
    // We aren't. Return the next free node
    freeptr = p->freenext;
    return(p);
  }
}
bool linked_list::return_old(list_node *used_one) {
  // Push it on top of the free list
  used_one->freenext = freeptr;
  freeptr = used_one;
  return(TRUE);
}
linked_list::~linked_list() {
char *foo = (char* ) pool;
  delete []foo;
}
bool linked_list::insert(int datum) {
  list_node *new_node;
  // Create a new list node with the data item inside
  new_node = grab_new();
  new_node->data = datum;
  new_node->next = NULL;
// cout << (int) &(new_node->data) << endl;
  // Insert the new node at the end of the list
```

(*Cont.*)

Figure 9.5 Modified linked list: code *(Continued)*.

```cpp
  if (last != NULL)
    last->next = new_node;
  else
    root = new_node;
  // Reset the last node pointer
  last = new_node;
  return(TRUE);
}
list_node * linked_list::find(int item) {
  list_node *q;
  // Start at the beginning of the list
  q = root;
  // repeat until end of list
  while (q->next != NULL) {
    // If q holds this data item, then return it
// cout << "—-" << (int)&(q->data) << endl;
    if (q->data == item)
      return(q);
    // Otherwise, go to the next
    q = q->next;
  }
  // Didn't find it? Return NULL
  return(NULL);
}
bool linked_list::remove(int item) {
  list_node *p, *q;
  // Start at the beginning of the list
  p = q = root;
  // repeat until end of list
  while (q->next != NULL) {
    // If q holds this data item, then delete it
    if (q->data == item) {
      p->next = q -> next;
      return_old(q);
      return(TRUE);
    }
    // Otherwise, go to the next
    p = q;
    q = q -> next;
  }
  // Didn't find it? Return FALSE
  return(FALSE);
}
void linked_list::dump() {
  list_node    *q;
  // Start at the beginning of the list
  q = root;
  // repeat until end of list
  while (q != NULL) {
  cout << q->data << endl;
  // go to the next
  q = q->next;
  }
}
```

In the initialize routine, a pool of list nodes is allocated. Each list node takes up 8 bytes: 4 bytes for the integer and 4 bytes for the next pointer. Presuming that the page size is 1024 bytes, we can allocate pools of 128 list nodes that will still live in the same page. As soon as the pool is allocated, all the nodes in the pool are pushed onto the free stack, thereby inserting them into the cache. Now, as new elements are inserted into the list, the nodes are already extant in the cache. Also, there is a likelihood that traversals of the list will also stay in cache. When there are no longer any free nodes on the free stack, a new pool (of which all the nodes come from the same page) is again allocated. Figure 9.6 shows a stack of list nodes.

As to the improvement in performance between these two implementations: on two different machines, there was at least a 30–40 percent increase in speed with the linked list code!

Even though this implementation cannot guarantee that all the nodes will be in cache, or even have their pages loaded into physical memory, there is a greater chance of locality of reference. Since linked lists are the basis for many other basic data structures (binary trees, priority queues, B-trees, k-d trees, hash tables, etc.) an efficient implementation of linked lists is critical to good performance.

Vector Multiplication A relatively simple example of code that shows up frequently is vector-vector multiplication, or a dot product:

```
sum = 0;
for (I = 0; I < N; I++) {
  sum = sum + A[I] * B[I];
}
```

The access pattern in this code is straightforward: there are two arrays, each of which is accessed in serial order across the single dimension. As we have discussed in previous chapters, the locality behavior of this loop is simple. For each reference to an array element the cache is checked to see if the element is already there. If not, the cache line holding that element is brought into the cache, and the computation will stall until the requested operands are available. Figure 9.7 shows sequential corresponding accesses to both arrays.

Matrix Multiplication The result of multiplying two matrices A and B together into matrix C ($C = A * B$) is computed by performing a collection of dot products of rows and columns from the two operand arrays. The ijth element of the resultant array C is computed as the dot product of row i from array A and column j from array B. As in our previous example, the access patterns are simple, yet in this case, there is much different behavior. Here is the code:

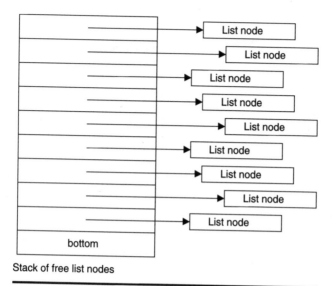

Stack of free list nodes

Figure 9.6 A stack of list nodes.

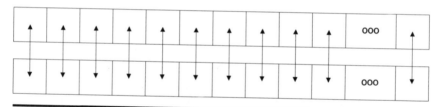

Figure 9.7 Sequential corresponding accesses to both arrays.

```
for (i = 1; i < N; i++) {
  for (j = 1; j < N; j++) {
    C[i][j] = 0;
    for (k = 1; k < N; k++) {
      C[i][j] = C[i][j] + A[i][k] * B[k][j];
    }
  }
}
```

Because each row must be multiplied by each column, every vector is
accessed N times. This would imply the existence of some degree of temporal locality along with the spatial locality mirrored in the vector-vector multiply. Yet, because the order in which the dot products are done, we lose the
benefits of the locality. In fact, under certain "wrong" circumstances,
the performance of this operation can be abysmal, considering the size of the
matrices compared to the size of the cache. In the next few chapters, we will
look at ways to transform these kinds of loops to take better advantage of
locality.

Data Dependence

Before discussing how to write and modify code for better memory performance, it is useful to understand something about the nature of performance enhancements via code transformations. Obviously, when modifying existing code for better performance, this is a useful skill. But why bother when writing new code? The reason is that most simple algorithms are enumerated in their most obvious-to-understand format. When describing a data structure, and the algorithms used to implement that data structure, most texts and guide books will be concentrating on clarity and not performance. When implementing these algorithms in performance mode, a clever programmer will need to do the performance analysis before the actual implementation.

When certain optimizations are to be performed, it must be determined that they are safe. A safe optimization is one that does not modify the outcome of the code being executed. Optimizations that are implemented as code transformations require that no interdependences in the execution sequence of the code are violated. For example, consider the following code segment:

```
x = y + 2;   // Statement S1
y = x * 7;   // Statement S2
```

The value assigned into y at Statement S2 depends on the value assigned into x at Statement S1 (Fig. 9.8). If the two statements were interchanged, the value assigned into y would be incorrect. In this example, statement interchange is not a safe code transformation. The issue above is an example of code dependence; Statement S2 depends on Statement S1.

Different kinds of dependence

We discuss two kinds of dependence: control dependence and data dependence. Control dependence involves the flow of execution based on the result of previous statements. Data dependence involves the flow and ordering of data variable assignments. As a conventional note, in the next sections, we will be referring to sequences of program statements, and tag them with names such as Statement S1.

Control dependence occurs when a statement is executed only under test of certain conditions. Statement S2 is said to be control dependent on Statement S1 if S2 is executed only if a condition tested at S1 is satisfied. A good example is a statement inside an *if* block:

```
if (foo == bar) {   // Statement S1
   x = x * 6;       // Statement S2
}
```

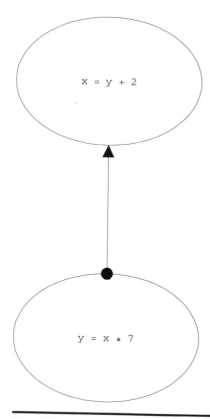

Figure 9.8 Statement 2 depends on Statement 1.

Optimizations must preserve the conditions of control dependence.

Another type of dependence occurs when a variable (or any memory location) is used in more than one statement. The order of occurrence of the uses in these statements defines the kind of data dependence. For example, consider the example from above:

```
x = y + 2;   // Statement S1
y = x * 7;   // Statement S2
```

In this case, the variable x is assigned a value at S1 that is read and used at S2. The assignment of a variable is referred to as the variable's definition. The read of a variable is referred to as its use. When a variable's definition (or "def") occurs before its use, we see a *forward*, or *flow, data dependence*. A forward dependence is also referred to as a *RAW*, or a read-after-write dependence.

Another kind of data dependence occurs when a variable's use occurs before its next definition:

```
y = x + 4    // Statement S1
x = 0;       // Statement S2
```

In this case, the assignment to variable x at Statement S2 must occur after the use of its previous value at Statement S1. When a variable's use occurs before its definition, we call it an *antidependence*. This is also referred to as a *WAR*, or a write-after-read dependence.

A third kind of data dependence occurs when an assignment of a variable in one statement is followed by an assignment of the same variable in another statement. Consider this example:

```
y = x + 2;   // Statement S1
y = z * 7;   // Statement S2
```

In this case, the variable y is assigned in Statement S1, and is then assigned again in Statement S2. When a variable is assigned in one statement and assigned again in a later statement, we call that an *output* dependence. This is also referred to as a *WAW*, or write-after-write dependence.

Data dependence restrictions must not be violated. In each of these examples, the data dependence prescribes the order in which the operations must take place. For a forward dependence between Statement S1 and Statement S2, the computation being stored in S1 must be completed before Statement S2 uses the value. For an antidependence between Statement S1 and Statement S2, the variable being assigned in Statement S2 must not be overwritten before its use in Statement S1. For an output dependence between Statement S1 and Statement S2, the assignment in Statement S2 must occur after the assignment in Statement S1.

There are algorithms that have been designed to investigate a code for its dependences; the investigation is called dependence analysis. While there are some very sophisticated methods for determining dependence, we will concentrate on a few simple methods, which may catch most of the important ones.

Dependence Analysis

What is dependence analysis? Before attempting to optimize code, we must first check that any transformations we will attempt to perform will not violate any correctness constraints. The constraints are centered around whether any dependences are broken by the attempted transformation. Dependence analysis is a set of methods to find out what dependences there are in a code sequence. Once these dependences are isolated, the optimizer may determine which code transformations are to be performed.

Dependence analysis can be quite complex. Optimizing compilers are built with many different tests for dependence. We will look at simple hints and tests for dependence. For the most part, in writing code, much of the dependences can be found by simple tests.

We can formalize the discussion of dependence analysis by describing the following sets of variables associated with Statement S using a modified form of the notation from Michael Wolfe's *High Performance Compilers for Parallel Computing*. The set *IN(S)*, called the IN set of a statement, is the set of variables that are read by Statement S. The set *OUT(S)*, or the OUT set of a statement, is the set of variables that are modified by Statement S.

Given two statements, S1 and S2, if any of the variables in OUT(S1) are also in IN(S2), there is a flow dependence between S1 and S2. If any of the variables in IN(S1) are also in OUT(S2), there is an antidependence between S1 and S2. If any of the variables in OUT(S1) are also in OUT(S2), there is an output dependence between S1 and S2.

Loop-carried dependence

Most of the optimizations we will be concerned with are performed on the code inside loops to make the overall loop runtime faster, and so we will look at dependence between statements inside loops. Identifying dependence in loops is more difficult than between any two arbitrary statements. Inside a loop, two statements may have a dependence inside an iteration of the loop, or there may be a dependence between the execution of a statement in one iteration of the loop on the execution of a statement during a different iteration of the loop. When one iteration of a statement depends on another iteration of a statement, the loop is said to have a *loop-carried* dependence. A loop-carried dependence may be between the same statement or between different statements in the loop.

As an example of a loop with a loop-carried dependence on the same statement consider the loop in Fig. 9.9.

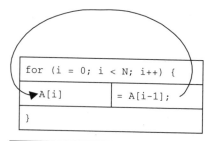

Figure 9.9   A loop-carried dependence.

```
for (i = 1; i < N; i++) {    // Statement S1
  A[i] = A[i - 1] * 2;       // Statement S2
}
```

In this loop, there is a loop-carried dependence on Statement S2. We can use a technique called *loop unrolling* to uncover the loop-carried dependence. Loop unrolling is used to cut down on the number of times the loop tests are executed, while still executing the correct number of iterations. This is done by "squeezing" two loop iterations into one loop body. During loop unrolling, the number of iterations of the loop is halved, while the body of the loop is copied once, and slightly modified to reflect the squeezed iteration. If the loop were to be unrolled once, the dependence would be immediately visible:

```
for (i = 1; i < N/2; i = i + 2) {    // Statement S1
  A[i] = A[i - 1] * 2;               // Statement S2
  A[i + 1] = A[i] * 2;               // Statement S2"
}
```

The loop-unrolling process has changed the number of iterations in this loop from N to N/2, since the loop induction variable I is incremented by 2 each time through the loop. To make sure that all the iterations are performed, the loop body was copied, and the copied line is changed to reflect the next virtual iteration having been added. Having unrolled the loop, we see that the array element read in Statement S2" is the same as the array element assigned in Statement S2, and this shows the loop-carried flow dependence.

Another way to see the dependence is to make a table of the iterations of the loop (see Table 9.1). By consulting Table 9.1, one can see that the value stored in each iteration is accessed during the following iteration.

As an example of a loop-carried dependence on two different statements, consider this loop:

```
for (i = 1; i < N; i++) {    /* Statement S1 */
  A[i] = B[i - 1];           /* Statement S2 */
  B[i] = B[i] * 2;           /* Statement S3 */
}                            /* Statement S4 */
```

TABLE 9.1   Iterations of the Loop

Iteration	Array element assigned	Array element accessed
1	A[1]	A[0]
2	A[2]	A[1]
3	A[3]	A[2]
4	A[4]	A[3]
⋮		
N	A[N]	A[N−1]

In this example, there is a loop-carried dependence between Statement S3 and Statement S2. To see this more clearly, let's unroll the loop:

```
for (i = 1; i < N/2; i = i + 2) {    // Statement S1
  A[i] = B[i - 1];                   // Statement S2
  B[i] = B[i] * 2;                   // Statement S3
  A[i + 1] = B[i];                   // Statement S2"
  B[i + 1] = B[i + 1] * 2;           // Statement S3"
}
```

As we can now see, the array element assigned in Statement S3 is the same one read in Statement S2". This shows the loop-carried flow dependence between Statement S3 and Statement S2.

With loop-carried dependences, the number of iterations that must execute before the dependence manifests itself is called the *dependence distance*. In our examples above, all the loop-carried dependences had a dependence distance of 1. Here is an example of a loop where the distance of the loop-carried dependence is 3:

```
for (i = 3; i < N; i++) {
  A[i] = A[i - 3];
}
```

The value assigned in iteration i is used three iterations later. One interesting feature of this loop is that the dependence does not "kick in" until the third iteration. That is, the values fetched during the first three iterations are not assigned inside the loop; only once the fourth iteration begins does the dependence manifest itself.

Detecting dependence

The basic question to ask when you are evaluating a loop is "Where, if any, are the dependent statements?" If there are no dependences, any correctness-preserving optimizations may be performed. If any dependences are found, the performance analyst may try to rearrange the code to break the dependences until the code is in a state where optimizations may be applied.

The question of dependence detection often boils down to asking whether any two array elements refer to the same memory location. For example, in this loop:

```
for (i = 0; i < N; i++) {
  for (j = i; J < M; j++) {
    A[i + j] = A[i - j+10];
  }
}
```

can `A[i + j]` ever refer to the same element as `A[i - j + 10]`, even in different iterations?

Loop index expressions and iteration space

To understand the issue more fully, let's look at this question more formally. We can configure the classification of loops in terms of levels of nesting, and accesses that are formed as a function of the indices of the loop nests. In other words, an n-level nested loop can be described as an assignment to an array when the index computations into the array(s) are functions of the loop induction variables:

```
for (i_0 = L_0; i_0 < U_0; i_0++) {
  for (i_1 = L_1; i_1 < U_1; i_1++) {

    for (i_{n-1} = L_{n-1}; i_{n-1} < U_{n-1}; i_{n-1}++) {
      A(f_0(i_0, i_1, . . . ., i_{n-1}), f_{n-1} (i_0, i_1, . . . ., i_{n-1}),
        . . . ., f_{n-1}(i_0, i_1, . . . ., i_{n-1})) =  . . . .;
      = A(g_0(i_0, i_1, . . . ., i_{n-1}), g_1(i_0, i_1, . . . ., i_{n-1}), . . . .,
        g_{n-1}(i_0, i_1, . . . ., i_{n-1}));
    }
  }
}
```

where f_i and g_i, for all values of `i`, represent functions of the loop indices.

The *iteration space* is the n-dimensional cartesian coordinate space representing the iterations of the n-deep nested loop. Each iteration is represented as a set of coordinates in the iteration space. For example, consider this loop:

```
for (j = 10; j < 16; j++) {
  A[j] = j * 2;
}
```

Here, the iteration space is a one-dimensional space representing the values that are assigned to the loop index `j`: (10, 11, 12, 13, 14, 15). If we institute a convention that all iteration space coordinate begin at the value 0, we will transform the iteration space into a *normalized* iteration space: (0, 1, 2, 3, 4, 5). As a graph, see Figs. 9.10 and 9.11. If the loop is doubly nested, the iteration space will have two axes; if there are three loop nests, the iteration space will have three axes, and so on.

Because there is an ordering to the sequence in which iterations are executed, we can define a lexicographic ordering of the points in the iteration space. As an example, consider this loop:

Figure 9.10 Iteration space.

Figure 9.11 Normalized iteration space.

```
for (j = 0; j < 5; j ++) {
    for (k = j + 1; k < 9; k++) {
        A[j][k + 1] = B[j][k];
    ;
;
```

The ordering of the iterations is as follows:

(0,1), (0,2), (0,3), (0,4), (0,5), (0,6), (0,7), (0,8)
(1,2), (1,3), (1,4), (1,5), (1,6), (1,7), (1,8)
(2,3), (2,4), (2,5), (2,6), (2,7), (2,8)
(3,4), (3,5), (3,6), (3,7), (3,8)
(4,5), (4,6), (4,7), (4,8)

Lexicographic ordering is important in discussing more complex loop transformations. We will see some examples of the use of the lexicographic order in the next chapter.

Our goal is to determine if there is a dependence between two statements in a loop. To do this, we need to determine whether anywhere at all in the sequence of statements, if we expand the loop, there exists a dependence between any two statements. This can be seen by looking at the set of all array references as if they had been expanded. We can represent the dimensional indices of a reference by a vector, denoted with letters of the Greek alphabet. Assume α and β are two sets of indices of two array references inside a loop, at Statements S1 and S2. There is a dependence between S1 and S2 if α is lexicographically less than β and this set of dependence equations is satisfied:

$$f_i(\alpha) = g_i(\beta) \ \forall i, 1 \leq i \geq m$$

That is, a dependence exists if α comes before β in the iteration sequence, but there is some instance where the actual array element referenced by α is the same as the array element referenced by β in another iteration.

For example, consider:

```
for (j = L; j < U; j++) {    // S1
   A[c * j + M] = . . . ;     // S2
   . . . = A[d * j + N];      // S3
}
```

In this example, is there a case where in two different iterations, where $j = x_1$, and $j = x_2$, such that $(c * x_1 + M) = (d * x_2 + N)$? If so, then if $L \leq x_1 \leq x_2 \leq U$, then there is a forward dependence between Statement S2 and Statement S3.

The equation $(c * x_1 + M) = (d * x_2 + N)$ can be simplified to more general format:

$$c\, x_1 = -M$$

$$d\, x_2 = -N$$

Renaming the constants c and d in this set of equations as a_1 and a_2, we get this set of equations:

$$a_1 x_1 = -M$$

$$a_2 x_2 = -N$$

Summing these two equations together, we get:

$$a_1 x_1 + a_2 x_2 = -M - N$$

We can collect the constant values that accumulate on the right-hand side of this equation into a single constant value C. This set of equations then, in general for i array references, can be summarized as:

$$\sum_{1 \leq i \leq N} a_i x_i = C$$

This summation represents the set of dependence equations for a collection of i array references. If there are more loop indices, then the dependence equations become more complicated. The above set of equations is known as a *linear diophantine equation*. Therefore, the problem of detecting dependence is equivalent to solving a set of linear diophantine equations. Clearly, though, solving this set of equations in one's head is out of the question. In fact, finding a solution automatically is basically computationally intractable as well, so we must rely on simpler tests.

The Greatest Common Denominator (GCD) test

One dependence test can be deduced by using the knowledge that a linear diophantine equation $\sum_{1 \leq i \leq N} a_i x_i = C$, where $g = \mathrm{GCD}(a_1, a_2, a_3, ..., a_n)$

(that is, g is the greatest common divisor of all the a_i's), has a solution if and only if g divides the constant C. Using our example from before:

```
for (j = L; j < U; j++) {    // S1
    A[2 * j] = . . .;        // S2
    . . . = A[2 * j + 1];    // S3
}
```

We find the linear diophantine equation is:

$$2x_1 = 0 \qquad \text{// equation 1}$$

$$2x_2 = -1 \qquad \text{// equation 2}$$

We subtract equation 2 from equation 1 to yield:

$$2x_1 - 2x_2 = 1$$

The GCD(2, -2) is 2. But 2 does not evenly divide the result 1, and therefore there is no forward dependence.

Eyeballing it

It is usually the compiler's job to detect dependence. While it is not the programmer's job to do this, as we have seen, there are language issues (particularly in the use of pointers in C and C++) that will prevent the compiler from being able to detect dependence. It is therefore a good idea to get into the habit of eyeballing code for loop dependences.

To eyeball a dependence, the programmer must have an understanding of the direction of data flow through the iterations. As we have seen, this is a simplified form of computing the iteration space, except that users will probably be able to do this only for simple loops (with nesting 1 or 2).

For most of our purposes, either eyeballing the loop or using the GCD test is sufficient to find the existence of dependence, although sometimes the GCD test is too restrictive (i.e., the conclusion is that a dependence exists, even though there really is none). A long-term research issue for compiler designers is to find better tests for dependence.

For the most part, if the programmer knows where the dependences are in the application, it will allow for code transformations that can help optimize for better access patterns. In the next chapter, we will look at code optimization in general, and at certain loop transformations in particular.

Summary

In this chapter, we looked at the issue of data access and how different data accesses are related within a program. We looked at an example of linked lists, showing that, depending on how the code was programmed, the memory access patterns could degrade or improve performance.

We also began to look at loop-oriented code such as vector and matrix operations. This led to a discussion of data dependence, of which we discussed three types: forward dependence, antidependence, and output dependence. This was followed by a discussion of dependence analysis and the issues regarding array indexing and loop nesting. We finished by looking at ways to determine if there are dependences in a loop.

Advanced Optimization

We have looked at simple code transformations that the compiler should perform. We have also looked at data dependence and how dependence analysis helps in deciding when certain transformations are legal. In this chapter, we discuss more advanced and complex code transformations that, if we are blessed with a good compiler, should be performed automatically when optimization is switched on.

If we are not so lucky, many of these transformations may be hand-coded by the programmer. These optimizations will require that dependence analysis be performed.

More Code Transformations

Statement reordering

Statement reordering involves the movement of one statement past another in the sequence of execution. There are a number of reasons to move statements, including attempting to increase locality. Another reason might be to amortize overhead during code scheduling; that is, if there is a significant latency involved in fetching an operand, moving the fetching of the data away from its use will allow other computation to overlap with the memory access, effectively hiding the memory latency. A third reason might be to move code closer together to improve the chance for other optimizations to take place.

As we have seen, in the P6 architecture, this is not as important an optimization. This is a result of the hardware's capability for out-of-order execution, which will automatically perform statement reordering dynamically. Even so, the ability to reorder statements during compilation will expose new optimization opportunities.

Note that before one statement may be moved past another set of statements, no dependences may be violated. Here is the first example in which dependence analysis comes into play. For statement reordering, both control and data dependences must be honored.

As an example of reordering statements to increase locality, consider this example:

```
a = x + y;   // Statement S1
b = v + w;   // Statement S2
c = x * 10;  // Statement S3
```

In this case there is a use of the variable x in both statements S1 and S3. Since there is no intervening assignment to x, we can reorder the statements to put the two uses of the variable closer to each other:

```
a = x + y;   // Statement S1
c = x * 10;  // Statement S3
b = v + w;   // Statement S2
```

Index set splitting

A transformation performed on a loop is to split the index set of the iterations of a loop into two parts. *Index set splitting* involves dividing the iterations of a loop into two groups, and then copying the body of the loop into both sets of iterations. The following code segment illustrates an opportunity for index set splitting:

```
for (i = 0; i < N; i++) {
  A[i] = B[i] + C[i];
}
```

The index set of this loop ranges from 0 to N. We can split the index set of this loop into two parts: from 0 to N/2 and from (N/2) + 1 to N:

```
for (i = 0; i < N/2; i++) {
  A[i] = B[i] + C[i];
}
for (i = (N/2) + 1; i < N; i++) {
  A[i] = B[i] + C [i];
}
```

Index set splitting (Fig. 10.1) is often used in a degenerate sense to remove the first (or last) iteration of a loop; this is called *loop peeling*. Loop peeling is a useful transformation for a few reasons. First, if there is an invariant expression computed within the loop, yet the expression would not be computed unless the loop is executed at least once, peeling an iteration from the loop can be used to remove the invariant code from the body of a loop.

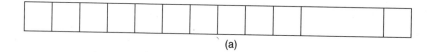

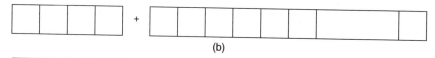

Figure 10.1 Index set splitting.

Consider this example:

```
for (i = 0; i < N; i++){
  A[i] = x * y + i;
}
```

The value of (x * y) is invariant, and needs to be computed only once. By peeling off the first iteration, we can compute (x * y) once, instead of (N + 1) times:

```
temp = (x * y);
A[0] = temp;
for (i = 1; i < N; i++) {
  A[i] = temp + i;
}
```

Other reasons for index set splitting are to enable other loop transformations, most particularly strip mining and loop fusion, both of which will be covered later in this chapter.

Loop unrolling

A simple loop optimization called *loop unrolling* consists of duplicating the body of a loop some number of times, and decreasing the number of iterations by a corresponding amount. If the loop's body is duplicated once, each iteration of the new loop corresponds to two iterations of the original loop, and in this case, the loop index would be incremented by 2 through each iteration, instead of just 1. As an example, consider this code:

```
for (i = 0; i < N; i++) {
  A[i] = A[i] + B[i];
}
```

This loop can be unrolled once, as long as any odd iterations are handled:

```
for (i = 0; i < N; i = i + 2) {
  A[i] = A[i] + B[i];
  A[i + 1] = A[i + 1] + B[i + 1];
}
// Handle the straggler
if ((N % 2) == 1) {
  A[N] = A[N] + C[N];
}
```

The loop body is still executed the same number of times, but the loop itself is executed half as many times. The result is that the test and branch code is executed half as much, which reduces the number of branches, thereby increasing the execution speed. Reducing the number of branches also accommodates any branch optimizations built into the processor.

A loop may be unrolled more than once, and as long as the odd iterations are executed, this can lead to a more advanced set of optimizations. As an example, the loop above can be unrolled yet again:

```
for (i = 0; i < N; i = i + 4) {
  A[i] = A[i] + B[i];
  A[i + 1] = A[i + 1] + B[i + 1];
  A[i + 2] = A[i + 2] + B[i + 2];
  A[i + 3] = A[i + 3] + B[i + 3];
}
// Handle the stragglers
for (i = i - 4; i < N; i++)
  A[i] = A[i] + C[i];
}
```

Remember that, in referring to two arrays, there may be some cache interference if the arrays are aligned along the same cache line mapping. If this is true, then the corresponding references to array elements in A and B will knock each other out of cache. This can be fixed by rearranging the sequence of statements inside the unrolled loop:

```
for (i = 0; i < N; i = i + 4) {
  t0 = B[i];
  t1 = B[i + 1];
  t2 = B[i + 2];
  t3 = B[i + 3];
  A[i] = A[i] + t0;
  A[i + 1] = A[i + 1] + t1;
  A[i + 2] = A[i + 2] + t2;
  A[i + 3] = A[i + 3] + t3;
}
```

The first access to an element of array B will bring the subsequent four elements into the cache. Storing those values in the temporary variables (t0, t1, t2, and t3) will have the effect of storing the values in registers. The next set of statements will load the values of elements in array A, (which may now overwrite B's elements in the cache), add the corresponding elements of array B from the registers, and store them back directly into the cache.

Loop fusion

Two loops that have an identical index set may be merged together into one loop, under the right circumstances. There are two major benefits to loop fusion. The first involves the reduction in loop overhead; instead of having two sets of loop index assignments and tests, there is only one. Enhanced scheduling possibilities and the potential for reuse are parts of the second major benefit. Both of these benefits can be illustrated by the following example:

```
for (i = 0; i < N; i++) {   // Statement S1
  A[i] = B[i] + C[i];       // Statement S2
}                           // Statement S3
for (i = 0; i < N; i++) {   // Statement S4
  D[i] = B[i] + A[i];       // Statement S5
}
```

which would be transformed into:

```
for (i = 0; i < N; i++) {
  A[i] = B[i] + C[i];       // Statement S2"
  D[i] = B[i] + A[i];       // Statement S5"
}
```

In the original set of loops, there is twice as much loop overhead than in the second loop. Note that there is a common use in both statements S2" and S5" of the ith element of the array B; this reuse avoids a memory reference per iteration. Also, note that in the transformed loop there is an immediate reference at Statement S5" of the value assigned into A[i] at Statement S2", effectively eliminating a memory reference, since the computed value can be held temporarily in a register within each iteration.

This optimization will also enable better code scheduling. Remember that any memory reference that is not in cache will force a cache reload; during the reload, any computation that does not ultimately depend on the fetched value can continue.

When can loop fusion be performed? Clearly, if a data dependence exists that would be violated by the fusion, the transformation is illegal. For example, consider this set of loops:

```
for (i = 0; i < N; i++) {      // Statement S1
   A[i] = B[i] + C[i];          // Statement S2
}                               // Statement S3
for (i = 0; i < N; i++) {       // Statement S4
   D[i] = B[i] + A[i + 1];      // Statement S5
}
```

In the second loop, there is an assumption that all the values of the array A have been assigned in the previous loop. If these two loops were to be fused, a spurious loop-carried antidependence appears:

```
for (i = 0; i < N; i++) {
   A[i] = B[i] + C[i];          // Statement S2"
   D[i] = B[i] + A[i + 1];      // Statement S5"
}
```

The value being fetched at Statement S5" (the reference to A[i + 1]) would be incorrect if the loops are fused. Before loop fusion, any dependence relationship must flow from the body of the first loop to the body of the second loop, except if it is carried by an outer loop. When trying to fuse loops, one must first test to see if the fusion would violate any dependence relations, such as in our example above.

Another requirement for loop fusion is that the loops be *compatible,* which means that the loops must execute the same number of iterations, and that they must be close to each other in the code sequence. As long as the number of iterations is the same, it does not matter if the induction variables are the same, or even if they refer to the same index set. The index set can be renamed to indicate that the number of iterations is the same. If the number of iterations is not the same, the loop peeling transformation can be applied to adjust the number of iterations. As an example, consider:

```
for (i = 0; i < N; i++) {        // Loop A
   a[i] = b[i];
}
for (i = 0; i < N - 1; i++) {    // Loop B
   c[i] = a[i + 1];
}
```

In this example, Loop A iterates N times, while Loop B iterates N − 1 times. We can peel off one iteration of the first loop, giving the following code:

```
a[0] = b[0]
for (i = 1; i < N; i++) {        // Loop A
   a[i] = b[i];
}
for (i = 0; i < N - 1; i++) {    // Loop B
   c[i] = a[i + 1];
}
```

These two loops now iterate the same number of times, and as long as no dependence is violated, the loops may be fused. We can see that the first element assigned to array A in Loop A is A[1], while the first element fetched in Loop B is A[1] also. Each corresponding reference to array A in Loop B refers to the element assigned in the same corresponding iteration in Loop A; the dependence is a forward dependence from Loop A to Loop B, which would not be violated by fusion:

```
a[0] = b[0];
for (i = 1; i < N; i++) {    // Loop A
  a[i] = b[i];
  c[i - 1] = a[i];
}
```

If the loops are not adjacent to each other, other optimizations may be applied to try to move the loops together. Particularly, if there is code between two loops, we can apply the statement reordering transformation to move code from between the loops.

Loop fission

Loop fission is the act of breaking a single loop into more than one loop. Loop fission can be said to be the inverse operation of loop fusion, and is performed to enhance locality of reference for both instructions and memory references. Loop fission can also be performed to enable other loop transformations that will enhance locality, such as loop fusion.

In terms of locality for instructions, when a loop contains many statements, loop fission can reduce the number of instructions that need to be loaded into the cache; with a processor with a small instruction cache, this differentiation becomes important.

An example of loop fission is the following:

```
for (i = 0; i < N; i++) {
  a[i] = b[i] * 10;
  c[i] = d[i] + 4;
}
```

In this case, we can divide this loop into two separate loops:

```
for (ia = 0; ia < N; ia++) {
  a[ia] = b[ia] * 10;
}
for (ib = 0; ib < N; ib++) {
  c[ib] = d[ib] + 4;
}
```

Dependence relations that are carried by an outer loop or are satisfied by an outer loop do not have to be preserved in fissioning a loop. When a compiler computes this, a graph is built that reflects the dependences between different statements in the loop body. If there are no cycles in the dependence graph, then the loop can be fissioned for each statement in the loop, and the subsequent loops can be reordered in the program in any order that preserves any dependence relations. For example, consider this modification of the loop above:

```
for (i = 0; i < N; i++) {   // S1
  a[i] = b[i] * 10;         // S2
  c[i] = d[i] + 4;          // S3
  e[i] = a[i];              // S4
}
```

The dependence graph for this loop is shown in Fig. 10.2. Since there are no cycles in the dependence graph, this loop can be fissioned into:

```
for (ia = 0; ia < N; ia++) {   // Loop A
  a[ia] = b[ia] * 10;          // S2"
}
for (ib = 0; ib < N; ib++) {   // Loop B
  c[bi] = d[ib] + 4;           // S3"
}
for (ic = 0; ic < N; ic++) {   // Loop C
  e[ic] = a[ic];               // S4"
}
```

Now, since the original dependence graph showed that there was a dependence between Statement S4 and Statement S2, the new loops can be reordered as long as the dependence between S4" and S2" is preserved:

```
for (ia = 0; ia < N; ia++) {   // Loop A
  a[ia] = b[ia] * 10;          // S2"
```

```
for (i = 0; i < N; i++) {        // S1

   a[i] = b[i] * 10;            // S2

   c[i] = d[i] +4;              // S3

   e[i] = a[i];                 // S4

}
```

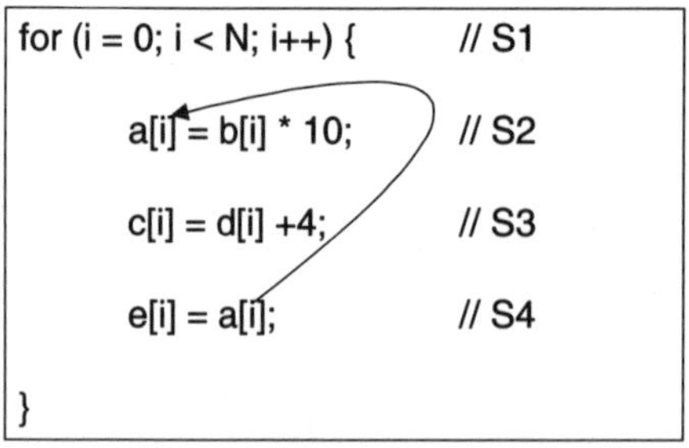

Figure 10.2 The dependence graph.

```
}
for (ic = 0; ic < N; ic++) {    // Loop C
  e[ic] = a[ic];                 // S4"
}
for (ib = 0; ib < N; ib++) {    // Loop B
  c[bi] = d[ib] + 4;             // S3"
}
```

Now that Loop A and Loop C are adjacent, the loop fusion transformation can be applied to enhance the locality of the reference to array A:

```
for (ia = 0; ia < N; ia++) {    // Loop A
  a[ia] = b[ia] * 10;            // S2"
  e[ia] = a[ia];                 // S4"
}
for (ib = 0; ib < N; ib++) {    // Loop B
  c[bi] = d[ib] + 4;             // S3"
}
```

If there are cycles in the dependence graph, then it does not mean that loop fission is not allowed. Cycles in the dependence graph imply the existence of loop-carried dependences. Statements involved in the loop can be separated out into their own loop body, while any other statements not involved in the cycle may be fissioned. To find all the statements involved in a cycle, use an algorithm to find the strongly connected components of a graph, an algorithm that can be found in many texts on graph algorithms.

Loop interchange

Loop interchange, which is probably one of the most important loop transformations, was originally developed to help with the discovery of parallelism inside loops, for the purpose of moving parallelism into the inside of a set of nested loops. If a loop-carried dependence is carried by an outer loop nesting, then the inner independent loops could be executed in parallel. Loop interchange consists of switching the nesting of loops. Loop interchange can be shown by an example. In a doubly nested loop such as this one:

```
for (i = 0; i < N; i++) {
  for (j = 0; j < M; j++) {
    A[i][j] = B[i][j];
  }
}
```

loop interchange would switch the loop nestings of the i loop and the j loop:

```
for (j = 0; j < M; j++) {
  for (i = 0; i < M; j++) {
    A[i][j] = B[i][j];
  }
}
```

Loop interchange (Fig. 10.3) is allowed as long as data dependence relations are not violated. If a dependence is carried by an inner loop, interchanging the loops must not change the loop carrying the dependence. Loop-independent relations must remain independent after the interchange.

A way to test for this is to compute the dependence distances for each loop nest. As long as interchanging loops does not create a situation where a dependence distance on one loop, when swapped, changes so that a new dependence appears earlier in the expanded statement sequence, the transformation is legal.

Loop interchange is not just used for finding parallelism. Other uses for loop interchange are to change the locality characteristics of a set of loops, to decrease the overhead of inner loops, and to increase the index-1 strides within a loop.

What is an example of a loop that can't be interchanged? A prime example is when the interchange would yield a dependence distance vector that is lexicographically negative—in other words, when modifying the loop nesting will affect the dependence relations, the interchange is illegal. For example:

```
for (i = 2; i < N; i++) {
  for (j = 2; j < M; j++) {
    A[i][j] = a[i - 1][j + 1];
  }
}
```

In this example, there is a forward dependence on the i loop and an antidependence on the j loop, and, with the loop nestings as shown, the dependence distance vector is (1, −1). The following table shows expanding out the sequence of assignments.

A[2][2]=	A[1][3]
A[2][3]=	A[1][4]
A[2][4]=	A[1][5]
A[2][5]=	A[1][6]
A[2][6]=	A[1][7]
⋮	
A[3][2]=	A[2][3]
A[3][3]=	A[2][4]

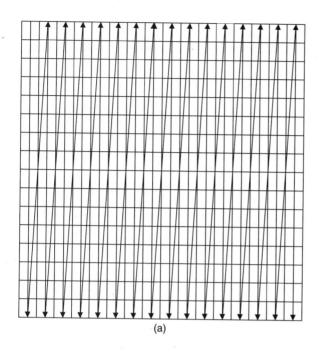

(a)

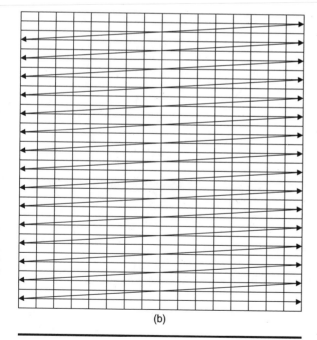

(b)

Figure 10.3 Loop interchange.

Should we interchange the loops, like so:

```
for (j = 2; j < M; j++) {
  for (i = 2; i < N; i++) {
    A[i][j] = a[i - 1][j + 1];
  }
}
```

then the dependence vector becomes (−1, 1), a lexicographically negative vector, indicating that the interchange is illegal. As a proof, consult the following table which shows the assignment sequence for the new loop.

$A[2][2]=$	$A[1][3]$
$A[3][2]=$	$A[2][3]$
$A[4][2]=$	$A[3][3]$
$A[5][2]=$	$A[4][3]$

Note that with the interchange, the array element $A[2][3]$ is used before it is assigned—a violation of the dependence relation, indicating that this interchange is not allowed.

Loop reversal

For any loop that has no loop-carried dependences, the iteration sequence can be reversed so that instead of iterating from the lower bound of the index set to the upper bound of the index set, the loop begins at the upper bound and iterates backward through the index set. This transformation is called *loop reversal*. For example, the loop:

```
for (i = 0; i < N; i++) {
  A[i] = B[i];
}
```

has no loop-carried dependences. It is therefore legal to reverse the iteration space to yield this loop:

```
for (i = N; i > 0; i--) {
  A[i] = B[i];
}
```

While legally reversing the loops does not have any effect on the correct behavior of the loop, loop reversal will (see Fig. 10.4) help in other transformations such as loop fusion. In particular, if the iteration space is reversed, a previously blocked opportunity to fuse loops may no longer be illegal. We saw in an earlier section that if there is a loop-

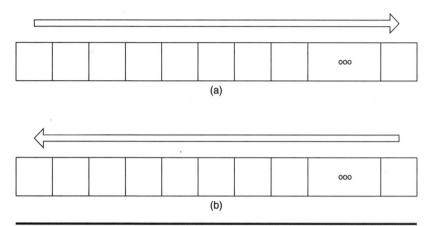

Figure 10.4 Loop reversal.

carried dependence introduced by an attempt to fuse loops that violates any previous dependence relationships between the bodies of the loops, the fusion is illegal.

By reversing a loop, what may have been introduced as a loop-carried dependence that violates the original dependence relationship may no longer be a violation. Consider this example:

```
for (i = 0; i < N; i++) {
   A[i] = B[i];
}
for (i = 0; i < N; i++) {
   C[i] = A[i + 1];
}
```

Attempting to fuse these two loops would result in the introduction of a loop-carried antidependence (i.e., reading element A[i + 1] before it is assigned in the next iteration), while the dependence relationship between the array references in the two loop nests is a forward true dependence (i.e., all elements of array A are assigned before in the first loop body being read in the second loop body). Loop reversal, however, will alleviate this problem. Let us apply loop reversal to the two loops:

```
for (i = N - 1; i > = 0; i--) {
   A[i] = B[i];
}
for (i = N - 1; i > = 0; i--) {
   C[i] = A[i + 1];
}
```

Now, except for the first iteration, the element of array A used in the second loop will always be the one that had already been assigned in the first loop. These two loops may now be fused:

```
for (i = N - 1; i > = 0; i--) {
  A[i] = B[i];
  C[i] = A[i + 1];
}
```

Strip mining

Strip mining converts a single-loop nest into a doubly nested loop. Strip mining, which is always legal, is used most notably for changing the locality characteristics of a loop, for vectorization, and for parallelization. Strip mining a loop consists of virtually breaking the loop into a loop of loops. For example, this loop:

```
for (i = 0; i < N; i++) {
  A[i] = B[i];
}
```

can be strip-mined into the following doubly nested loop:

```
for (It = 0; It < N; It = It + S) {
  for (i = It; i < min(N, It + S - 1); i++) {
    A[i] = B[i];
  }
}
```

In this example, the strip size S is used to block the set of references to both arrays A and B.

In strip mining, because the loop is changed from a single-loop nest to a double-loop nest, the dependence vector will necessarily change as well. (See Fig. 10.5 for an example of strip mining.) If the dependence distance of the original loop is d, then the new dependence distance is (d div s, d mod s). Also, if the loop cannot be converted to an even number of inner loops (that is, d mod s is not 0), then the dependence relation (d div s + 1, $-$((s $-$ d) mod s) is also generated.

An example of the use of strip mining in improving performance involves the notion of the "cache register." As we have seen, the cache is typically small in size, and if we make too many references to memory, we will find lots of cache turnover, especially in a loop that reads many distinct array elements:

```
for (i = 0; i < N; i++) {
  a[i] = b[i] + c[i] + d[i] + e[i];
}
```

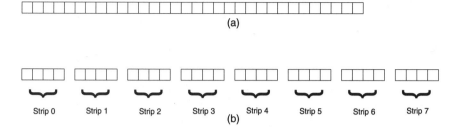

Figure 10.5   Strip mining into strips of size 4 elements.

In this case, we have references to five arrays in each iteration. The cache and memory access behavior here, if N is large, will not be conducive to good performance, since after a certain point, the cache will be saturated and each reference may force a line refill. Also, the many references to different arrays in sequence will have a serious DRAM paging latency, causing an additional decrease in speed at that physical level of the memory hierarchy.

Since strip mining is always legal, though, we can think of the cache as a set of vector registers, and operate our loop on vector chunks that we know will all fit into the cache simultaneously:

```
for (It = 0; It < N; It = It + S) {
  for (i = It; i < min(N, It + S - 1); i++) {
    a[i] = b[i] + c[i] + d[i] + e[i];
  }
}
```

Then, knowing that streaming data into the cache while maintaining good locality of reference will improve memory access performance, we can effectively load the vector strips into the cache as virtual registers:

```
for (It = 0; It < N; It = It + S) {
  // Cache line size is 4 elements: touch every fourth element
  // and the whole vector strip is brought in
  for (i = It; i < min(N, It + S - 1); i = i + 4) {
    t = b[i];
  }
  for (i = It; i < min(N, It + S - 1); i = i + 4) {
    t = c[i];
  }
  for (i = It; i < min(N, It + S - 1); i = i + 4) {
    t = d[i];
  }
  for (i = It; i < min(N, It + S - 1); i = i + 4) {
    t = e[i];
```

```
  }
  for (i = It; i < min(N, It + S - 1); i++) {
    a[i] = b[i] + c[i] + d[i] + e[i];
  }
}
```

If the cache line size is four integers, by loading every fourth element of each array in sequence we are loading in the whole strip as a direct stream, which will alleviate the DRAM paging pressure. In addition, with the vector strips loaded into the cache, the inner loop no longer has any memory stalls, since all the elements are known to be sitting in the cache.

Loop tiling

Strip mining is useful for single-nested loops. Loop tiling is the corresponding transformation for multiply nested loops. Loop tiling is performed to "block" the execution of a loop for the purpose of better spatial locality. A prime example where loop tiling (which at times is also referred to as "blocking") is beneficial, consider the classic matrix multiplication example:

```
for (i = 0; i < N; i++) {
  for (j = 0; j < N; j++) {
    for (k = 0; k < N; k++) {
      C[i][j] = C[i][j] + A[i][k] * B[k][j];
    }
  }
}
```

Here, each row of array A is fetched along with each column of array B. The dot product of the two vectors is assigned as the additive value into array C. Yet, when the matrices are large, there is no temporal locality, even though elements of arrays A and B are accessed multiple times throughout the loops. As we have seen in earlier chapters, if the arrays are large enough, each reference will turn out to be a cache miss, or even a TLB miss, which will cause a serious performance bottleneck. Instead, we can view the matrices as a collection of submatrices, as shown in Fig. 10.6. Each submatrix of array C can be computed as a sum of the multiplication of the submatrices of arrays A and B: submatrix $C^{21} = A^{21} * B^{12} + A^{22} * B^{22} + A^{23} * B^{32}$.

Breaking the arrays into blocks is an example of tiling. When tiling, each loop is adjusted to represent the tiling characteristics. The tile size ts represents the extent of the iterations for each loop index. The tile offset *to* is chosen such that each tile will start at an iteration *i* such that i mod $ts = 0$. In general, the rule for transforming a loop like

```
for (i = Lo_value; i < Hi_value; i++)
```

is to change the loop index to:

```
for (It = floor((Lo_value - to)/ts) * ts + to;
  It < floor((Hi_value - to)/ts) * ts + to;
  It = It + ts) {
    for (i = max(Lo_value, It); i < min(Hi_value, It + ts - 1); i++)
{
```

Applying this to the matrix multiplication code, we can choose a tile size of *s:*

```
for (It = 0; It < N; It = It + s) {
  for (Jt = 0; Jt < N; Jt = Jt + s) {
    for (Kt = 0; Kt < N; Kt = Kt + s) {
      for (i = It; i < min(It + s - 1,n); i++){
        for (j = Jt; j < min(Jt + s - 1,n); j++){
          for (k = Kt; k < min(Kt + s - 1,n); k++){
            C[i][j] = C[i][j] + A[i][k] * B[k][j];
          }
        }
      }
    }
  }
}
```

The three outer loops are the tiling loops, while the inner three loops are the original loops. By tiling the loops, we can take advantage of the locality of the fetched segments of the arrays as they fit into the cache.

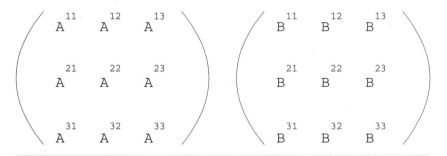

Figure 10.6 Submatrix decomposition of arrays A and B.

Instead of generating a cache miss on each access, sections of each array are loaded into cache and the elements in the cache are reused to compute partial results, which are then accumulated in the result array. As a result, the temporal reuse of elements is increased, which leads to much more efficient execution.

Scalar expansion

When there is a scalar variable inside a loop that is assigned and referenced inside the loop, this dependence may restrict an opportunity for optimization. For example, consider this loop:

```
for (i = 0; i < N; i++) {   // Statement S1
  temp = A[i];              // Statement S2
  B[i] = temp + temp/2;     // Statement S3
}
```

In this example, there is a flow dependence on the variable temp between Statement S3 and Statement S2, as well as a loop-carried antidependence from Statement S3 to Statement S2. The loop cannot be split, as a result of this dependence. Yet the dependence can be viewed as a transparent one; the final result assigned to temp is the one that is the most important; the rest are manifestations of output dependence.

A way to handle this is to promote the scalar to a vector. In other words, expand out the scalar variable into an array:

```
for (i = 0; i < N; i++) {                      // Statement S1
  temp_array[i] = A[i];                        // Statement S2
  B[i] = temp_array[i] + temp_array[i]/2;      // Statement S3
}
temp = temp_array[N - 1];
```

The loop has been transformed into one without the loop-carried antidependence. This loop may now be transformed by using some of the other loop transformations.

Summary

In this chapter we looked at more advanced and complex code transformations that should be performed automatically when compiler optimization is switched on, although many of these transformations may be hand-coded by the programmer. We discussed the use of dependence analysis as a tool for further optimizations, and how these optimizations improve the execution of the code. These optimizations, some of which require dependence analysis, include statement reordering, index-set splitting, and scalar expansion. We also looked at loop transformations such as loop unrolling, loop fusion, loop fission, loop interchange, loop reversal, strip mining, and loop tiling.

Advanced Optimizations for Concurrency

In this chapter, we will look at a different way to optimize code, both for computational improvements and for memory access improvements. The optimizations we consider in this chapter touch on the issue of simultaneous operation, or concurrency.

With the imminent appearance of multiple processor computers accessible to the desktop user, the notion of computational distribution becomes more important than ever. While traditionally, concurrent operation has been reserved for the world of supercomputing, shared-memory multiprocessor machines are increasingly available and affordable. When the symmetric multiprocessor machine becomes commonplace in the office, concurrency will be important for both memory and computational efficiency to take advantage of multiple processors.

Evidence of this trend can be seen in the increasing importance of the thread programming paradigm. Clearly, thread programming in Windows-based products can help with efficiency in dealing with event handling in an event-driven system. Also, threads are useful for controlling multiple GUI-based applications that require processing power behind the nice windows. But threads are important in high-performance applications on SMP machines, so hopefully the software trend will enable SMP hardware to comfortably sit in a desktop PC.

Also, an increasingly familiar computational paradigm is that of networked workstations. This framework consists of distributed workstations connected by network. Often, a fast network technology such as ATM (asynchronous transfer mode) is used for the interconnection to try to speed up data communications. Layered on top of this network is a layer of middleware: software to handle fast communication between processors. Applications can be built as a collection of processes running on top of distributed machinery.

In this chapter, we will discuss concurrency, and then look at different ways that concurrent operations can be implemented and taken advantage of during the execution of a program. We will look at the topic of scheduling, which is the mechanism of determining which operations will take place in what order. Also, we will look at threads, and how some of the loop transformations discussed in the previous chapter can be applied to create code for threads. We will also look at some more advanced issues on the parallelization of nested loops, as well as statement- and instruction-level parallelism achieved through code scheduling and software pipelining.

What Is Concurrency?

Concurrency may be defined as multiple operations taking place at the same time. Concurrent operation has been around for a very long time within the operating system. Early time-sharing and multiple-user machine systems made use of the virtual machine concept to give the impression that concurrent operations were taking place, although the granularity of the concurrency was on a user-by-user scale.

Concurrency reached a finer granularity with the implementations of *multiprogramming,* where multiple programs could be loaded as processes on a machine, operating simultaneously. *Processes* are individual entities, which do not share any memory. An even finer granularity can be reached with *threads,* also known as *lightweight processes.* Threads are individual execution "strands" that share a memory address space. The thread level is the obvious level where the types of analysis that we have discussed in this book are appropriate; we will show how data dependence analysis can be used to determine where code can be broken into threads suitable for a multiple-processor shared memory system.

At an even finer granularity, concurrency can be isolated inside small code sequences. In computer systems with multiple instruction issue processors, concurrency can be implemented by using a sequence of machine instructions. Particularly in certain matrix arithmetic algorithms, instruction-level parallelism can increase the execution speed significantly. Again, we will look at ways that data dependence can be used as a tool for the detection of instruction-level parallelism.

In any event, the detection of concurrent code is useful even in a computer system without any architectural support for parallelism. In particular, when the latency in memory accesses is an issue, the detection of concurrent code can be useful in scheduling the operations to overcome the latency limitations inherent in the memory organization. In a nutshell, the detection of parallelism can be very useful for explicitly defined parallelism or implicit parallelism in the execution of a program.

Concurrency, Threads, and Synchronization

Code can be broken into regions of sequential operation and regions of parallel operation. During the sequential operation, a single control process executes. At a parallel region, a collection of slave threads that will execute in parallel are initiated.

As each thread completes its portion of the parallel operation, it no longer continues to execute. Because the control process may not be able to continue execution until all the threads complete, all the threads must *synchronize* with the control process upon completion. The point of synchronization is called a *barrier*. At the barrier, either the threads may be destroyed, or, if thread start-up overhead is heavy, the threads may be idled until they are required for the next parallel region.

Even on a multiple processor system, if the system is not completely dedicated to a single application, the threads are still scheduled by the system scheduler. Because of this, it cannot be guaranteed that all threads will definitely execute simultaneously. Rather, if the threads can be assigned specifically to individual processors, an additional degree of performance can be achieved. The assignment of threads to processors is a scheduling issue.

Scheduling

Given a set of resources and a collection of tasks that require the use of those resources, a *scheduler* assigns the resources to the tasks in a way that makes efficient use of the resources. As a simple example, consider the general problem of scheduling processes on a CPU, where the processes have both computational and I/O requirements. Given two processes, as described in the table below, there are different choices for the scheduling.

Task	CPU requirements	I/O requirements
1	1 unit	2 units
2	2 units	1 unit

In Fig. 11.1, we can see two choices. In choice 1, the total time for both tasks to complete is 5 units, while in choice 2, the total time is 4 units.

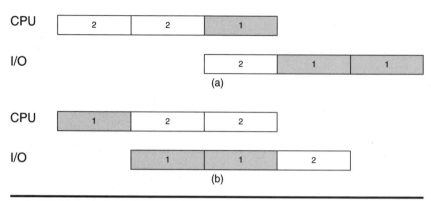

Figure 11.1 Scheduling choices.

Similarly, in our discussion of performance, the issue of scheduling appears both at a macro level (assigning tasks to processors), at a middle level (slave-thread scheduling for loop parallelism), and at a micro level (the ordering of instructions). On the high end, we must have faith in the operating system's ability to juggle jobs. At the middle level, we can make use of an operating system's thread capability to spawn lightweight processes to execute parts of parallel loops; on the other hand, we still may have to rely on the operating system to successfully schedule the threads. In some dedicated systems, we can actually assign threads directly to specific processors, where "dedicated" means that all the processors are to be exclusively reserved for the execution of a single process at a time. While it is possible to schedule parallel jobs on a dedicated system, often the system is completely allocated to a single job which runs to completion. For example, in a dedicated multiple-processor system, the protocol may allow for distinct processor allocations; in this case, the programmer (or the compiler) has the control over the scheduling.

At the low end of scheduling for parallelism is the topic of instruction scheduling. In most modern microprocessors, most instructions may take one or two clock cycles, including loads, as long as the data items required are sitting in the cache. Some instructions may take more time, such as floating-point multiplication or addition. Since superscalar superpipelined processors have multiple functional units, more than one instruction can be executed at the same time. In these processors, scheduling the instructions so that individual instructions can be issued simultaneously is a level of scheduling that we expect the compiler to provide. Nonetheless, the programmer can take steps to hint to the compiler the right way to schedule instructions.

Additionally, knowing that cache misses will take significant amounts of time, and also knowing that different kinds of access patterns will result in decreased locality of reference, the amount of time it may take for values to be accessed from memory is high, even if the instruction execution time is fast. In these cases, another form of scheduling can be used that attempts to overlap the memory reference latency with computations that can be performed. In particular, statements that are users of data items fetched from memory must wait until the values have been brought into the register set. When an instruction cannot execute because it is waiting for a value to be fetched from memory, the situation is called a *stall*. If we can rewrite our code so that the stalls are minimized, or overlapped with other computation, we can hide the latency, thereby increasing performance. This is done by using techniques called *code scheduling* and *software pipelining*.

Threads

Threads, or lightweight processes, are individual code strands that operate simultaneously within the address space of a parent process. Threads differ from individual processes in that processes all execute within individual address spaces. Processes take up their own context, and as a process is swapped in or out of the CPU, the entire context must be swapped as well. These context switches take significant amounts of time. Because thread execution is subsidiary to a specific process within the address space, threads do not require the same context-switching overhead as processes—thus the name lightweight process.

Threads are suited for concurrent execution over different portions of a shared memory object. In addition, given a set of threads that are to be assigned to a finite set of processors, we can look at the way that the threads are scheduled to the processors.

How are iterations assigned to threads? They are either scheduled ahead of time (statically), or at runtime (dynamically). In order to statically schedule iterations to threads, the programmer must have all the information about the division of work ahead of time.

Doling out the iterations to threads can be done as blocks of consecutive iterations (known as *block scheduling*) or by assigning each successive iteration to a different thread (known as *cyclic scheduling*). Examples of block and cyclic scheduling are shown in Fig. 11.2. In multiprocessor systems with shared memory and caches, it is wiser to use block scheduling if inside the loop the array references are index 1. If the loop is cyclically scheduled, each iteration must bring the referred memory location into the cache; if two successive iterations allocated to two different threads refer to the same cache line, there will be two copies of the cache line sitting in the caches of different processors. As we have seen elsewhere, having multiple copies of the same cache line sitting in different caches, even though the memory locations being accessed are different, will lead to false sharing. Modifications to elements in that cache line will force cache line invalidations across the bus, causing significant bus traffic that will form a bottleneck for other memory accesses.

We can easily build software that will behave the same as a statically scheduled allocation of iterations to threads. A class definition of a parallel loop is shown below:

```
class Threadifier {
    private:
        int _numprocs;
        int _lower_bound;
        int _upper_bound;
        int _stride;
    public:
        Threadifier(int number_of_processors=1);
        virtual void Loop(int index);
        ExecuteLoop();
        MakeThreads(int lb, int ub, int stride);
};
Threadifier::VirtualLoop() {
    p_lb = 0;
    p_ub = N/_numprocs;
    for (procs = 0; procs < _numprocs; procs++) {
        // Critical section wait
        wait (mutex);
        _lower_bound = p_lb;
        _upper_bound = p_ub;
        threads[procs] = create_thread(procs, p_lb, p_ub, LoopFunc);
}
Threadifier::Looper() {
    start = _lower_bound;
    end = _upper_bound;
    // let the threadifier start the next thread . . .
    signal(mutex);
    for (i = start; i < end; i++) {
        LoopFunc(i);
    }
}
```

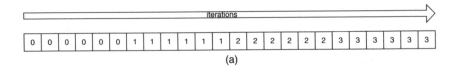

(a)

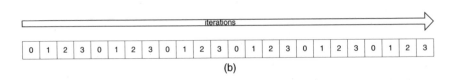

(b)

Figure 11.2 (a) Block scheduling. (b) Cyclic scheduling.

As long as there are the same number of processors as there are threads, static scheduling will provide a relatively balanced execution. On the other hand, if there are more threads than processors, the operating system allocation of threads to processors may lead to a *load imbalance*. A load imbalance indicates that some processors are working while other processors are idle. An example of an imbalanced allocation of work can be seen in Fig. 11.3.

To alleviate the load imbalance, we can allow *dynamic scheduling* of iterations to threads by "advertising" small units of the available work and allowing threads to compete for the next piece of work, until all the work is completed. This can be implemented by using a critical section, through which each thread must pass to be allocated a work unit. Through this scheme, all worker threads will be occupied at the same time, and if the threads execute at different speeds, this dynamic scheduling will let the faster threads take on more work, leading to a more balanced system.

The granularity of the size of the work unit in a dynamic scheduling scheme depends on different factors. Dividing the work into a very fine grain (e.g., one iteration per work unit) will lead to more balance, but will incur more scheduling overhead. Larger numbers of iterations in a work unit will reduce the scheduling overhead, but imbalance becomes more likely.

One answer to this conundrum is to dynamically modify the size of a work unit as the work is being completed. For example, a scheme could be to allocate to the next thread an amount of the remaining iterations proportional to the number of threads. The result is that faster threads will take on more work while the slower threads continue to execute, and as more work is completed, the rest of the work is handed out in smaller chunks to more threads.

Transforming Loops for Concurrency

Using the transformations described in the previous chapter, it is easy to design code that can trivially spawn threads to execute in parallel. But sometimes there are conditions that inhibit parallelization. In particular, some of those conditions are:

- Multiple branches inside the loop
- Calls to function or procedures inside the loop (including I/O)
- Loop-carried dependences

If the function call can be removed from inside the loop, then the possibility of parallelization is there again. For example, consider this loop:

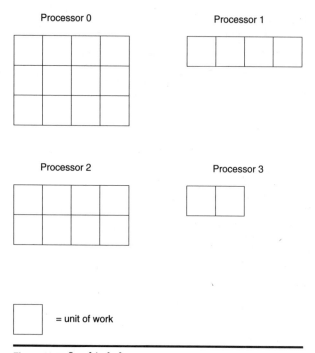

Processor 0   Processor 1

Processor 2   Processor 3

= unit of work

Figure 11.3 Load imbalance.

```
for (i = 0; i < N; i++) {
  A[i] = A[i] + foo(A);
}
```

In this example, the function foo() is called on every element of A before it is assigned. Because the call to foo() is in the loop, the loop cannot be parallelized, especially because the function may modify the contents of the array before the value is assigned. If we knew that the function is pure, and did not modify its arguments, then we could pull the calls to foo() out of the loop, and the results assigned into a temporary:

```
for (i = 0; i < N; i++) {
  TEMP[i] = foo(A);
}
for (i = 0; i < N; i++) {
  A[i] = A[i] + TEMP[i];
}
```

In loops with no loop-carried dependences, there are no constraints on the order of execution of the iterations. Because of this, the iterations could all be executed in parallel. In practice, subsets of the iterations are peeled off and collected into individual threads.

But what about loops that do have loop-carried dependences? Because of these dependences, the programmer is constrained from being able to parallelize the loops. There are two directions to go to solve this. One is to try to remove the loop-carried dependences, while the other route is to make use of synchronization primitives.

Removing dependence

One answer is to use the transformations discussed in the previous chapter to remove the offending dependences.

In this loop:

```
for (i = 0; i < N; i++) {
  A[i] = A[i] + B[i - 1];    // Statement S1
  B[i] = C[i] * 10;          // Statement S2
}
```

there is a loop-carried forward dependence from Statement S2 to Statement S1, and this prevents threading of the iterations. But, using the loop fission transformation, we can break the loop into two independent loops, making sure to adjust the iteration indices to not violate the dependence:

```
for (ib = 1; ib < N; ib++) {
  B[ib] = C[ib] * 10;
}
for (ia = 0; ia < N - 1; ia++){
  A[ia + 1] = A[ia + 1] + B[ia];
}
i = N + 1;
```

Note that because the dependence in the loop was between the assignment of an element from array B to the access of the same element in the next iteration of the loop, we must guarantee that the assignments take place in the right order. Yet, the element of B that is used to compute the value of array A is the value that had been stored on the previous iteration. Knowing this, we can break the loops using fission, which still has the loop-carried dependence in the first new loop, but not in the second loop, which can then be parallelized.

Another example is this loop:

```
for (i = 1; i < N; i++) {
  for (j = 2; j < M; j++) {
    A[i][j] = A[i][j - 1] + B[i][j];
  }
}
```

There is a loop-carried dependence in the inner loop from the assignment to element A[i][j] to the next iteration. Because of this dependence, the inner loop cannot be parallelized. Instead, if we use loop interchange to swap the loops, we get this:

```
for (j = 2; j < M; j++) {
  for (i = 2; i < N; i++) {
    A[i][j] = A[i][j - 1] + B[i][j];
  }
}
```

In this transformed loop, the dependence has been transferred to the outer loop. This allows the iterations in the inner loop to be executed in parallel.

A third example shows a loop with a more simple dependence:

```
for (i = 0; i < N; i++) {
  T = A[i] + B[i];
  C[i] = T + 1/T;
}
```

In this example, there is a loop-carried antidependence and a loop-carried output dependence on the scalar variable T. These dependences prevent the parallelization of the loop, even though the dependence is evidently avoidable. This can be alleviated by using another transformation, scalar promotion:

```
for (i = 0; i < N; i++) {
  T[i] = A[i] + B[i];
  C[i] = T[i] + 1/T[i];
}
```

In this example, we have eliminated the dependences on the scalar value by turning it into an array. Now that the dependences are gone, the loop may be parallelized.

Review of Loop Transformations

Below is a review of loop transformations and when these transformations are used:

Index-set splitting

- To remove invariant code
- To adjust loop indices for loop fusion
- To create iteration parallelization

Loop fusion

- To increase locality of reference
- To reduce loop overhead
- To enable more effective scalar optimizations

Loop fission

- To make the instructions in a loop fit into the instruction cache
- To expose opportunities for parallelism
- To separate references that may lead to cache interference

Loop reversal

- To reverse the dependence direction
- To enable loop fusion

Loop interchange

- To increase locality of reference
- To uncover opportunities for parallelization
- To decrease loop start-up costs
- To make certain inner loop array references invariant so that they may be removed

Strip mining

- To allow for parallelization when the dependence distance is greater than the strip size
- To increase locality of reference

Scalar expansion/scalar privatization

- To remove scalar loop dependences
- To allow for parallelization

Synchronization

The other way to handle dependence in the parallelization of loops is to insert synchronization primitives to guard the dependences. To do this, we must insure that the iteration with the dependent target does not execute until the iteration with the source of the dependence has executed.

Let us assume that we have at our disposal the standard mutual exclusion semaphores, *wait()* and *signal()*. These semaphores are applied to mutual exclusion variables, which are also referred to as *mutexes*. When wait() is applied to a mutex, the code stream executing the wait() stalls (or sleeps) until the mutex variable is set. In turn, the mutex is set by the signal() semaphore. When the signal() is executed, the first thread to have executed the wait() on that mutex is then free to continue processing. Since we know that, in a multiprogrammed system, interrupts may break the execution sequence of code, we must ensure that the wait() and signal() semaphore operations are performed *atomically;* i.e., the semaphore operations cannot be interrupted.

Given these semaphore operations, we can guard iterations by using an array of semaphores that span the iteration space. For a loop with a loop-carried flow dependence like this one:

```
for (i = 0; i < N; i++) {
  A[i] = A[i - 1] + 10;
}
```

we would want to make sure that iteration i does not execute until iteration i - 1 has completed. The code for the body of the loop would look like this:

```
register1 = fetch(A[i - 1])
register1 = register1 + 10
store register1 into A[i]
```

To guarantee that the parallel iterations do not violate the dependence, we must insert semaphore actions inside the code:

```
wait(iteration[i - 1])
register1 = fetch(A[i - 1])
register1 = register1 + 10
store register1 into A[i]
signal(iteration[i])
```

A vector of semaphores referred to as iteration[] is used here to implement the synchronization. In this example, the thread executing iteration i waits until the thread executing iteration i − 1 has completed. When the signal is performed, the thread executing iteration i may then continue.

Strip mining

Strip mining can also be used to help in breaking the dependence, if the dependence distance of the loop is greater than 1. If the distance is enough that the loop may be divided into strips shorter than the distance, then the iterations inside the stripped inner loop may be executed in parallel, with synchronization required for the new outer loop. For example, consider this loop:

```
for (i = 10; i < N ; i++) {
    A[i] = A[i - 10] * B[i];
}
```

In this example, there is a loop-carried forward dependence between the assignment to A[i] and the use of that element 10 iterations later. With a dependence distance of 10, we can strip this loop using 10 as the strip size:

```
for (is = 0; is < N; is = is + 10) {
    for (I = is; I < min(N, is + 10 - 1), I++) {
        A[I] = A[I - 10] + B[I];
    }
}
```

Inside the new inner loop, we know that none of the elements being assigned is going to be referenced during the execution of the inner loop. Therefore, each of the iterations may be executed in parallel, and the only need for synchronization is between iterations of the outer loop which now carries the dependence.

Loop tiling, being similar to strip mining, is also useful in alleviating dependences inside inner loops. The combination of loop skewing, which involves adjusting the iteration bounds, and tiling will potentially block the iteration space of a doubly nested loop in a way that can achieve both parallelism and spatial locality for iterating over areas of memory that are held in cache.

Instruction Scheduling

We have discussed the organization of a superpipelined superscalar processor. Even at the instruction level, there is still concern about latency and locality. In this section, we will look into ways to take advantage of the latency in instruction computation and in memory accesses to achieve a high degree of parallelism at the instruction level. Again we have concepts of overlapping parallel computations, and overlapping computation with communication.

Building on what we have learned about dependence, we can look at the implicit parallelism at the instruction level. For example, consider this code fragment:

```
r0 <- fetch(A[i])   ; instruction 1
r1 <- r0 + r2       ; instruction 2
store r1, B[i]      ; instruction 3
```

In this example, `instruction` 1 fetches a value from the array A, `instruction` 2 uses the fetched value to compute a new value, and `instruction` 3 stores the computed value back into array B. There is a forward dependence of `instruction` 2 on `instruction` 1, and a forward dependence of `instruction` 3 on `instruction` 2. Because of these dependences, these instructions cannot be performed in parallel, even with a superscalar architecture. Alternatively, this code example:

```
r0 <- fetch(A[i])    ; instruction 1
r1 <- r3 + r2        ; instruction 2
store r4, B[i]       ; instruction 3
```

does not have the same dependence relations as the previous example. In this case, all three instructions are independent. On a processor whose CPU has multiple functional units, one integer unit could be loading the element of array A, an addition unit could be adding the two registers, and a third unit could be storing the register value into array B. This is an example of instruction-level parallelism.

Given a code segment like the first example here, there is probably not much that can be done. But if the code in that example is included as part of a longer instruction sequence, such as:

```
r0 <- fetch(A[i])    ; instruction 1
r1 <- r0 + r2        ; instruction 2
store r1, B[i]       ; instruction 3
r8 <- r9 + 1         ; instruction 4
r3 <- fetch(X)       ; instruction 5
r4 <- r5 * r6        ; instruction 6
store r8, Y          ; instruction 7
```

then we can evaluate the dependences between the different instructions and determine if any of the instructions may be computed in parallel. In this case, the same dependences exist for instructions 1 through 3, but the only dependences in instructions 4 through 7 are between instructions 4 and 7. This absence of dependence allows the instructions to be reordered. Reordering the instructions will open the opportunity for concurrent execution on multiple functional units. A sample reordering could be:

```
r0 <- fetch(A[i])    ; instruction 1
r8 <- r9 + 1         ; instruction 4
r1 <- r0 + r2        ; instruction 2
r3 <- fetch(X)       ; instruction 5
r4 <- r5 * r6        ; instruction 6
store r8, Y          ; instruction 7
store r1, B[i]       ; instruction 3
```

What this reordering has done is move the dependences away from each other. In this instruction ordering on a dual-functional unit machine, instructions 1 and 4 can be executed simultaneously, instructions 2 and 5 can be executed simultaneously, as can instructions 6 and 7, followed by the final instruction in the sequence. Reordering instructions in this manner is called instruction scheduling, and all good optimizing compilers for superscalar RISC machines should implement this. Often, though, some scheduling opportunities are missed or prevented by compilers because of "roadblocks" in the code. For example, in a function with arguments passed by reference, the compiler cannot know if any of the arguments are aliased (i.e., refer to the same location). The possibility of aliasing will prevent instruction scheduling in a function like this:

```
function foo(int *a, int *b, int N) {
  int x, y, z;
  for (int i = 0; i < N - 1; i++) {
    z = x + 2;       //Statement S1
    x = a[i];        //Statement S2
    a[i] = x + z;    //Statement S3
    b[i] = i;        //Statement S4
  }
}
```

In this loop, it would be nice to move the assignment to `a[i]` away from the calculation of x and z. Yet the only statement that could be moved up would be the assignment to `b[i]`. If the assignment to `b[i]` were moved to between Statement S2 and Statement S3, then we might have a dependence violation, since a and b may point to the same array. It is in code like this where the user's knowledge of the code must supplement the compiler's inability to distinguish aliases.

How do we schedule code? Choosing the optimal way to schedule a sequence of instructions is actually an exponential problem, and is best achieved by using a heuristic algorithm. Most heuristics involve weighting each instruction with its expected time of execution and trying to fit the instructions together without violating any dependence constraints into the tightest possible fit. A good schedule might be:

```
r0 <- fetch(A[i])    ; Fetch may be stalled due to cache line fill
   r8 <- r9 + 1      ;
r4 <- r5 * r6        ; No dependence here!
   r3 <- fetch(X)    ;
r1 <- r0 + r2        ; Hopefully, r0 will be ready by now...
   store r8, Y          ; result of two instructions
                        ; earlier should be done now
store r1, B[i]          ; store result of previous operation.
```

Software Pipelining

Knowing the sequence of instructions within a loop, we would like to apply the same instruction scheduling techniques described in the previous section. Scheduling dependent operations inside a loop by attempting to overlap independent computations should increase the speed of the inner loop.

As long as there are no loop-carried dependences inside the loop, we know that the iterations may be performed in any order. So if we were to reorder the suboperations within each iteration, to overlap computations, as long as we can guarantee that all iterations are completed, we may rearrange the code freely. This rearrangement is called software pipelining, and the effect of this transformation is that multiple iterations of the loop are being computed simultaneously.

Consider a simple loop like this:

```
for (i = 0; i < N; i++) {
  A[i] = B[i] * x;
}
```

During each iteration of the loop there is one array element fetch operation, one scalar access, a multiply, and an array element assignment. We know that if the arrays are not in the cache, all accesses will result in a cache line fill. Also, the multiplication operation may take a few cycles. In this loop there is a dependence of the multiplication operation on the access to B[i], and a dependence on the assignment to A[i] on the completion of the multiplication. These computation dependencies may stall the operation of the processor, and software pipelining can avoid these delays. The idea is to unwind the iterations of loop in sequence, then try to rearrange the operations inside the loop:

0	1	2	3
$t0 = $ fetch $B[0]$	$t1 = $ fetch $B[1]$	$t2 = $ fetch $B[2]$	$t3 = $ fetch $B[3]$
$t0 = t0 + x$	$t1 = t1 + x$	$t2 = t2 + x$	$t3 = t3 + x$
store $t0$ to $A[0]$	store $t1$ to $A[1]$	store $t2$ to $A[2]$	store $t3$ to $A[3]$

To pipeline this loop, we want to separate the computational dependences. We can do this by pushing each one into the next iteration:

0	1	2	3
$t0 = $ fetch $B[0]$	$t1 = $ fetch $b[1]$	$t2 = $ fetch $b[2]$	$t3 = $ fetch $b[3]$
	$t0 = t0 + x$	$t1 = t1 + x$	$t2 = t2 + x$
		store $t0$ to $A[0]$	store $t1$ to $A[1]$

The upshot is that in each iteration from iteration 3 and on, the inner loop looks like this:

```
for (i = 3; i < N - 3; i++) {
  t(1) = B[i];
  t(i - 1) = t(i - 1) * x;
  A[i] = t(i - 2)
}
```

We don't really need to promote the scalar temporaries to an array; the values are recycled through the loop as scalars by reassigning each one in sequence. Since the loop was unwound three times, we will need three temps, although we can be pretty sure that these values will live in registers:

```
for (i = 3); i < N - 3; i++) {
  temp_i = B[i];
  temp_im1 = temp_im1 * x;
  A[i] = temp_im2;
  temp_im2 = temp_im1;
  temp_im1 = temp_i;
}
```

Summary

In this chapter we introduced the concepts of concurrency and parallelism. We talked about the differences between the heavy processes and lightweight threads, followed by the notion of thread synchronization.

Then we looked at scheduling for processes and threads, and how thread scheduling interacts with memory allocation and data distribution. We showed an example of thread programming.

We then looked at how transformations from Chapter 10 could be applied to identify and separate opportunities for concurrency, as well as how dependence analysis could show where concurrency is prevented. We finished with a discussion of fine-grained parallelism at the instruction level, including instruction scheduling for superscalar processors and software pipelining.

Final Thoughts

12

Where Do We Go from Here?

What we have tried to do in this book is provide a framework for understanding the issues regarding data flow across the memory hierarchy. We have looked at architectures and organizations of caches, TLBs, memories, operating systems, disks, networks, etc. We have seen that the self-similarity of the different layers of memory can lead us to the same conclusions: that maximizing the use of spatial and temporal locality will improve application performance. Whether we talk about register allocation, cache-line misses, or disk reads and interprocessor communication, the notions are the same.

Yet, the universe of the memory hierarchy is much larger than the scope provided in this book. Code optimization research moves forward on many fronts. On the one hand, hardware architects try to design systems that echo the way that data move through an application. On the other hand, compiler designers study new ways to optimize code and detect opportunities for increasing locality and overlapping computation with communications.

In this final chapter, we will look at two areas of interest with respect to memory hierarchies and performance programming. The first is the area of networked, communicating machines, and the second is advances in hardware development.

Cooperating Processes

Another common memory hierarchy level appears when data are shared between cooperating processes. Any time communication takes place between two processes, there is a protocol for sending and receiving data to which the processes must adhere. Whether the communication takes place at the same physical processing node, through a memory location that is shared among more than one physical processing node, or across a network, involving distinct processing nodes, the movement of data mirrors the movement of data at higher hierarchy levels.

Modern software systems, be they operating systems or user applications, depend on the ability to transfer information between different processes. The interprocess communication may take place between processes executing on a single processor, between processes that are executing on different processors that share some set of resources, or between processes that are connected only via a network system. Typically, the transfer of information between processes involves a number of copies of data from one memory location to another; at some point, the transfer of data during interprocess communication resembles the movement of data across different levels of the memory hierarchy. This would allow us to consider interprocess communication as its own memory hierarchy level, with its own characteristics for latency as well as locality. We will see in later examples that in some applications, the information that is transferred between processes often exhibits recognizable access patterns, which will allow the programmer to take advantage of the locality to gain better performance.

When processes organize their communication around a set time during each execution, and each process waits to rendezvous with the other, the communication is said to be *synchronous*. A process that expects to communicate synchronously will reach a barrier in the code that checks if the communication partner is prepared to exchange data. If so, the process must wait until its partner reaches it barrier as well, causing a potential delay in the execution. More often interprocess communication is *asynchronous*; that is, one process sends a message to another with no particular schedule. This is manifested through the sending of signals to a process, through an event-driven system, or through a protocol for requesting information and servicing those requests.

Network Communications

As internetworked computer systems become more popular, and software systems are built to take advantage of distributed computing, the issue of performance of passing information between machines on a network becomes important in building applications. We can view nonlocal computers on a network as an additional level in the memory hierarchy.

An application that communicates across a network needs to involve the computer hosting the application, the network connecting the computers, and the computers hosting the processes that are the destinations of the communications. The organization of information exchange between processes can be divided into three basic layers:

- The network access layer
- The transport layer
- The application layer

The *network access layer* is concerned with the actual exchange of data between the computer and the network. At this layer, messages are packaged and labeled with the recipient computer's network address. This layer is not concerned with the content in the messages; data messages are presented to this layer in a standardized format for the transport layer.

It is the *transport layer* that deals with the reliability of the transmissions along with packetization of the data into the standard format. When a message is presented to the transport layer, the data are split up into a set of data transmission blocks of the same size, and a message header is attached to each block. Each header contains information about the destination machine's address, the destined recipient process, and a tag that identifies the source of the message. Also included in the header is a block identification number that indicates the order in which the blocks of the message were split, so that when the messages are delivered, they can be reassembled. The message header also contains information reliability checking. This is usually some kind of cyclic redundancy check value that can be computed as a function of the data in the message.

The *application,* then, can simply present a message and a destination to the transport layer. At the source computer, the transport layer breaks the message into its transmission blocks, and then presents those blocks to the network access layer. At the network access layer, each block is tagged with its header containing the network address of the destination computer, and then the block is injected into the network. At the destination computer, the blocks are received by the network access layer, stripped of the network header, and presented to the transport layer.

At the destination, the transport layer performs a reliability check on each block, and then collects all the data blocks and reassembles the messages. If any of the individual blocks' transmission was faulty, a request can be made to resend the erroneous block. When a message is completely reassembled, the reliability of the entire transmission is checked. If there was an error in the transmission, the sender is notified to resend the message. Otherwise, the complete message is then forwarded to the destination application.

Client/Server Computing

With the ability to transmit information between computers, the work of an application can be divided among the computers on the network.

Client/server computing involves both the splitting up of tasks of an application, as well as the determination of which machine in the network is best suited for which task. For example, many database applications are broken up so that a large-capacity machine (the *server*) provides the database storage and the data accessing capability, while many desktop machines (the *clients*) provide the presentation and user interface part of the application.

Depending on the exact type of application, different tasks may be divided in different ways between the server and the clients. In a *host-based* application, all the tasks are performed by a single computer. In a *server-based* application, all the application work is performed by the server, while the presentation work is performed by the clients. In a *client-based* application, most of the work is done at the clients, relying on the server only for basic services (such as serving files from a file server, or delivering data from a database). In a *cooperative-based* application, some of the application tasks are performed by the server and some are performed by the clients.

In any internetworked application, the remote site's data repository appears as a new layer in the memory hierarchy. Transactions of requests for data from remote applications can be viewed as data accesses to a very far away memory. In many ways, a server in a client/server application or the remote site in the network can be treated the same way as the other layers in the hierarchy.

This is a good point to discuss how three-tier client/server applications reflect the memory hierarchy. In a *three-tier* application, an intermediate broker sits between the server system and a thin client. A thin client operates only as the presentation layer, providing the user interface and event drivers. The middle-level broker operates as the delivery layer, accessing the data from the enterprise storage location (the server tier), potentially transforming the data along the way, as well as caching information for multiple clients. Since the broker can act as a serving station for information, potentially avoiding the reference back to the server, any data that have been fetched by the broker that have not been modified at the server can be delivered to the clients. Does this sound familiar? It should, since this is the same memory hierarchy model as the cache!

Optimizing for locality

Clearly, adding this dimension of communication into a data transfer framework would indicate a significant test to any attempt to optimize for locality. Because message passing between processes involves the multistage procedure of transferring data between layers of communications code, it is difficult to not have applications stalled, waiting for remote data.

This problem becomes more acute in distributed memory multiple processor systems. As more systems are built to harness unused cycles of desktop machines, the strain on the communications system grows. But, as we will see, a goal of performance analysis and enhancement leads us to this conclusion: if an application can anticipate its communications requirements, and request its data ahead of the needed time, then the application can overlap computation with its communication, thereby hiding the latency.

RPC

One programming paradigm that makes use of communication protocols is the remote procedure call (RPC). The remote procedure call is a way to implement distributed computation by allowing the functionality of different procedures to execute on multiple processors. In other words, part of an application may execute as one process, while another part of the same application may execute as another process. It can be made clear that even though RPC itself is a name of a mechanism for communicating, the RPC idea is the basis for all modern broker-serviced applications in heterogeneous computing, such as CORBA, COM, and DCOM.

As an example, different portions of an application may be separated and doled out to machines that are better suited to each particular piece of the application. Graphics applications are a good example; the heavy mathematics needed to render an image may be better suited to a high-performance machine, while the processing to display the image on a terminal screen may require a processor that is tuned for graphics I/O. In general the RPC paradigm forms the basis of many client/server applications.

Another good general example is the automated teller machine (ATM) application. The user interface portion of the application may execute at the ATM machine itself, but the verification request may be implemented as a call to the remote bank's computer. The request to the remote bank can be implemented by an RPC call. When the user desires a cash withdrawal, the local program executing at the ATM machine will generate a request to the remote bank via RPC, then wait for that request to be executed. When the remote bank performs the verification, the answer is sent back to the ATM, which can then dispense the cash and log the transaction.

RPC: Implementation

RPCs are implemented as a collection of layers on top of the communications system. There are three issues that are addressed in any discussion of RPCs:

- The caller side
- The callee side
- The cross-platform representation of data

The notion of the RPC is to request remote execution using the familiar syntax of a procedure call. In a system implemented with remote procedure calls, the appearance of the network communication is transparent to the application; for the most part, the RPC looks and feels just like a local procedure call.

RPC is implemented by using *stubs*. A stub is a routine that looks like it implements the API; instead, it packages the arguments together and sends them on their way. In an RPC system, any routine may be specified as a remote routine. For each remote procedure, an entry point is generated for two locations: the host machine and the remote machine. At the host, the entry point *marshals* the data together and packages it up. The argument package is then presented, as a message destined for the callee machine, to the transport layer of the caller machine. The message is fed out over the network and is received at the callee location. At the destination machine, another stub layer receives the message and unpacks the arguments. The arguments are then forwarded to the called entry point on the server machine. When the procedure has completed, the result values are packaged up again, to be sent to the caller. The message is sent out over the network, received at the caller site, and the result is then unbundled and forwarded back to the caller.

This describes both caller and callee side operations; one question remains. What happens when data are represented in different formats on different machines? For example, there is a difference between little-endian and big-endian representations of integers. Also, in some systems, certain kinds of data types have padded space to force alignments. In an RPC system, there must be some standard for transporting data. This standard, described by Sun Microsystems, is the XDR format (for eXternal Data Representation). At each machine, a set of XDR routines is used to transform each data item into a standard representation. Also at each site are the reverse operations: converting a standard form back to the local representation.

RPCs, while being a powerful mechanism for distributed computing, also form a different view of the network in the memory hierarchy. Again, since the running application makes an RPC call the same way as a local procedure call, the running program may stall until the RPC returns. This synchronous activity of *blocking* while waiting for the return can nullify the effect of the cooperative operation.

Because of this delay incurred, there has been development of non-blocking forms of interprocess communication for remote operation.

An asynchronous RPC, or a nonblocking RPC, will allow the caller to make the call, then proceed to other tasks while waiting for the return values.

The Internet

We have looked at internetworked computers; the popularity of the global interconnections of computers referred to as the Internet has become quite a phenomenon in the lives of many home computer users unacquainted with multicomputer operations. The explosive use of the Internet can be viewed as a case study of how reducing memory latency can empower computer users.

The Internet itself is not new. Research funded by the Defense Advanced Research Projects Administration (DARPA) established the backbone of what is now called the Internet about 30 years ago. Over time, the ARPAnet merged with other national, then global, networks to form a worldwide set of connections that allow data to be passed from one machine to another, until a destination is reached.

Yet it is only recently that home users have made use of these networks. In the past days of home computing, the speed of the hardware available to connect to other machines was prohibitively slow. Even with the fast 2400-baud, then 9600-baud modems, intercommunication was unbearably slow. This is an example of where the memory latency was so overwhelming that it did not pay to make use of the remote data. In order to support the kind of commercial traffic needed to foster widespread Internet usage, local communication hardware needed to be upgraded.

It was not until modems with speeds of 14.4 and 28.8 KB (and greater) baud rates were generally available (i.e., at a reasonable price) that the latency was reduced. As the data delivery bottleneck opened up, more data could be pumped into the home computer at faster rates. This has led to the utilization of the Internet at a tolerable level to the user: an example where decreasing memory latency allowed for better resource usage.

Hardware

Multiprocessor caches

In a multiprocessor shared memory system [also referred to at times as a *symmetric multiprocessor (SMP)* system], one main memory is shared among more than one processor. If each processor has its own cache, sharing memory can be made more efficient by having each processor keep the memory it needs resident in its own cache. Yet at times, it is possible that there are areas of memory that reside in more than one cache, and different processors may want to both read and write to these memory addresses. Because of this, the view of memory in each cache needs to remain consistent with the views in all the other caches. This is referred to as *cache consistency,* or *cache coherence.* As an example, consider a dual-processor shared-memory machine, each processor having its own write-back cache. If the first processor (processor 0) reads a shared variable *foo,* that address is loaded into its cache. When the second processor (processor 1) also reads the same shared variable *foo,* a copy is loaded into its cache as well. If processor 0 then executes an instruction that writes into *foo,* because it is resident in its cache the value will be updated there. At this point, there are three copies of that variable: one in the cache of processor 0, one in the cache of processor 1, and one in main memory. The value in processor 1's cache is consistent with main memory, yet neither holds a current value of the variable. This demonstrates the cache consistency problem.

To attack this problem, shared-memory multiprocessors are designed with cache coherence algorithms to ensure that cache copies are consistent across the system. There are two basic schemes for ensuring cache consistency: *directory-based* schemes, and *snooping* protocols.

A directory is a logical repository of all the information about each block of physical memory; this includes information about which caches hold copies of the block and about whether that block has been written, among other things. When a cache copy is modified, all caches that have a copy are notified. The details of this notification are the same as in the snooping protocols, which are discussed below. While the directory is a logical collection of information, the physical representation may be distributed among all the processors.

In a snooping scheme, processors "snoop" the shared bus; when a transaction is initiated by one processor that affects copies of variables that are resident in other processor caches, those caches must update their own copies in some way, be it through strict updating or by invalidation. On a cache write, all caches that have a copy must either snoop the new value from the bus and update their own version, or (in a simpler way), they may invalidate the cache line that holds their copy (by setting the valid bit to 0). Through this invalidation, when a read of that variable takes place, the line is seen as invalid, and a read miss takes place. If a read miss occurs, all caches check to see if they have an updated version of the read address. If so, the data are provided to the missed cache.

There are two kinds of snooping protocols. With the first kind, called *write-invalidate,* an "announcement" is made via the bus to all caches to invalidate the line to be written before the write actually takes place. Only after all other caches have invalidated their copies will the writer's cache be updated. If another processor wants to write to the same address, it must reload the line into its own cache, and then proceed with the write-invalidate protocol. With the second kind, called *write-broadcast,* the writing processor broadcasts the new value, and all processors that hold that address update their own version with the new value.

A problem with shared-memory multiprocessors happens when two completely separate variables happen to be allocated to the same cache line. For example it is possible that processor 0 exclusively uses a variable x that happens to have been allocated to the same cache line as the variable y, used exclusively by processor 1. As these variables are read, they are both loaded into both caches. When x is written by processor 0, the cache line is updated, which requires a broadcast, and an invalidate in the cache line for processor 1 takes place. When processor 1 executes a write to variable y, the same cache line is written, also causing a broadcast and an invalidate. Since each alternating write invalidates the other's cache, each immediately subsequent read misses in the cache, even though no actual overwriting has taken place. This is called *false sharing,* and there is currently research going on to analyze applications to determine if false sharing is happening, and if so, to reallocate the distribution of variables in order to prevent it.

In programming for multiple processors, the goal is to build an application that loads as much locally used data into each processor's cache, and avoid shared variables as much as possible except when they are needed for synchronization or for message passing. When all of a processor's memory references are made to the cache, the demand on the main memory and on the shared bus is decreased, while the bandwidth of data to the processor is high. The use of snooping protocols that grab updated copies out of other caches can give the image of the other processor caches as an additional level in the memory hierarchy, something that lies between a particular cache and main memory.

COMA: Cache-only memory architecture

A problem we have encountered in looking at multiprocessor systems that share memory is that of shared copies lingering in caches around the system. In a distributed-memory multiprocessor system, the data-sharing issue is more acute; when data objects have been allocated across the memories of the different machines, accesses to particular parts by a nonlocal processor results in a request for the movement of data across the network. In either system configuration, as the communication requirements grow, the scalability of the system decreases, meaning that there is a limit to the benefits that can be attained by adding resources in the system.

One way to address the data-sharing issue in a multiprocessor system is to dissociate the data from a particular memory address. In a regular distributed shared-memory system, as data items are fetched they are brought into the processor caches, where they live until they are flushed, or the underlying memory is modified by another processor's cache flush. In a cache-only memory architecture, each processor's memory acts as a cache for data in the system. When a process requires data, its memory is queried for the item. If the data item is not there, it makes a request to the other processor memories to forward a copy of the data item if any has a copy. As data items are needed, they migrate to the processor that will be using the data. In a COMA system, all pre-allocated memory items begin their life in one memory location, but eventually all migrate to and are replicated at the processor locations where they are needed and used.

The main issue in a COMA machine is the coherence among the processor memories. In a regular multiprocessor system, signals to invalidate cache lines need to be articulated to all processors whenever the underlying memory is changed. In a COMA system, the same holds true for memory data blocks, but there are additional issues. For example, when a processor requests a data block that needs to be accessed from another processor's memory, what happens if the requesting processor's memory is full, and the only blocks that can be ejected are the only valid copies of data? Also, in a COMA machine, the processor memories act differently as levels in the memory hierarchy; each processor will still have a hardware cache, with the processor memories being queried only if there is a miss in the hardware cache. Because of this, the way that data items are referenced may be an issue.

NUMA: Nonuniform memory access

In contrast to the COMA design, multiprocessor machines can be built where the available memory is both shared among all the processors and distributed among the processors. In this model, each processor has its own cache, and access to its local memory is performed the same way as access is made to any part of the global memory. The difference is that, when data items that are not local are accessed, the processing node that holds that part of the memory is accessed to fetch the data. In other words, if the data requested are not available locally, then the time to access the data differs, depending on where the data has been located in the system. This implies that the amount of time it takes to access memory is nonuniform, depending on the data location.

In a *nonuniform memory access (NUMA)* architecture, processing nodes are typically clustered together as groups, then the clusters are interconnected as well, by a high-bandwidth bus. The shared memory space is distributed across all the processor memories, and the processors' caches are kept coherent by a directory-based protocol. If a memory address is referenced, first the local cache is checked; if the data are not present in the local cache, a second-level cache that may act for the entire cluster is checked. If the data item is not present at that level, the reference must be performed by accessing memory. At this point, because the address space is shared, a memory access can be made directly to any of the processors, without having to send a message asking for the data. If the data item can be accessed at the cluster level, the access time is shorter than if the data item must be accessed at a remote memory. This accounts for the name nonuniform memory access.

The goal of the NUMA architecture is similar to that of the COMA: to have frequently accessed data items migrate to their location of need. While in the COMA system there may be multiple copies of data blocks, in the NUMA system the intention is that local caches maintain copies, even though each block has its own address location. Since clusters have their own caches, the memory hierarchy of a NUMA system is more complex than that of a standard symmetric multiprocessor (SMP) machine, yet the goal is to reduce the bus traffic between nodes when it comes to cache coherence. Because of this, the NUMA system is more scalable than an SMP system, which should lead to better performance.

Predictive caches and prefetching

As we have seen, outside the realm of loops and array references there are many applications that exhibit spatial locality that cannot necessarily be discerned automatically. For example, while we have tried to modify our linked-list code to behave well with respect to both the cache and virtual memory, it would be better if the programmer did not have to jump through hoops to get good performance. One attempt to address this is to build caches that prefetch memory locations on the basis of prediction. A predictive cache is a cache that uses transaction tracking and pattern matching to determine the memory locations that are probably going to be hit soon.

To continue the linked-list example, it should be clear that linked lists are traversed repeatedly, usually visiting each node in the same order as the list is traversed, or back and forth through the list if the list contains back-links. If a particular algorithm makes use of a linked list in an idiomatic way, the access pattern can be tracked in a small, fast memory buffer, and queried as new references are made. If the current sequence of references matches in one of the available patterns, the next block in the pattern is prefetched into the cache if it is not already there, even though a reference has not yet been made.

The idea of predictive caching is useful in that it maps well to any layer of the memory hierarchy. Predictive caching may be built into hardware for memory accessing, or can be applied at the file system level as well. The concept boils down to four pieces:

- *Transaction tracking*: Having an efficient way to keep track of the events.

- *Pattern matching*: Having an efficient way, based on the way that the transactions have been logged, to check whether the current sequence matches any of the known patterns.

- *Prediction strategy*: Presuming that a pattern has been identified, what is the next step?

- *Prefetch mechanism*: This includes the initiation of the events to access the memory that should be next in the access pattern.

Conclusion

We have now looked at many levels of the memory hierarchy and we can come to two conclusions. The first is that no matter what level of the hierarchy we look at, locality of reference is the key to high performance. The second conclusion is that when we are forced to wait for data to arrive, if instead we can maximize the locality characteristics of the access patterns, we can hide some of the data access latency inherent in data movement.

Hopefully, this book will have helped in understanding about memory hierarchies, locality of reference, and program performance. We have looked at hardware architecture, and machine organizations of CPUs, caches, memory, virtual memory, disk memory, and interprocess communication in the context of the memory hierarchy. We have also looked at performance analysis, program timing, and benchmarking. Lastly, we looked at data dependence analysis, program transformations, and code optimization. With this understanding of the ins and outs of data movement across the levels of the hierarchy, hopefully the reader can go on to write efficient programs understanding the nature of data flow. Here's wishing you the best of performance!

Bibliography

Bloomer, John, *Power Programming with RPC*, O'Reilly & Associates, Inc., 1992.

Cragon, Harvey G., *Memory Systems and Pipelined Processors*, Jones and Bartlett Publishers, 1996.

Dowd, Kevin, *High-Performance Computing*, O'Reilly and Associates, Inc., 1993.

Handy, Jim, *The Cache Memory Book*, Academic Press, 1993.

Hennesy, John L., and David A Patterson, *Computer Architecture: A Quantitative Approach*, Morgan Kaufman, 1990.

Hwang, Kai, *Advanced Computer Architecture*, McGraw-Hill, 1993.

Intel Corporation, *Intel Architecture Optimization Manual* (downloaded from *www.developer.intel.com*).

Letner, Charles, "Loop Splitting under Windows NT," *Dr. Dobbs Journal*, July 1996.

Meyers, Scott, *Effective C++*, Addison-Wesley, 1992.

Schimmel, Curt, *UNIX Systems for Modern Architectures*, Addison-Wesley, 1994.

Sedgewick, Robert, *Algorithms in C++*, Addison-Wesley, 1992.

Sun Microsystems, *UltraSPARC Programmer Reference Manual*, Sun Microsystems, 1995.

Wolfe, Michael, *High-Performance Compilers for Parallel Computing*, Addison-Wesley, 1996.

Index

ABOUT THE AUTHOR

David Loshin was associated with Boston University for five years, teaching graduate-level courses in Computer Science (including Operating Systems, Compilers, and Computer Architecture). He is the author of *High-Performance Computing Demystified*, an expository book on supercomputing architectures, software, and applications. David currently works for a major New York financial firm creating data mining software.